BOB AND RAY
KEENER THAN MOST PERSONS

BOB <u>AND</u> RAY
KEENER THAN MOST PERSONS

THE *BACKSTAYGE* STORY OF BOB ELLIOTT
AND RAY GOULDING

DAVID POLLOCK

WITH A FOREWORD
BY DAVE LETTERMAN

APPLAUSE
THEATRE & CINEMA BOOKS

An Imprint of Hal Leonard Corporation

Published in 2013 by Applause Theatre & Cinema Books
An Imprint of Hal Leonard Corporation
7777 West Bluemound Road
Milwaukee, WI 53213

Trade Book Division Editorial Offices
33 Plymouth St., Montclair, NJ 07042

Printed in the United States of America

Book design by UB Communications
Unless otherwise noted all photos are from the personal collection of Bob Elliott.

Library of Congress Cataloging-in-Publication Data

Pollock, David.
  Bob and Ray, keener than most persons : the backstage story of Bob Elliott and Ray Goulding / David Pollock.
     pages cm
Includes bibliographical references and index.
  ISBN 978-1-55783-830-8 (hardcover)
1. Elliott, Bob. 2. Goulding, Ray. 3. Comedians—United States—Biography.
4. Radio broadcasters—United States—Biography. 5. Actors—United States—
Biography. I. Title.
  PN2287.E418P65 2013
  791.4402'80922—dc23
  [B]
                            2012049815

www.applausebooks.com

To Jillzy

CONTENTS

FOREWORD BY DAVE LETTERMAN

Bob and Ray became a part of my life when I was a young boy. The weekend NBC Radio program called *Monitor* was my first exposure to Bob and Ray. Each hour the broadcast would feature a "report" from Bob and Ray. Even as a youngster I could tell these guys were not hooked up right. The ridiculous was taken for normal. Silliness was reality. They would state the premise and off they went. They were both loons. This is a pretty irresistible form of comedy. Bob and Ray began on radio or perhaps whatever people did before radio. As I grew up their many appearances on radio and television shows was something my father and I looked forward to and enjoyed. I thought it was very cool that my dad loved Bob and Ray.

Later in my life when I was thoughtlessly given a television show of my own Bob and Ray made several appearances. This was thrilling, hard to believe and funny. Wait a minute, maybe it was just Bob. Or maybe it was just Ray? Maybe I never had a show. I'm so old I can hide my own Easter eggs.

Anyhoo, so here we finally have a book about Bob and Ray. David Pollock has done a wonderful job writing this book. Someone had to write it as sadly, I think Ray is dead and Bob is illiterate. Also good Christ, when are we going to stop wasting trees? On the other hand, what's a couple hundred board feet of lumber compared to a book that guarantees a solid night's sleep? Well I could go on all day about Bob and Ray, but I need to get back to my own private hell. Let me finish here by saying: Bob and Ray, gay? Read the book then flip a coin.

God bless you, and good night.

PROLOGUE

He reached over to the shelf in his cramped dressing room and, with a little tap, launched the handcrafted wooden Italian clown into another round of perpetual somersaults. The mesmerizing, brightly colored figure, a gift from his wife, Lee, had done all that Bob Elliott could ask of it to keep him nicely distracted from the anxiety-filled realities of that sweltering, September 24, 1970, opening night of *Bob and Ray—The Two and Only*.

The large, brightly lit make-up mirror he seated himself in front of symbolized the alien world in which he now found himself. Elliott had been informed by the conventions and rhythms of broadcasting—radio guys did not slap on make-up and become Broadway actors; they performed comedy bits mocking Broadway actors, a responsibility he never shirked. Could tonight, he wondered, be some kind of cruel payback?

In AM radio's twilight decades, Bob Elliott and Ray Goulding were snapped up by every major network still standing, some stretches on the air seven days a week. Their comedy, said Groucho Marx, reminded him of Robert Benchley: "They have that same *Alice in Wonderland* philosophy. . . . I'm just crazy about them." Johnny Carson called them "two of the funniest—and most influential—humorists of their time." But that was history now, as was their original nightly fifteen-minute NBC television series. Only some of the Broadway first-nighters in the John Golden Theatre would remember that Elliott and Goulding had been TV pioneers, on NBC five nights a week.

Next door, in equally Spartan quarters, separated only by a common bathroom, sat Ray Goulding, mindful of his voice—all of his voices, in fact. As there were no understudies, if he had a cold, all of his characters had a cold. "It becomes an epidemic," he liked to say. And he was in a constant state of worry that he might catch one. According to his widow, Liz, "He lived on Vitamin C." For Goulding, it would take more than a somersaulting toy clown to allay anxiety.

Like every New Yorker that night, he and his partner were victims of the fiendish Indian summer heat wave. Johnna Levine, co-producer of the show, had advised the two that if it got impossible to keep the theater comfortable, "Take off your goddamn jackets and tell everybody in the audience to do the same."

The usual opening-night angst was peppered by the fact that the two were not used to the theater, Johnna pointed out. "They were full of trepidation about this new milieu. It was not something they had ever done before and they were very uptight, but friendly and malleable, let's say, in terms of what had to be done."

Johnna's co-producer husband, Joseph I. Levine, the salesman of the two and a longtime Bob and Ray fan, had initially written them years earlier, proposing "a most exciting and delightful evening in the theater." It was an overture that most performers only dream of, plopped in their laps by the co-producer of a recently successful two-man show, *At the Drop of a Hat*—a point Levine was careful to slip in. The warm, emphatic producer, when teamed with his equally enthusiastic wife, was not an easy man to say no to, especially when he was lavishing praise. But Elliott and Goulding managed to do it.

And they persisted in their refusals throughout seven years of arm-twisting by the Levines. They were "disinterested or apprehensive," Johnna said, with the idea of performing on stage. "They had never been and didn't want to try." In truth, disinterest masked apprehension. Following a disastrous nightclub engagement in Buffalo a decade earlier, Elliott and Goulding had intuitively avoided placing themselves in harm's way. Removed from their radio studio comfort zone, insecurities lurked. "They had to be dragged to Broadway kicking and screaming," Johnna said.

"Jeez, we can't memorize two hours of stuff," Goulding had repeatedly told the two producers in a series of yearly meetings. "We never do the same thing twice." But his partner knew that was not necessarily true. Elliott had not exactly leapt at the opportunity either, though the idea had secretly intrigued him.

In the end, however, it was not the Levines' persistence that did the trick. The guys had a change of heart, Johnna said, "but I think the change of heart realistically was the fact that nothing else was happening. That's the reality. They didn't have a specific radio outlet; there was no show. It was time to try another venue."

The stage manager, Don Koehler, stepped to the bottom of the narrow stairs leading to the second-floor dressing rooms and shouted, "Five minutes, gentlemen." He, too, was anxious over the evening's outcome. This was his first job in nearly a year.

Elliott and Goulding, in sports jackets and ties, headed down the long, straight stairway to the Golden's drab, forbidding backstage. The theater on West Forty-Fifth Street, they had been told, had been selected because of its rich history of intimate two-person revues. But force-fed tales about the successes of A Party with Comden and Green, Flanders and Swann's At the Drop of a Hat, and An Evening with Mike Nichols and Elaine May, did not particularly put the two at ease. Nor, for that matter, were they reassured when they learned that the Golden's biggest smash was a 1929 hit called Rope's End, based on the team of Leopold and Loeb.

Near the wings, the two spotted Bob Hodge, who had been featured in a playbill ad proclaiming The Two and Only as "the only funny comedy on Broadway in years." Though grateful for the endorsement, they knew what the public did not: Hodge was the show's stage doorman. Barely thirty-one, Hodge harbored dreams of becoming a comedy writer and was seldom without a note pad for jotting down ideas. Neither Elliott nor Goulding, however, could ever recall seeing anything actually written on the pad.

Crossing behind the cyclorama they could hear the expectant murmur of the audience, infiltrated by a platoon of critics, including Ted Kalem of Time, Jack Kroll of Newsweek, Brendan Gill of The New Yorker, Henry Hewes of the Saturday Review, Richard Watts of the New York Post, and John Simon of New York, each and every one a potential knife thrower. There were also reviewers from the wire services, plus Leonard Harris of WCBS-TV and Edwin Newman of WNBC television.

But most feared of all was the powerful New York Times man, Clive Barnes, who, in the opinion of playwright and two-time Academy Award–winning screenwriter William Goldman, was "the most dangerous, the most crippling critic in modern Broadway history." Elliott and Goulding knew that any sort of pan from Barnes would mean *The Two and Only* would fold faster than their fictional Mary Backstayge disaster, *Lament of the Locust*.

As unnerving as Barnes's opening-night presence could be, an even worse fate was the stigma of his non-presence. It could slam the brakes on advance sales. How good could a thing be (so the logic on the street went) if it was not even worth Barnes's time? And that was his original reaction to *The Two and Only*. In his defense, by 1970, Elliott and Goulding had only been in the game for a quarter of a century. They would ultimately be teamed longer than such enduring comedy twosomes as Laurel & Hardy, Burns & Allen, Abbott & Costello, and Martin & Lewis.

In 1970, in fact, Barnes did not even know who Bob and Ray *were*. "It was some kind of vaudeville act as far as he was concerned," Johnna said. "He was not going to come; he was going to send a second-stringer." Only when the producers unleashed the show's terrier of a press agent, Leo Stern, on him, was Barnes finally convinced the show was a full-scale production and agreed to attend.

Clive Barnes was unpredictable, but his pieces could be scathing and were frequently laced with acidic asides. In a then-recent review he had written, "One sure gauge I have of telling whether a play is boring me is when a telephone rings in the last act and I start in my seat and hope it's for me."

Also adding to opening-night jitters was the fact that Barnes was, first and foremost, the paper's dance critic. Only in the last few years had he also been assigned the Broadway beat. The charm of Elliott and Goulding's identifiably American characters lay in their sheer ordinariness. Exposing them to the whims of a British ballet reviewer with a known English bias struck at a fundamental reality of the entire enterprise. Bob and Ray, clearly, were not for everybody. Their humor existed in its own self-contained universe, a product of a unique, on-air chemistry that even *they* never seemed able to explain.

During previews, Johnna had commented to Lee Elliott about a woman who had approached her at intermission. "Look," the woman remarked, "this isn't going to go because not everybody gets them. But *I* adore them. I think they're the greatest thing in the world."

"That's the story of our lives," Lee responded. "Everybody thinks *they* adore them and nobody else will get it."

As their friend Andy Rooney would later observe, "Fortunately, there are a lot of people who think, as I do, that they appreciate Bob and Ray more than anyone else does."

Only minutes from now, there would be no call from Koehler for "curtain up!" There was no curtain. William Ritman's set, already visible to the audience in the semi-darkness, depicted the cluttered "attic of America," as Johnna put it, "the United States' collective consciousness of radio and what had gone before." As the theater filled, objects in the attic began to take shape, triggering outbursts of happy anticipation.

Slowly, lighting director Tom Skelton's inventive placement of "spots" and "pins" focused on a bookcase, numerous pieces of furniture, a canary cage, an antique Philco radio, and a trapeze hung from somewhere above. There was a Flexible Flyer, a glass-domed stock ticker, some canoe paddles and skis, and a microphone bearing the call letters of NBC's original New York flagship, WEAF. A coat rack held several bits of costume pieces, topped by a gray fedora with a press card in its band.

Director Joseph Hardy, balding much too early for his forty-one years, had already begun to pace at the back of the house. Next door at the Plymouth Theatre, *Child's Play*, for which he had earned a Tony Award, was in its sixth month of sold-out performances. And a few short blocks away, Joe Orton's *What the Butler Saw*, which he also directed, was an off-Broadway smash.

Hardy had been hired, Johnna said, because she and her husband "most emphatically" had concerns as to exactly how spontaneous, frozen moments-in-time radio sketches would play on the stage. Transposing the material into script form was "very difficult," Johnna said. "All we had was their renditions of it."

As Goulding would later describe the process, "We had to transcribe it onto paper from tape so that eventually we had to memorize what we had originally ad-libbed."

"It became a question of how you presented this on stage and made it theatrically viable," Hardy said. "It had to be a piece of theatre, not a piece of radio . . . not a static kind of recitation piece. . . . Otherwise you're doomed." He had confronted similar challenges with another revue, *You're a Good Man, Charlie Brown*, and, the previous season, grabbed a Tony nomination for bringing an imaginary Humphrey Bogart to life in Woody Allen's *Play it Again, Sam*.

Gore Vidal, with whom the Levines were involved on another project, was one of the producers' opening-night guests. The three took their seats, fifth-row center. "Johnna, stop fretting," Vidal had been telling her all day. "They're going to do wonderfully, just wonderfully." His words had not been comforting to Elliott and Goulding. If critics could be brutal, they feared, the insular theater community was worse when it came to petty jealousies, and hardly could be expected to embrace a couple of ex-radio-announcers-turned-Broadway party crashers. Yes, there had been an exception: Bumping into Elliott on Madison Avenue, Tony Randall had enthusiastically flashed two tickets just purchased on the strength of the show's early buzz. But at Downey's, an actor's hangout around the corner from the theater on Eighth Avenue, James Coco, then riding the crest of his *Last of the Red Hot Lovers* Tony nomination, spotted Elliott and walked past his booth with a dismissive glance.

A few rows behind the producers were the stars' wives, Lee and Liz, and their families, numbering eleven children between them. Given the long-established freeform nature of the team's comedy, Liz's concerns centered on their being able to adapt to the confining routine of *The Two and Only*, calling it "one of their most rigid adventures."

With all these imponderables swirling, the duo headed down another set of stairs to a room directly under the stage, essentially a musicians' bullpen just off the orchestra pit. *The Two and Only* would begin with the audience hearing Bob Elliott's familiar voice (as Wally Ballou) reporting on some of the last-minute, backstage "color and excitement." They then would appear coming up into the "attic" in which, the *Saturday Review*'s Henry Hewes later reported, "The distinguishably undistinguished comics seem just a couple more leftovers." It was high praise.

At a microphone stand was assistant stage manager Richard Thayer, waiting to cue them into the opening Wally Ballou bit, after which they would scurry up a small, circular staircase, entering the set through a trap-door. At the last second, as they stepped to the mike, Elliott heard his partner say something that sounded to him like "house in Boundbrook." He had no idea what it meant; nor would he the following night, nor the night after when Goulding would repeat the exact same words. Over the following months Elliott would consult a few books and ultimately piece together that Goulding was trying to say *"hulse im brücke,"* German for the theater's traditional good luck wish: "Break a leg" (originally, in German, "Break a neck and leg.") This was not something Goulding had known on his own—just miscellaneous information he had picked up from the show's production assistant, Iris Merlis. Goulding had assumed that Elliott, having spent time in Germany during the war and having mastered some of the language, would understand. But Elliott did not. And, furthermore, he did not want to let his partner know that he did not. And Goulding was not about to ask him if he knew. Such was the complex offstage, personal relationship of Bob and Ray.

When not working, the two rarely saw each other. Perceiving themselves more as businessmen than personalities, they resisted even being labeled comedians, and never considered themselves an "act." Upon meeting Elliott and Goulding, a first impression was their total lack of show-biz swagger. On the streets of Manhattan, they could easily have been mistaken for two Wall Street portfolio managers or out-of-town-buyers on their way to the garment district. Their four-decade partnership was that of two introverts trapped in an extrovert's business.

1

THE ELECTRIFIED FISH HOUSE

The era when the Hotel Touraine's French Renaissance architecture and furnishings were compared to the glories of the world-famous Château de Blois, and its guest register was signed by royalty (as it was, in 1897, by Prince Albert of Flanders, heir apparent to the Belgian throne), had long since vanished. A half-century later, the biggest names entering the Boston landmark at Boylston and Tremont appeared to be the occasional crooked politician and, incongruously, visiting cowboy bands.

The lobby's winding, wide, marble staircase led to the mezzanine level and the studios of radio station WHDH, crammed into what was once the presidential suite. The place looked like it sounded on the air: old and musty. A center hallway separated studios A and B and was lined with uncomfortable wooden benches for guests of the station's few audience programs, conveying the feeling of a bus depot waiting room. The newsroom's wire-service machines were located in the bathroom. *The Boy from Ireland*, featuring Terry O'Toole's Irish songs and stories, and organ concerts, together with those cowboy bands, set the tone for the station's music policy.

WHDH first signed on in Gloucester in 1929, under the ownership of John J. Matheson, a Nova Scotian fishing master from Cape Breton, who relished his reputation as a "mackerel killer." However, Matheson—who never discouraged associates from calling him "Captain"—was not as successful when it came to hooking radio listeners.

By the end of 1930, the station had settled in Boston with the transmitter on a salt marsh just north of the city, in Saugus, effectively increasing the power and reach of the thousand-watt signal. However, the beam was strictly directional; it did not go anywhere west, but had a tremendous carry to the east, out over the Atlantic. It could be picked up halfway to the Azores. That nobody lived halfway to the Azores mattered little to the captain, who had discovered an untapped captive audience. His fanciful plan was to broadcast the current Boston fish prices, enabling the skippers at sea to hurry in if the quotes were favorable, or remain at the fishing banks if they were low; in effect, turning the fleet into speculators. Following Captain Matheson's death, in March 1940, the reins passed to his sons, Ralph and John, Jr.

Three times a day WHDH announcers called a private number at the Boston Fish Pier to ascertain the up-to-the-minute boat arrivals and prices prior to broadcasting each early-morning, midday, and late-night *Fisherman's News Service* half-hour program ("The *Stellar B* arrived with twenty-two thousand mixed fish, sixteen thousand halibut, eighteen thousand hake . . ."). So that the mariners could scribble down the figures, the reports were read on the air at a tediously slow, dictation-like speed. It was the most despised assignment at the station. WHDH became known as "the voice from home for fishermen at sea," but, in private, it was "the electrified fish house." Comedian Henry Morgan, once one of those announcers, claimed WHDH stood for, "We handle dead haddock."

Another announcer burdened by reading fish prices in addition to other assignments, including morning and afternoon DJ blocks, was twenty-three-year-old Bob Elliott. The trim, fair-haired, five-foot-ten-inch Elliott was in the middle of the noontime edition of the *Fisherman's News Service* in late spring 1946, when George Watson, WHDH's short, fortyish, bustling program director, stuck his head in Studio B. With him was a twenty-four-year-old, six-foot-one-inch New Englander with black hair and a mustache. "He resembled a thin Oliver Hardy," recalled Elliott, "and wore a new-looking postwar suit and sported a hard straw hat like Van Johnson wore in *In the Good Old Summertime*."

Watson motioned for the man to follow him in. "Bobby, little chum," he said during a recorded commercial, "this is Ray Golding. He'll be working with you on your shift doing the news."

"*Goulding*," Ray corrected.

After the commercial break, when Watson returned to his office, Goulding remained. Elliott continued with the morning Fish Pier arrivals:

"There were two draggers . . . four trawlers . . . and five net seiners, with a total of one hundred and sixteen thousand pounds of mixed fish." He then turned off the mike for a couple of seconds, allowing fishermen to jot down the information.

"This is what you do for a living?" Goulding asked, fully aware that as the newest member of the staff, he, too, would be saddled with the fish reports. Some minutes later, Elliott concluded the half-hour by cueing the engineer for the pre-selected recorded music, known affectionately as "fish fill."

To the extent that the birth of Bob and Ray as a team can be traced at all, it happened moments later when Goulding stayed on during Elliott's afternoon record show and the two chatted briefly, both on and off the air. "I liked him immediately," Elliott said. "He was a breath of fresh air; it was a stodgy place. . . . We had a lot of laughs that first hour or so he sat in with me."

How funny it really was—or was not—matters little; what does matter is that it seemed funny to Elliott and Goulding. In their minds, they were merely entertaining each other. And with the approval of management— approval in the sense that nobody told them to stop—they kept doing it every morning following Goulding's newscasts on Elliott's *Sunny Side Up* program. It was cobbled together on the fly at the fortuitous intersection of serendipity and happenstance. There was no field manual to consult; they were already on the air. As Elliott would later comment, "It was pure necessity. It wasn't always funny, but it was *something*."

The two discovered they had much in common: Both were ex-GIs, born in March, raised near Boston during the Depression, caught in the gravitational pull of radio. Neither came from privilege nor went to college, and each had fathers who had passed away at age fifty-four. And both started working in the medium while still in their teens.

But it was marked differences that would spark their comedy.

2

GRABBED BY THE MEDIUM

Inevitably, a crowd gathered in front of the Metropolitan Theatre on Tremont Street, attracted by the earphone-wearing man-on-the-street program's glib young announcer. Such shows were ubiquitous at the time, and Boston had three or four. As the curious looked on, the cheerful host wagged his microphone between himself and random passersby, on this occasion, a Back Bay housewife, a salesman from Dedham, and a young high-school kid from the suburbs. The announcer was Roland Winters, and the young kid was named Bob Elliott, who only moments earlier had pushed his way in front of another station's man-on-the-street microphone at Copley Square. He and his Winchester High pal, Arthur Harris, Jr., would regularly take the train to Boston and insinuate themselves into all the man-on-the-street shows. One way or another, they would fight their way to the front, hoping to be picked. "If we went separately," Elliott reflected over a half-century later, "we'd call each other at night and say, 'How did I sound?'"

Most of the interviewees hoped to win a silver dollar, but for Bob and Arthur there was a more powerful overriding imperative: "It was the act of talking into a microphone," Elliott said, "and having our voice go over the radio. We were just grabbed by the medium. . . . A lot of times, we'd go from one show to another, and never get on one. It was that desire."

When not stalking man-on-the-street programs, Bob was playing multiple roles in Sunday-evening radio broadcasts. So what if the studio was the sunroom of his parents' Dutch colonial home, near the crest of Symms Hill at 16 Ledyard Road in Winchester, and the microphone fashioned from a piece of wood? As a kid, Bob was highly motivated and creatively and mechanically gifted. Between guitar lessons and art school, he captured a couple of soapbox-derby medals with cars he built himself.

Robert Brackett Elliott, the only child of Fred and Gail (née Brackett) Elliott, was born in Boston, Massachusetts, on March 26, 1923. Gail—like her mother, brother, and two sisters—had been born in the family house, built in 1814, in Brooks, Maine, and now owned by the local historical society. She was very artistic, with a particular talent for needlepoint.

His father, Fred, originally from East Somerville, Massachusetts, was an insurance man, initially for John Hancock, before becoming a general agent whose duties included writing policies for several companies. He liked billiards, baseball, and was on the John Hancock bowling team. Fred had a warm personality and wielded a pointed sense of humor, mandatory in the mortality business. He also introduced his son to two of his favorite humorists, Fred Allen and Robert Benchley. Fred studied the cornet as a kid, and played the piano by ear, but could claim no part of his son's mechanical skills. "He gave me enthusiasm," Elliott said, "but didn't know an axle from a tire."

The modest and accommodating Fred and Gail were popular members of their weekly bridge group. Fred, to his credit, never complained about being dragged to endless antique markets, and Gail put up with her husband's 7-20-4 cigars. In the summer, the family would take off in Fred's '32 Essex Super Six for two weeks, usually at Swan Lake, Maine, near Belfast. It involved "a ten-hour drive," said Elliott, "and a couple of flat tires."

Bob's fascination with broadcasting was a product of the period; both he and radio came of age at the same time. It was the new entertainment, with its own unique cast of performers. Audiences discovered their favorites; Bob discovered his. For some reason, Elliott recalled, "I was inspired by the announcers more than the actors. . . . I thought the announcers were superstars when I was a kid." Seated in the large, brown mohair chair in the living room, Bob listened closely to such then-familiar voices as Pierre Andre, Kelvin Keech, and Alois Havrilla. These polished, silky-voiced, tuxedo-clad gentlemen evoked a magical world, one far removed from the Great Depression. "We just ruled out college," he said. "My family couldn't afford it."

But they did foot the tab for family field trips to New York, where they encamped at the Winthrop Hotel at 47th and Lexington, strategically selected for its proximity to the network studios. Fred and Gail and their young aspirant attended live broadcasts of Rudy Vallee, Fred Allen, and a special favorite, Ray Knight's *The Cuckoo Hour*.

When Fred was later transferred to New York, the family, through his connections, rented an apartment in Parkchester in the Bronx, which had just been developed by Metropolitan Life as one of the first model residential communities. Bob enrolled in the Feagin School of Drama and Radio. His fellow students included Angela Lansbury, John Lund, Gordon MacRae and his future wife, then known as Sheila Stevens. Two others, Ira Grossel and Jack Chakrin, both of whom had acting scholarships, met there and became a handful for the teachers as a self-appointed classroom comedy team. They would later become renowned as Jeff Chandler and Jack Carter.

"We were constantly plotting things," Carter recalled, "changing lines in plays, having a sub-laughter of our own in the middle of a scene—yeah, we were different. It was a very gentile school; we gave a touch of color to it." Even then, not one to downshift his "electric personality," as he called it, it was impossible for classmates not to notice Jack Carter, as opposed to Bob Elliott, who kept an exceedingly lower profile. "I don't remember Bob being there," Carter said. "Isn't that funny?"

As for teachers, the school had some great actors that were then appearing on Broadway. And for radio, Charles Starke, a top announcer, taught classes. "We did scenes and stuff," Carter continued. "You learned voice and you did speeches. You got information in Radio City about where to go to 'make the rounds,' as they called it. You had to go to every shmucky casting office until you got a break." Elliott also worked nights as an usher at Radio City Music Hall; this proved to be invaluable experience for his next job as a page at NBC.

After about a year and a half in New York, Fred was diagnosed with cancer of the esophagus, and he and Gail returned to Boston and moved in with her parents, Bertha and Charles, in Somerville. Visiting his father in the spring of 1941, Elliott auditioned at WHDH. A month later a telegram from George Watson arrived at the Feagin School. The job was his. "I was out of this world," he said. Elliott was a staff announcer for $18.50 a week. He was eighteen.

On Armistice Day, November 11, 1941, shortly before the attack on Pearl Harbor, the cancer overtook Fred. Bob secured a draft deferment and helped support his mother. At WHDH, he conducted a daily man-on-the-street program of his own from Boston's North Station, *Depot Dialogues*, and emceed afternoon band remotes from smoke-filled, beer-smelling bars like the Silver Dollar, on Washington, where the leader was a young piano player named Keith Bennett. The group always took a twenty-minute break after the show, and for "some reason never explained," Elliott noted, an authentic Hawaiian group would take over. The engineer would then repack and lug two thirty-pound suitcases of equipment around the corner to the equally enchanting Ort's Grill. Cab fare was provided for the two on longer hauls out to the Hi-Hat Club in the South End (a local draw if for no other reason than its two-dollar barbecue chicken dinners), and to the Essex Hotel, opposite South Station, for six-thirty-in-the-evening broadcasts of Jack Manning and his "Strings of Romance." A plum Elliott gig was announcing the major traveling black bands of the day, including Lionel Hampton, Fletcher Henderson, and Andy Kirk and his "Clouds of Joy," on eleven-fifteen-in-the-evening pickups from a cavernous dive called the Seven Seas. The name had been changed from Gundlach's Hofbrau when the war broke out.

Political speeches occasionally involved Elliott introducing Boston's Irish scoundrel of a mayor, James M. Curley, who served four terms, one while in prison on a fraud conviction. He also knew how to avoid paying for purchased airtime, requiring, on one occasion—as per program director George Watson's orders—Elliott's refusal to let the mayor into the studio until he got the money first. "I'm eighteen years old and standing up to this guy, and his cohorts are grouped around," Elliott recalled. "At the last minute, he took the money out and peeled off whatever the price was, like four-hundred bucks." Dealing in cash was Curley's preferred MO, although it usually flowed in the opposite direction.

Another assignment, *The Holland Butter Dairy Maid Program*, was a weekday hour of innocuous household tips and family issues. Off the air, a not-so-innocuous attraction developed between Elliott and the program's

16

hostess, Jane Underwood, a pretty, enterprising young brunette from Newton. The two began spending more and more time together, eventually sharing an apartment on Pinckney Street in Beacon Hill. Keeping the romance a secret from listeners was a snap. The real performances occurred off the air, as their colleagues and families were also kept in the dark.

When, at nineteen Elliott received a second deferment, the two sneaked off to Salem and were secretly married. In 1943, now out of deferments, Elliott was ordered to basic training at Camp Campbell, the Army's charming bed-and-breakfast straddling the Kentucky–Tennessee border, where he ended up in an evacuation unit specializing in pulling tanks and heavy machinery out of ditches. This was not work he felt particularly qualified for, an opinion the U.S. Army would eventually share. What Elliott *was* qualified for was doing funny voices and dead-on impressions, skills evidently not in heavy demand at Camp Campbell in 1943. Next stop: 26th Division HQ, 104th Infantry Regiment, at Fort Jackson, South Carolina, where he was assigned to Special Services. He had barely unpacked his duffle bag before being ordered to four weeks of intensive training in entertainment, sports, and recreational activities at the Army's Special Service Unit at Washington and Lee University in Lexington, Virginia. Overnight Elliott went from towing an 85-millimeter gun-equipped Sherman tank to running a 16-millimeter Bell & Howell movie projector. His buddy, "Fitz" (William Fitzsimmons from Philadelphia), was put in charge of maintaining athletic equipment.

In the late summer of 1944, the 26th—"The Yankee Division"—was deployed overseas, embarking from Staten Island on a heavily overcast Sunday, August 27, aboard the S. S. *Argentina*. With maneuvering to avoid German U-boat lanes, the passage took the convoy eleven days. On September 7 Bob and Fitz, duffle bags on their backs, were warmly welcomed to France, scrambling down a cargo net on the side of the ship to an LST in the devastated port of Cherbourg. Navy frogmen were still clearing the mangled wrecks. They then headed by truck through the hedgerows of the Cotentin peninsula, establishing headquarters in the little Normandy village of St. Martin-d'Audoville. The various units set up in nearby farms and fields. Elliott's 104th Regiment Service Company bivouacked in an apple orchard just a short hike from the north end of the

Utah Beach invasion zone, a section easily spotted by the continual presence of mine-removal squads.

As long as the troops and their curious neighbors, a shell-shocked herd of Norman cows, stayed within cordoned-off perimeters, they would not step on unexploded ordnance. As newly liberated local cheese makers and cider houses reopened, the group began feasting on hunks of Camembert, washed down with Calvados. Fitz had the baseball gloves out every day, and Elliott's movie projector flickered at night on a large screen tied to two trees. A favorite was the MGM musical *Ship Ahoy*. The blaring Sinatra numbers did not seem to bother the cows, but, then, they had survived D-Day.

The days of Camembert and Calvados would not last long. On October 4, the division headed clear across France by truck convoy to consolidate with General George Patton's Third Army in the Vosges Mountains of Lorraine. The 104th had arrived on German-held soil. Clusters of bloated livestock killed during earlier shellings dotted the fields, as did the crumpled bodies of dead enemy soldiers, lying where they dropped. The weather was as unwelcoming as the scenery. It was cold, wet, and miserable. Elliott's service company bivouacked in Hoéville, on the eastern outskirts of the city of Nancy.

Only six kilometers further east were the frozen and muddy Moncourt Woods, from which the 104th was ordered to clear dug-in German forces. On October 22, artillery flashes suddenly lit up the sky. As Elliott recalled, "It sounded like slamming doors echoing down a hotel corridor." The fighting, in and around the woods, raged on for days.

"That was the first action," recalled Ralph Shirak, then a twenty-two-year-old rifleman with Company A. "It was furious and very, very costly. We lost almost half of Company A, including its company commander." Shirak, a music buff, had been "a big fan" of Elliott's WHDH record shows, which he picked up in his hometown of Clifton, New Jersey, thanks to a twelve-foot aerial attached to his vintage 1920s Atwater-Kent radio. He would soon meet Elliott for the first time.

On November 8, in a chilling rain, the unit captured Vic-sur-Seille and then drove toward Morville and Hampont. "All familiar names," said Elliott, "particularly Vic-sur-Seille. . . . I have that name etched in my memory." The Lorraine Campaign—as it later came to be known—proceeded to slice a wedge, north and east, between Nancy and the German border. Once an enemy stronghold was cleared, Elliott explained, the advance pushed on so rapidly that key battles at Château Voué, Conthil, and Albestroff became just "names on signs" as his service company convoy raced forward through the increasingly sloppy terrain. Both he and his film cans emerged unscathed.

By December, Elliott was in the city of Metz, in northern France, where the division enjoyed some R&R—that is, until events quickly interceded. On the 16th, German armored columns mounted a surprise counteroffensive, overrunning thinly stretched American lines across the Ardennes encircling the 101st Airborne in Bastogne, Belgium. The Battle of the Bulge was on. Elliott and Fitzsimmons and the 104th were trucked to an assembly area at Hobscheid, Luxembourg, near Belgium's eastern border.

On the 22nd, in a clinging morning mist, the 1st Battalion of the 104th Infantry advanced north on foot through the slushy, frozen hills and woods. Bob and Fitz's service company truck was to the rear. The suddenness of the operation precluded any viable intelligence about the enemy, other than that it was there—somewhere. By mid-morning, it had turned colder and was snowing. The objective was to reach the village of Buschrodt by nightfall.

After roughly sixteen miles, the advance was halted by heavy snow and an extremely dense forest. Its trails were not only confusing, but, by then, barely visible. The battalion commanding officer and a reconnaissance party—inexplicably, not including a radioman—went ahead in three Jeeps to scout out the terrain. About twelve hundred yards outside of the nearby tiny hamlet of Pratz, the lead Jeep halted at a small rise, with a clear view of the route forward. Suddenly, a blast of machine gun fire from the east raked the patrol, killing one and wounding another.

The sound was unmistakable to the CO's ears: the burst of the American Browning 30-caliber machine gun. Positive that it must have come from the 2nd Battalion of the 104th advancing on a parallel course to their right flank, he walked in the direction of the attack and shouted, "We are Americans, too! Stop firing!" When this was greeted with another salvo, the group dove for cover in a shallow roadside ditch.

Only then discovering they were without a radio, one of the men volunteered to crawl back to Pratz for help. After moving a short distance, he was spotted and wounded. Their only hope was to wait for darkness. It never came. A full, bright moon reflected off the glittering snow and lit up the night like a minor-league ballpark. All remaining options seemed to involve crawling. After a few tentative test moves, the men managed to slowly retreat into some woods about five hundred yards to the west and, after daybreak, found their way back into Pratz. So ended Day One of the 1st Battalion's exploits at the Battle of the Bulge. The command post was moved to Pratz, where Elliott and Fitz set up their PX operation in a barn behind a family's house.

The next day, weapons collected the previous night near Buschrodt from a surrendering German patrol—elements of the same unit that fired on the reconnaissance party—revealed why their machine guns sounded like American Browning automatics: That is exactly what they were.

To disrupt German intelligence, Elliott and the troops were ordered to rip off their blue and olive, Yankee Division YD patches. A complement of enemy Mark IV and Panther tanks lurked in the sector, as did columns of the *Volks Grenadier Division* and two companies of the elite *Führer Grenadier Brigade*. Rumors swirled of atrocities at the hands of German SS troops.

"I probably was in danger more than I realized," granted the unfailingly modest Elliott, adding that he had it "relatively easy and never fired a gun."

"I didn't have much chance to shoot a rifle there, either," Ralph Shirak recalled. "We were being shelled. . . . You were more aware of the snow and sleet and the ice than you were about anything else. The forest was so thick that many of the casualties were caused by shells hitting these giant trees and people getting killed by huge branches that came down."

The PX barn was packed with shipments of cigarettes. The supply line kept coming, Elliott recounted: "Toothbrushes, shaving cream—everything—and these poor guys were in foxholes up there, freezing to death." Supply sergeant Joe Gebo would return from the front every day to grab additional forty-carton cases of Luckies and Chesterfields. "They were using the unopened cigarette cartons," Elliott said, "not for smoking, but to pack around them as insulation in their frigid foxholes. They couldn't smoke; the pinpoint light of a cigarette could be seen a quarter-of-a-mile away." Sergeant Gebo also delivered daily reports of pitched battles in nearby villages of Eschdorf ("a meat-grinder," in Elliott's words, "terrible!"), Arsdorf, and Esch-sur-Sûre. All commanded approaches to vital bridge-heads on the Sure River, roughly seven miles forward.

Walking guard-duty shifts in sub-zero temperatures through Pratz's few desolate blocks in the middle of the night was lonely and creepy, Elliott recalled. There was a town hall, a church, very few stores, and no street lights. "There were long periods of no sound and then there'd be a flurry of exchange—probably artillery, mostly. Occasionally it would get a little closer. . . . That was scary."

Guard duty demanded constant vigilance against a tenacious enemy: fatigue. It was ever-present, as was the knowledge that, at any point, an officer could come by and check to see if you were awake. "You wouldn't know whether he would or not," Elliott said. "Often, he slept through the night." Like everyone, Elliott discovered his own methods to avoid falling asleep. Sometimes the sound of his chattering teeth kept him awake. Other nights, the powerful concussion from the new German rocket artillery known as *Nebelwerfer*—or, more technically, "Screaming Mimi"—helped.

The Bulge was finally pinched on January 25, 1945. As the enemy withdrew, the 26th hastily pulled out to follow Patton's push southeast. The crates of cigarettes were left stacked to the rafters; there were no available trucks to move them out.

The 104th crossed the Rhine on March 24, near Oppenheim. Special Services kept the film cans coming, sometimes not only the same titles, but the exact same prints, only with fewer and fewer sprocket holes re-maining. The unit's projector whirred on, with troops, by turns, nodding off and snapping awake as Tech-5 Elliott desperately fought to keep *Girl Crazy* in-sync, despite endless dropped frames. When the YD secured the city of Fulda, including its movie house the first week of April, GIs saw *Strike Up the Band* in the presence of some unexpected familiar touches of home: comfortable theater seats and sticky floors.

The 26th continued across central Europe, and, when the fighting stopped on the 7th of May, had already reached the Danube. After some occupation duty in Czechoslovakia, Elliott was assigned to the Armed Forces Radio station, KOFA, outside of Linz, Austria. It was in nearby Wels that Ralph Shirak, of A Company, recognized him from a sheet-music cover he had back in New Jersey.

He was walking near a truck, Shirak recalled, when "I walked up to him and shook his hand and said, 'You're Bob Elliott.' And he said, 'Yeah, I know.' . . . He had that same smile, which is half-smile, half-smirk. You could tell this is a guy you would really like to get to know; a gentle, kind person, but with a wit."

Sailing home from Marseilles in January 1946 on the deck of the converted Panamanian cruise ship S. S. *Christobal*, rough seas and fog in the Straight prevented Elliott from catching even a glimpse of the Rock of Gibraltar. "I was never in heavy battle, personally," Elliott said, reflecting on his days in uniform. "I was no hero. I gave out cigarettes." For this he earned the European Theater of Operations medal with four battle stars, a Good Conduct medal, the French *Fourragère de Croix de Guerre*, and a Regimental Bronze Star, on which is inscribed, "To Robert B. Elliott—For Distinguished or Outstanding Achievement."

"It must have been for 'Distinguished,'" he said, "not 'Outstanding'—maybe for splicing a piece of broken film." One almost unheard of achievement he is proud of is never once getting the reels of a movie out of sequence in a war zone.

There is "a bit of a cone of silence in terms of the past," said Bob's youngest son, Chris, sensing that his dad was "playing down" his contributions. The comedian and writer said his parents talked little about themselves, and certainly not about his father's war years. He added that he can only imagine the entire experience must have been more frightening than his dad has led him to believe, and that "possibly there were things he doesn't want to talk about. It's like how the Greatest Generation views what they did," Chris said. "He's not going to say anything he didn't do. But personally, just knowing him, I'm sure he saw things that were pretty horrific and just chalks it up to what everybody else was experiencing, and, probably in comparison, not as horrible."

In her husband's absence, Jane maintained a small public-relations business. Upon his return from the war, Bob resumed his WHDH staff duties, soon to be assigned an additional role of hosting the seven-to-nine morning slot, already bearing the title *Sunny Side Up*.

Raymond Walter Goulding grew up amid the textile factory smokestacks of Lowell, Massachusetts, in an Irish-Catholic family of five children. His dreams of becoming a sports announcer had been stoked by his five-year-older brother Phil's passion for radio and his own boyhood love of the Boston Red Sox. It was a love that sprang naturally from hours spent as a kid on the ball field at Hyland Park, just down the street from the family home at 323 Parker Street. During Ray's formative early years, the team's copious losing—twelve straight second-division finishes, nine of them dead last, including six consecutively—nicely laid the groundwork for a lifetime of perennial anguish and heartache. "On my headstone," Ray would later say, "has to be: 'Cause of death: Boston Red Sox.'"

Four of the Goulding kids attended Lowell High School, where Ray was in the same 1939 graduating class as Jack Kerouac. A campus legend, Kerouac was revered for having snatched a tipped pass inches from the ground and racing for the Red and Gray's winning touchdown in their annual Thanksgiving Day game against neighboring Lawrence.

Having had scarlet fever and high blood pressure as a kid, Phil's fragile health was a constant concern. "It's not that Phil wasn't well," his younger sister, Ann, said. "We always *thought* he wasn't." When Phil marched in the annual Lowell High School parade in his full ROTC uniform, a family member was strategically posted at each block in case he got sick. "Even after I got married," Ann added, "if the phone rang late at night, I'd say, 'Oh, my God, I hope it's not Phil!' I just had that feeling."

By winning a school public-speaking contest in connection with WLLH in Lowell, Phil landed an announcing job at the station. A few years later, Ray—possibly assuming the judges would be disinclined to select another winner from the same family—entered the contest using the name "Dennis Howard." He, too, won, nosing out fellow Lowell High student Ed McMahon. With his brother putting in a good word, Ray joined him on the WLLH announcing staff. He was seventeen; Phil, twenty-two.

Ann and her sister, Mary, nineteen years older, bracketed three middle brothers, Joe, Phil, and Ray, the latter born March 20, 1922. Ann came along nine years later, which, according to Ray's widow, Liz, was "kind of a shock." Their parents—Tom, a chief dyer in a woolen mill, and Mary (but always called "Mae"), a second cousin to Philip J. Philbin, fourteen-term Democratic U.S. Congressman from Massachusetts—were from the neighboring towns of Lancaster and Clinton, respectively.

Mae, who had only to touch her cheek to bring the children over for a kiss, was a sensational cook. So much so that her sister-in-law Ruth's family often dropped in after dinner to see what Aunt Mae had left to eat, a fact that says less about Mae's gastronomic delights than Auntie Ruth's disasters. Conversely, when Mae's kids visited their aunt and uncle (also named Phil), it was with a wary nose for a culinary calamity lying in wait. One especially unappetizing memory involved the Thanksgiving dinner at which Ann and Ray had some difficulty slicing a mincemeat pie Ruth had served them. "If you're having a hard time cutting it," Uncle Phil told them, "just hold it down with your foot." When Auntie Ruth's kitchen was painted, years of uneaten food furtively scraped off plates by her children was discovered stashed between the radiator and the wall.

Ray's paternal grandmother, after whom Ann had been named, had given birth to her first four children in the U.S. But, for Tom's arrival, she impulsively returned to the village of Portumna, in Galway. Thanks to this affection for the "old sod," no end of bureaucratic headaches ensued, with her youngest child forever deprived of U.S. citizenship.

Tom was never one to let an opportunity to be funny slip by, even—or especially—if it involved the use of props. A favorite family story had him preparing breakfast for Ray and Ann on school mornings and serving ridiculously tiny portions on his little sister's dollhouse dishes. The proud owner of the first radio on the block, Tom would set it on the front porch on a warm summer afternoon for the neighbors' listening pleasure.

Ray's second son, also named Tom, today a Connecticut chiropractor, fondly recounted that his dad and Phil once rigged a microphone in another room, leading out to the radio's speaker. According to Tom, when everyone was gathered around and their uncle Walter was visiting, "My dad said, 'Will Uncle Walter please go home!' It came out of the radio, so Walter got up and just took off. It was like he heard from God. . . . Dad also said he blew the radio out and got holy hell for that."

There was always a radio on in the house. One evening, as a teenager, Ray was babysitting Ann, and each insisted on listening to a different program on their father's new push-button model. It was an entire half-hour of pushing buttons, Ann said. "He'd push it for what he wanted and I'd pushed it for what I wanted. I was the brat."

Phil and Ray devoured Amos 'n' Andy, Jack Benny, Fred Allen—riveting voices in an exciting new world, and all the more alluring when balanced against Lowell's bleak 1930s reality. In the textile mills, the Depression, like a freeloading relative, showed up early and hung around forever. For Phil and Ray, the glamorous lure of broadcasting easily supplanted any career dreams of toiling in boiling acid dyebaths and inhaling polymer fiber lint.

One November day, WLLH's audience heard the rich, resonant voice of staff announcer Dennis Howard reading a commercial for a brand of tidies (round lace doilies), advising listeners "to decorate their Thanksgiving table with Aunt Tilley's gaudy titties." But only Tom and Mae knew that Dennis Howard was really their son Ray. Not wanting two Gouldings on the air, the station had insisted he keep his pseudonym. If not the family's proudest moment, it was certainly one of the most remembered.

At WLLH, Dennis Howard was tapped for all the usual beginners' tasks, such as emceeing movie theater dish-giveaway nights. Remotes involved Ray hauling all the equipment to the various sites himself. Another live report involved covering a possible suicide by someone threatening to leap off a building. Shielding his microphone was a struggle. "There was some guy in the crowd going, 'Jump, chicken! *Jump!*'" Ray's son Tom said. "That really galled him."

Another involved his play-by-play broadcast of a hockey game. "He didn't know a damn thing about the rules of hockey," his oldest son, Ray, Jr., recalled. "He said it was the worst thing he ever had to do." But Goulding would always claim his greatest WLLH embarrassment was taking his fifteen-dollar-a-week checks to the bank.

The tough times turned tragic at the start of 1941. On January 3, Ray's father died of a sudden heart attack. He had been cleaning the floor when he began to experience chest pains. Ray never believed in the veracity of that diagnosis. "My dad was not a big fan of doctors," said Tom, a doctor himself. "I always felt that he felt someone missed something." Then, only four and a half months later, Mae died of kidney disease (then called Bright's disease). Kidney ailments would shadow the family for generations. Phil, Ray, and Ann moved in with their older sister, Mary, and her husband, Paul, and their four kids. Adding to the family's tragic period of loss, just two days before Mae's untimely passing, Mary and Paul lost their five-month-old baby.

In August 1942, WEEI, the CBS-owned affiliate in Boston, suddenly had an opening on their announcer's staff. Phil, for the past year a WEEI employee, tipped his brother off; Ray auditioned and got the job. His replacement at WLLH was Ed McMahon. Six months later, when Phil auditioned at CBS in New York, the network had no openings. But impressed by his warm voice, they hired him anyway, initially assigning him to a couple of sustaining (unsponsored) programs, one starring Frank Sinatra.

Among Ray Goulding's WEEI duties were newscasts and local-station IDs between network shows, programs he would be spoofing just a few years later. For Ray, WEEI was definitely the Big Time. And, best of all, he was finally allowed to use his real name—or, at least half of it. He was now "Ray Howard." WEEI, like WLLH, did not want two Gouldings on the air. Only with his next assignment would he finally be permitted to go by Ray Goulding, thanks to a more compassionate employer—the U.S. Army.

Drafted before Thanksgiving 1942—a gig Ray landed without Phil putting in a word for him—he was off for basic training at Camp Pickett, Virginia, a converted CCC camp named after a Confederate general who graduated last in his West Point class, and whose division was annihilated at Gettysburg. Ray Goulding's attempts to get overseas were continually thwarted by a certain high-ranking officer, Colonel Moose, a career military man and an astute judge of character. Impressed with the young soldier's intellect and work ethic, Moose ordered Goulding, following basic training, to a succession of courses at prestigious universities. In one of these places of higher learning, he was the only student without a master's degree or doctorate. Other than increasing his knowledge, Liz Goulding commented, each course "did nothing for Ray. . . . It went on Colonel Moose's record and he retired as a two-star general, I believe."

Attending OCS at Camp Barkeley, a newly constructed post on 77,000 acres of dust in west central Texas, Goulding was commissioned before he was twenty-one. Like Bob Elliott, Ray Goulding was unfailingly modest, rarely discussing his military career. But, in 1943, Ray finally engaged enemy forces, no less than members of Hitler's elite Africa Korps. Never mind that they were German POWs at Fort Knox, Kentucky. His youngest son, Mark, recalled his father telling him that the prisoners under his command had believed that all of America had been leveled by bombing, and, upon entering New York Harbor, these misguided men thought the skyline was made up of false-front cutouts to deceive them.

"Dad was not a fan of Hitler," stated Mark's brother Tom, pointing out that when Ray bought his green Porsche in '58—a car he really enjoyed— it was "stretching his comfort zone."

Recalling her late husband's account of the Germans at Fort Knox, Liz added that a particularly arrogant POW assigned to Ray's office once called his attention to a magazine ad for Dutch Boy paints. It featured a picture of a beautiful house with a nice garden in front. "The POW," said Liz, "pointed to the photo and said: 'Someday *me*'—meaning here in America when the Germans win."

Captain Goulding was assigned to the camp's armored division's administrative medical corps at the Fort Knox hospital, where he taught medical protocol and procedures. It was the last thing any of his family would have expected, Liz said. "He couldn't even stand the sight of blood." His fellow officers and roommates were all professional men, including physicians and surgeons with extensive backgrounds. Most were in their forties, at least, according to Liz. Ray was viewed as their equal, but no one actually knew his age, she said. "At one point they even started a pool to guess how old he really was. No one ever guessed under thirty-one, and he never enlightened them. This was 1944; he was about twenty-two."

It was at Fort Knox that Ray met Liz, an elegant, stylish, tall, slim, engaging second lieutenant with warm eyes and shoulder-length dark brown hair. Mary Elizabeth Leader, a medical dietician with a master's degree from Ohio State, had grown up in Springfield, Ohio, where her father managed the GM bumper factory.

Liz had joined the Army, she said, in order "to go places and see the rest of the world." Kentucky, one state away, would be the extent of her military travels. The couple was fixed up on a blind date at an officers' club dance. Ray never managed to get her name straight the entire evening, calling her Lieutenant Lee, instead of Lieutenant Leader. On Sunday dates, she would sometimes accompany him to Louisville, where Ray moonlighted at a radio station. It was essentially a record show, but interspersed with a batch of what Liz described as "syrupy" poems that management forced him to read. Frequently, after reading one, Ray would switch off the mike for a second to make an appropriately inappropriate comment for Liz's benefit. Years later it would evolve into the concept for Ray's uncontrollably laughing character, Charles the Poet.

She was a very naïve and gullible twenty-two-year-old, Liz said, recalling a night when, working late, she received an urgent call from the post's CO, demanding that she open the officers' mess to feed a group of hospital brass who just got in from the West Coast. "I just blew my stack," Liz said. "At that hour of the night, there was nothing I could do. . . . Well, I said more than you should to an officer, but this was such an absurdity. . . . Of course, it turned out to be Ray, and there was no such thing. But he really got me furious."

She had a similar reaction the day they applied for their wedding license and Ray had to state his date of birth. "I was completely knocked over," she said. "He was like four months younger than I was. I wanted to kill him." On their wedding day, May 18, 1945, at the Fort Knox chapel, Ray was left at the altar—by his best man. At the last minute, Phil was bumped from his flight by a military priority traveler.

The following year, while expecting their first child, Liz experienced a bout of food poisoning, necessitating a frighteningly bumpy, labor-inducing ride in a vintage Army ambulance whose suspension system had itself been a battlefield casualty. "I just bounced and bounced," she said. "It was very rough." At the post hospital, Liz gave birth to a son, Raymond, Junior. The Gouldings brought him home when he was two months old. "He was a preemie baby, and so it was kind of touch-and-go there for a while," Liz said.

When Ray was discharged in the spring of 1946, he accepted an offer in Boston from WHDH, and the new family moved into "The Stork Club," a Lowell apartment house, so called for its exclusive occupancy by young marrieds with children. All Ray Goulding knew at that point was that, along with other staff assignments, including reporting the daily fish prices, he would be reading newscasts on the station's early morning program, *Sunny Side Up*, hosted by somebody named Bob Elliott.

3

THE OPPORTUNITY TO BE BAD

As Goulding's spontaneous on-air kibitzing with Elliott increased, what listeners heard was not a comedy team but, essentially, two neighbors talking over a fence. Where each of their riffs would lead was anybody's guess, including the ad-libbers' themselves, which was part of the attraction. Not only was it infectious, it was clearly at odds with the station's stuffy reputation.

In the years of Elliott's absence, WHDH continued tacking the old sea captain's programming coordinates of multiple, daily fish reports, cowboy bands, and programs heavy with Irish lore and songs. But that was about to change. In 1946, a buyer appeared in the name of the Herald Traveler Corporation. (The *Herald* was then the company's morning newspaper; the *Traveler*, the afternoon edition.) The publishing empire saw a lucrative broadcasting future; the Matheson family, getting on, saw a good deal.

Seeking a general manager to reinvent their new acquisition, the firm turned to New York, where, in the country's largest radio market, the pacesetter in taking on the networks had long been WNEW. The visionary behind its success was Bernice Judis, who had built the music-and-news format around a smart, cosmopolitan mix of engaging on-air personalities. "Tudie," as she was called, and who also had a share in ownership, had introduced radio's original disc-jockey program, Martin Block's *Make Believe Ballroom*. The day-to-day operation was in the hands of Tudie's program director, Ted Cott, and his protégé, a tall, imperially slim New Yorker named William B. McGrath.

Given a chance to run his own station, McGrath leapt at the opportunity. His mandate from the Herald was clear: Make over their musty, old "electrified fish house" in the image of WNEW. Once tuning in, McGrath did not need much convincing. The cowboy bands were the first to be tossed, followed by *The Boy from Ireland*, Terry O'Toole. Irish tenor Adrian O'Brien and his wife, Alice O'Leary, were also sent packing, as was the very British Jeffrey Harwood's ponderous late-night commentaries, and Robert Shimmel's uplifting, philosophical readings. But dumping the onerous *Fisherman's News Service* proved to be a bit thorny. When it was pointed out that these broadcasts had been the FCC's proviso for the station's license to boost the power to five thousand watts, McGrath was forced to compromise. The fish-market reports remained, though banished to just the early-morning and late-night hours.

The antiquated Hotel Touraine setup was deemed a pathetic match to WNEW's sparkling Fifth Avenue home. Certainly, McGrath could not recall WNEW newsmen ever having to race into the men's room every time they needed wire copy. He talked the company into acquiring spacious new, state-of-the-art studios on the eighth floor of the Paine Furniture Building in Park Square.

Navy veteran and WHDH music director, Ken Wilson, was commissioned to build the most complete record library in Boston radio, which, in turn, required personalities to introduce them. McGrath brought in Fred B. Cole, who had enjoyed a long run at Boston's WBZ, and, for a time, had traveled with Tommy Dorsey as the announcer on the band's dance remotes. Cole's *Carnival of Music* from ten o'clock in the morning to noon would be a fixture at the station for twenty-one years.

With Cole's show in place, McGrath invited staffers to submit concepts. Elliott presented a demo for *Back Bay Matinee*, based on a program he had heard in the Army, *Music Made in the U.S.A.* McGrath bought it. Elliott hosted *Back Bay Matinee* every afternoon from two to four, as well as a twelve o'clock-noon *Bing Crosby Show*, using his own Crosby record collection. Unlike the morning banter with Goulding, there was no pretense of comedy. He was strictly the genial, upbeat DJ—informed, cheerful, and a master of all segues. With *Matinee* and *Sunny Side Up*, Elliott had gone from staff announcer to disc jockey and a raise from $28 a week to $35, plus a share of the commercial spots.

Another staff man, former attorney Bob Clayton, also proposed a DJ concept: At four o'clock every afternoon, Benny Goodman's signature tune "Let's Dance" introduced Clayton's *Boston Ballroom*. If the obvious link to WNEW's original *Make Believe Ballroom* was lost on Clayton's largely teenage audience, it certainly was not lost on McGrath, who, as Fred Cole put it, tailored his programs to ones "that he'd heard elsewhere." WNEW's New York transmitter functioned as a virtual GPS for many radio stations.

Publishers, song pluggers, and name bandleaders stroked the jocks' egos by plying them with gifts and plastering their pictures on sheet music. Elliott made the covers of "Heartaches" and "Underneath the Arches," among others, and, he added, never succeeded in getting the floating picture of Sammy Kaye out of his transparent, liquid-filled, gift cigarette lighter.

Listening to Elliott and Goulding's byplay each morning, Bill McGrath sensed that he had found something he could develop. Before the year was out, he sold a short-lived fifteen-minute portion of *Sunny Side Up* to the National Biscuit Company, spotlighting "those two zany characters—Bob Elliott and Ray Goulding." This segment, beginning at seven-fifteen in the morning, interspersed with records, featured the twosome essentially playing themselves. Their characters were still in the wings. They were genial, quippy, and even sang an occasional duet. The pace was fast and the material was mostly one-liners ("The Pentagon building—Texas with washrooms"), and mostly borrowed.

To Ray Goulding's delight, pennant fever gripped New England throughout the summer of 1946. His beloved Red Sox jumped out to a 21–4 start, including a fifteen-game winning streak—the longest in the team's history—capturing the American League flag by twelve games. In the process, many WHDH listeners found their way to rival WNAC, since 1925 the town's baseball station, carrying the Braves and Red Sox home games. However, the following year, McGrath wrestled the broadcast rights—including the popular play-by-play team of Jim Britt and Tom Hussey—away from WNAC, starting with the 1947 season. It was a real coup, and, given the ad bundle from longtime sponsors, the Narragansett Brewing Company and Atlantic Refining Company, WHDH was eager to promote its new baseball package.

Bill McGrath had the uncanny ability of walking down the hall just as someone was about to leave the studio. His standard salutation was, "Got a minute?" Cornering Elliott and Goulding one morning, he proposed a regular slot for the two, a structured, twenty-minute pre-game show, *Baseball Matinee*, featuring the pair's on-air repartee. And instead of records, there would be live music. Not incidentally, a premium rate would be charged for advertisers. Familiar with McGrath's M.O., Elliott and Goulding assumed that the notion sprang from his desire to emulate WNEW's success with Jack Lescoulie and Gene Rayburn—*Jack and Gene*. The operative word for McGrath being "team."

The premiere of *Baseball Matinee*, the debut of Elliott and Goulding's first real program as a billed team—but not yet called Bob and Ray—went on the air at one-thirty-five, on Friday afternoon, April 11, 1947, preceding the first game of the city's annual weekend exhibition series between the Red Sox and Braves. The official season opener four days later would be a date for the ages. By taking the field against the Braves on April 15, the Dodgers' Jackie Robinson—in baseball's "noble experiment"—integrated the game forever. No one singular contest in any sport has had such a lasting cultural impact. It was all McGrath could have asked for to inaugurate his new baseball package—except for a revised contract. Because the Braves game was in Brooklyn, Jackie Robinson's debut was not heard in Boston. Locked into airing only the home team's games, WHDH was obliged to carry the Red Sox Fenway Park opener, by contrast a yawner against the lowly Washington Senators.

If you wanted baseball in Boston in 1947, you had to tune to 850 and WHDH, where fans also stumbled into Elliott and Goulding and their freeform parodies, voices, dialects, and crudely fashioned, live sound effects. If they stumbled in the first or second time, they started tuning in again soon after.

"It just evolved, really," Goulding told *Encore*'s Danny McCue in 1987. "We'd use a voice, or do a character. . . . We just talked and stumbled on to something, and if we didn't, so what? People knew you were off the top of your head so they were kind of *with* you anyway, if they listened to you at all. I often wondered if we were talking to ourselves." Unlike many performers starting out today, Goulding pointed out, "We had the opportunity to be bad."

With all of their other station assignments, there was simply not enough time to prepare material, or even to steal it. When they had a few minutes, they did write—Elliott typed, Goulding paced—brief sketches and spoofs of commercials, as from an April 18, 1947 script: "Be sure to stock up on several bottles of that cool, refreshing thirst-quencher, DRAWROF. Remember, DRAWROF spelled backwards, reads FORWARD."

Among the team's embryonic fictional characters was Mary McGoon, then called Mary Margaret McGoon, a composite of all radio women's editors. Liz said that her husband patterned the character after the long-time afternoon radio talk show hostess, Mary Margaret McBride. "It was a complete takeoff on her."

Elliott always pictured *The Cuckoo Hour*'s Mrs. Pennyfeather as the Mary McGoon template, noting that many comedians have since done similar characters. Ray's was more of "a real person," he said, yet she could also be "completely wacky." Goulding's textured falsetto completely embodied the character. Every word out of Mary's mouth—as she offered recipes for "imitation grape drink" or "fried rice popsicles"—was grounded in her own giddy reality. More than once, according to Elliott, his partner had remarked that Mary McGoon also served as the voice of their collective conscience. "There were times," he said, "when we were skidding along and it was Ray, hearing something that wasn't going well, and *she* would get us out of it."

Elliott's twangy-voiced cowboy, Tex Blaisdell, whose chief talent seemed to be performing rope tricks on radio, was also one of the originals. Sincere and good-natured, Tex, along with his Smoky Valley Boys, was a creature of the rodeo circuit, often pointing out, "I'm not with the rodeo—I'm *behind* it." Elliott patterned the voice after cowboy singer and actor Ray Whitley, who, like Jimmy Wakely and others, stopped by WHDH to plug his yearly Boston Garden Rodeo appearances.

Since the new program was a prelude to the afternoon's Red Sox or Braves broadcast, a sportscaster character, Steve Bosco, was introduced. Voiced by Goulding, Bosco's high-pitched voice matched his high-strung personality. The premise was in place from the beginning: Phoning in, Bosco would abruptly interrupt his flimsy baseball report, always a pretense for his real motive—a desperate need for cash (the result of some financial scrape, usually involving bad checks) to be wired to him immediately "in care of the most expensive hotel" in whatever city from which he was calling.

At the time, Arthur Godfrey's easily identifiable voice was all over the CBS radio dial, so Elliott's Arthur Sturdley character was a natural. "I smoked like a chimney in those days; we both did," Elliott said. "And that gave me a better Godfrey voice than I could ever do now." Many performers were imitating Godfrey then, and a few were exceptionally funny, but *nobody* did Arthur Godfrey like Bob Elliott. The characterization was devastatingly accurate, right down to Godfrey's ever-present little chuckle and his question mark-like "huh" tacked onto the end of every other sentence. The bits were always accompanied by Goulding mimicking Godfrey's pretentious, trumpet-voiced announcer, Tony Marvin, doing his best to stay out of the star's way ("Sorry, Arthur . . .").

Other enduring characters would soon follow, including the blundering reporter Wally Ballou (Elliott) and his occasional, equally incompetent "broadcasting partner," Artie Schermerhorn (Goulding); but these four belong in the founders' circle. Their voices would suddenly appear out of nowhere, offer a comment or two, and then disappear just as quickly. However, in sharp contrast to what would later evolve, the more promi-nent characters on *Baseball Matinee* were Elliott and Goulding as Elliott and Goulding—irreverent, antic, and incorrigible. Their spontaneous, playful interaction and camaraderie was the drive shaft of the program. More often than not, they intuitively grasped each other's rhythms; other times they stepped on each other's toes. It didn't seem to matter. Advertisers climbed aboard.

Two additional characters—real, not imaginary—were Ken and Bill, who provided the live music. Ken Wilson had been WHDH's musical director and staff organist dating back to the early Matheson days. Pianist Bill Green, possessor of a sharp sense of humor, was a local fixture, for years performing standards and show tunes at the Ritz-Carlton and Copley Plaza hotels. He was also an arranger and member of Sammy Eisen's band at the Somerset Hotel. In addition to being excellent musicians, the two, perhaps even more importantly, proved to be excellent comedic foils.

Elliott and Goulding were perfecting an identity and style, but, by early July, key elements, as *Boston Herald* columnist Rudolph Elie, Jr., then observed, were already in place, noting "their sense of the ludicrous, of the satirical, of the nonsensical."

Baseball Matinee was starting to make some noise, unquestionably goosed by an exciting summer with Sox slugger Ted Williams becoming only the second player in history to win a second triple crown. At the end of the season, McGrath, not wanting to upset listening habits, kept the pair in the same afternoon time slot. By so doing, and thanks to an easy rhyme, Elliott and Goulding's billing was forever set. Beginning on Monday, September 29, 1947, the now-half-hour-long program became *Matinee with Bob and Ray*. Full-page ads declared it: "Your date with daffiness!" Hereafter on these pages, in addition to the journalistic "Elliott and Goulding," and the more familiar "Bob and Ray," the pair will also be referred to—just as they were by broadcasting colleagues for over four decades—as "B&R," or, affectionately, "the boys."

On a visit to New York, where Phil was now at WMGM, Ray had been impressed by his brother's brand-new Packard. Soon after, he had one, too. If anyone could sell a product, it was Phil Goulding. "For young marrieds," Liz said, "it was kind of a big step. We had Packards until they stopped making them."

The Elliotts purchased a home on Boston's south shore. Fred Cole, a resident of Hingham, and Phil Goulding's equal when it came to a sales pitch, talked them into buying in neighboring Cohasset. The Gouldings' first house was in Lexington.

Commuting to WHDH from opposite sides of the city, B&R relied on their car radios for inspiration for parodies of popular network shows. The world of broadcasting was the controlling principal. Radio was not only their medium, it was their subject matter—radio about radio; it was what they knew. Their *John J. Agony's Bad Will Hour* mocked the smarmy John

J. Anthony and his guests' personal problems. (*Guest:* "I came to the city six-months ago with my life savings in a pillow case . . ." *John J. Agony:* "Hold on! Let me see if I have your story straight to this point . . .") *Dr. O.K.—The Sentimental Banker* took aim at the popular quiz show, *Dr. I.Q.* ("Congratulations! A box of Snickers to that lady! What size Snickers do you wear?") Daytime audience high-jinx shows, such as *Breakfast at Sardi's* and *Ladies Be Seated*, were more or less the starting points for *Ladies Grab Your Seats*, with Ray as the fluttery, elderly women contestants interviewed by Bob as the bubbly, hyper-genial emcee, an amalgam of Tom Breneman, Bud Collyer, and Johnny Olson, with a nod to Dennis James, the inspiration for his occasionally addressing the women as "Mother."

The team's first continuing soap opera, *The Life and Loves of Linda Lovely*—a title selected simply for its alliteration—lampooned all aspects of the genre, including the dramatic device of contriving an arbitrary significance to a certain object, then referring to it for weeks before shamelessly making it available as a premium offer to hype ratings. ("Linda, what a beautiful simulated sterling, heart-shaped, genuine imitation love brooch you're wearing. I'll bet your friends would love to have one of those.")

The parodies, and many others, had been incubating before the two even met. In addition to discovering the Fred Allen, Jack Benny and Vic and Sade mainstream, they had also ferreted out and studied favorite lesser-known, rank-and-file performers. "I think I emulated Stoopnagle and Budd [Frederick Chase Taylor and Wilbur Budd Hurlick] more than anyone else," Ray once observed. "Those guys were hysterical."

"They were like a radio Laurel and Hardy to us," Bob said. "They did far-out stuff. Stoopnagle's the one who originated, 'An eleven-foot pole for people I wouldn't touch with a ten-foot pole.'" He was impressed, too, by Phil Cook, who, beginning in 1929 on numerous series on the NBC Blue and, later, on CBS quarter-hour programs, nimbly darted between dozens of character voices and dialects; he even sang and accompanied himself on the ukulele. Other inspiring voices included Gene and Glenn (Gene Carroll and Glenn Rowell), a close-harmony singing-and-comedy act who performed on early radio, in vaudeville, and on records; their 1930s fifteen-minute NBC Red programs featured sketches centered on a fictional boarding house, with Glenn as himself, and Gene voicing the characters. B&R were also devotees of the British comedy-and-singing twosome, Flanagan and Allen, (Bud Flanagan and Chesney Allen), whose discs Bob later played so often on *Sunny Side Up* that his picture ended up on their sheet music. Bob and Ray also enjoyed the popular New England radio, vaudeville, and nightclub song-and-patter double-act, Hum and Strum (Max Zides and Tom Currier), who, accompanying themselves on ukulele and piano, performed comedy songs and standards. Hum and Strum, both Boston natives, became instant *Matinee*-parody fodder.

Growing up, Elliott and Goulding had absorbed all of broadcasting's conventions and nuances. As teenagers, they were perfecting impressions of the personalities, characters, correspondents, and announcers. They not only knew the shows and all the trappings, they knew what was funny about them. *Matinee's* takeoffs were conjured from their own individual fascinations.

The audience's familiarity with what was being lampooned was not a prerequisite. One need never have endured NBC's long-running *Mr. Keen, Tracer of Lost Persons'* clumsy exposition to appreciate *Mr. Trace, Keener Than Most Persons* ("You, standing there behind that heavy purple curtain with your feet sticking out, casting the silhouette of a gun!"). For that matter, the listener did not need to be familiar with CBS's *Aunt Jenny's Real Life Stories*, with Jenny and ebullient announcer Dan Seymour's non-stop savoring of her baked delicacies, the chief ingredient being (sponsor) Spry shortening, to connect with *Aunt Penny's True-to Life* stories ("Help yourself to another gingerbread cookie, Danny. They're made with light, digestible chicken fat. It'll sit in your stomach like a half-dollar piece").

The takeoffs neither pretended to be meticulously faithful to their source, nor even finely crafted. They were of the moment, created at the same time they were being broadcast and, as Rudolph Elie wrote in the *Herald*, about "anything that pops into their heads." If they sensed that a bit was tanking, they would bail out in the middle, or even weave the copy of the next commercial into the plot. A sound effect of a howling dog in an episode of *Jack Headstrong, All-American American* might reflexively trigger Bob to pivot into his Basil Rathbone voice, which, in turn, would launch Ray into his Nigel Bruce, and suddenly they would be off on a *Sherlock Holmes* jag. That a sketch would suddenly be aborted never violated the integrity of the piece because it had no integrity. It was a lark, a fanciful tangent. By mocking the subject's pretensions, Bob and Ray, themselves so unpretentious, made it inherently comical. When it worked, that is.

"Those shows sound so amateurish today," Elliott reflected. "It was sloppy—very sloppy. I mean, I'm embarrassed, but nobody cared, particularly."

Signing off over their theme music one day, Ray shouted, "Write if you get work," a phrase long familiar to readers of *Billboard* magazine's personal ads—a message-forwarding service for traveling performers. Another afternoon, he happened to say it again, and, from out of nowhere, added, "And hang by your thumbs." Other than filling out the show's closing seconds, it had absolutely no significance. Ray continued to say it—except on days when he didn't. Only later, as B&R's format became tidier, would it become their regular sign-off. Significant or not, it ultimately turned up in *Bartlett's Familiar Quotations*. It was Ray, too, who out of the blue came up with "sturdley," which in the team's early years became an all-purpose word used as a proper name, an adjective, or anything.

On the coattails of another magical baseball season, WHDH's billings' soared. The Braves, perennial doormats since the first Wilson administration, won their first pennant in thirty-four years. The American League race came down to an anguishing Red Sox one-game-playoff loss to the Indians, denying the city a 1948 all-Boston World Series.

In addition to *Matinee*, B&R soldiered on with their other staff duties. For a period, Goulding hosted a musical program with Tommy Dorsey, chatting with the bandleader between numbers—in this instance, on records—another legacy of the McGrath-WNEW pipeline. The New York station was steeped in the Big Band sound. Ray also briefly joined Tiny Ruffner—onetime pitchman for Fred Allen and Al Jolson—on a morning, housewives-targeted, half-hour comedy, *Kitchen Kapers*, a plum assignment paying an extra twenty dollars a show.

It remains murky as to whether it was Elliott or McGrath who hatched the concept for *Breakfast with the Elliotts*, in which listeners supposedly eavesdropped on Bob and Jane around the breakfast table. Such husband-and-wife programs had long been the rage in New York, notably with

Breakfast with Dorothy and Dick (Dorothy Kilgallen and Dick Kollmar) on WOR, which suggests it was McGrath's idea. If so, it also suggests that he was open-minded enough to lift a concept from a station other than WNEW.

Bob found an obscure Alvino Rey tune, "Breakfast for Two," recorded by a boy-girl duo (often assumed by listeners to be Bob and Jane) to introduce the show. Each morning Bob and Jane traded views on a few shallow subjects and threw in a record or two. McGrath sold the show to Boston's venerable department store, Jordan Marsh. But after a few weeks, it became apparent that Jane suffered from one serious shortcoming for such a program: She hated to get up in the morning. "And things were kind of falling apart personally," Bob added.

Finally, Jane's late arrivals, together with some complete absences, led to the hiring of an actress, Dolly Springer, to portray Jane. Springer proved ideal for the role and soon was even contributing scripts for the show, which continued for the better part of a year. Listeners never noticed the change.

In New York, WMGM, "The Call Letters of the Stars," was in need of a one-time fill-in for comedian Morey Amsterdam's nightly show. In yet another deal with Phil Goulding's unseen fingerprints all over it, Bob and Ray got the call. Phil, then in his fifth year at WMGM, just happened to be the program's announcer. He was kind of "a smaller version of Ray in size," Bob said of his partner's next-oldest sibling. "I think I would have picked him out as Ray's brother. . . . Phil was a very funny guy—he had a similar sense of humor. It was always fun when Phil was around, and Ray really adored him."

Friday evening, January 14, 1949, in front of a packed audience at the station's just-renovated 711 Fifth Avenue studios, backed by Joel Herron's orchestra, Bob and Ray made their New York radio debut. The sketches, introduced by Phil, included "Dr. O.K.," "Linda Lovely," and a mock offer for a beginner's burglar kit. All sparked screams. We were "very warmly received," Ray later wrote to a friend, calling the show "our stab at being discovered." Before heading home, the group adjourned around the corner to L'Aiglon on East 55th for a celebration dinner.

The two now began to reconsider public appearances. When visiting song pluggers raved to them about Martin & Lewis killing the crowds at their recent Copacabana debut, the boys could never really see themselves pulling off Dean and Jerry shtick, tossing glasses of water in each other's face and careening around the room, knocking over busboys' trays and smashing stacks of dishes. But they were now less reluctant when bandleader Sammy Eisen urged them to work up an act for Boston's Somerset Hotel. They started throwing together some material, mostly converted radio bits they had tried out at college appearances. Within weeks, an opening date was set.

In his Cohasset garage, Elliott built a wooden frame on a stand to represent a television screen in which they would perform some early TV spoofs. Not included in the preparations was a careful check of the calendar. The sudden discovery that opening night was not just any Wednesday, but Ash Wednesday, came as a total shock. All but a handful of the hotel's kitchen staff was promised that they would be allowed to leave early. In Boston, Lent was a time for doing penance, not going to nightclubs, unless, the boys rationalized, seeing their act *was* doing penance. Still, there was no shortage of choices for those seeking nightlife: Chandra Kaly and His Dancers at the Copley Plaza, Johnnie Johnston at the Latin Quarter—and Archbishop Richard Cushing packing them in at St. Cecilia's.

Wednesday, March 2, 1949, a large and expectant audience in the Somerset's Balinese Room greeted the two in their rental tuxedos as Eisen played them on with their *Matinee* theme, "Collegiate." Bob's Arthur Godfrey impersonation was surefire, as was his Harry Truman, coming only weeks after his inaugural. The show-stopper, however, was Ray's being interviewed as the man behind the huge Camel cigarette billboard at Kenmore Square, blowing smoke rings from three lit cigarettes between paroxysms of convulsive coughing. "You had to see him do it," Elliott said. "It went over tremendously. . . . He couldn't talk afterwards." The engagement was extended an additional week, ending shortly before the birth of the Gouldings' second child, Tom, on April 7.

At the station, chairs were set up to accommodate listeners who began showing up to watch the broadcasts. Their laughter served as an open invitation for others to stop by. The ratings continued to skyrocket. Of course, it did not hurt that WHDH's major independent rival, WORL, had its FCC license revoked for knowingly concealing information—specifically, the names of the station's owners. McGrath signed the boys for an additional two years. In August, they rejoined Sammy Eisen and his band for a one-night-only appearance at The Casino at Magnolia, a popular North Shore summer destination, and, conveniently, a *Matinee* sponsor. These things happen. Promoting the event on the air, B&R urged Casino patrons to approach Eisen with their musical requests. "You'll easily recognize Sammy," they said, "by the coin changer on his belt."

Such appearances, they felt, would further advance Bob and Ray as a double-barreled commodity, if only a local one. Somehow, they figured it would all pay off. But precisely how, they did not have a clue. There was no game plan, or business model. They had no agent (unless you count Phil Goulding), no manager, or even an attorney. If they had, they would not have performed so many free college dates before discovering that there was serious money to be made, especially in a university town like Boston.

They would also have avoided being exploited by slippery, small-time promoters, including one Roger Sass, who was seeking investors in a pre-stuffed-frozen-lobster enterprise. Tapping into B&R's WHDH popularity, Sass hired the team for a Friday- and Saturday-night appearance, at twenty-five dollars each, for both nights at the Sportsman's Club. This was "a roadhouse," Bob called it, "way the hell off in the woods" somewhere outside of Attleboro, Massachusetts, near the Rhode Island line. It took each of them forever to find the place, which had about fifty tables and featured a large supermarket-type freezer case along one wall.

Sass was thrilled with the Friday night turnout, Bob said. "Usually, if we played a place two nights in a row, we'd get paid each night. The tip-off with this guy was he said, 'I'll pay you both tomorrow after the second show,' which we didn't want to do. We needed the twenty-five bucks apiece whenever we could get it. But, we said, 'Okay,' and found our way home, late. And then we're down there the next night, and [there was] another good crowd. . . . So then he wants to give us a check. We were usually paid in cash; we were very upset. He was going to give us some lobsters, too. We didn't take them."

In retrospect, they should have. Not surprisingly, Sass's checks bounced, and the local police—a couple of whom B&R suspected had been present at one of the shows and signed up as investors—did nothing. "We never did get the money that I can remember," Bob said. "What could we do? We weren't going to go to McGrath because half of these things we did, he never knew about."

In their hearts, the pair could not foresee nightclubs in their future. Becoming recording artists seemed similarly alien, though occasionally on *Matinee* they continued to sing vocals of standards, such as "How About You?" and "Who's Sorry Now?" But in the fall of 1949 they took a chance, the catalyst being a parade of "cover" records of the Frankie Laine hit, "Mule Train." Versions were issued by Vaughn Monroe, Bing Crosby, and others, including Mary McGoon.

After first performing it live on the program, requests poured in for Mary to repeat the number; some even suggested that she put it on record. Finally, Ray recorded it in Mary's voice, joined on the choruses by Elliott as Tex Blaisdell. Bill Green provided the piano accompaniment. On the flip side, Mary sang, "I'd Like to be a Cow in Switzerland," with music and lyrics by Charles and Nick Kenny. ("I'd like to be a cow in Switzerland / Where the grass is always green / Where the hunters hide behind the trees / Shooting holes in good ol' Switzer cheese.") With McGrath's okay—in exchange for a cut—the record was highly promoted on the station. But when the pressed discs arrived shortly before Christmas, there was no shipping operation in place. Finally, Sam Clark, an owner of a small Boston record distributorship with a taste for offbeat labels, let the boys use his basement. Night after night, after their regular WHDH shifts, the two processed all mail-order requests themselves, including packaging and mailing, in Clark's garage. Everyone involved—including McGrath—made out okay. Sam Clark went on to become the head of ABC Records.

Participating in broadcasting's culture of inspired practical jokes demanded one prerequisite: the ability to channel one's mind-set to that of a fiendish thirteen-year-old. Few failed to qualify, including B&R. One of their early victims was Bob DeLaney, an ex-Marine and WHDH's late-night host. Before later becoming more identified as a play-by-play man for the Red Sox and New York Giants, DeLaney's recorded spots for Slippery Elm throat lozenges were played incessantly on *Matinee*, provoking the pair to advise listeners who were not completely satisfied with the product to "simply return the remaining portion of your lozenge to: Bob DeLaney, care of WHDH, Boston." Listeners happily complied.

Following a college appearance one night, the two tuned in to DeLaney's late-night program of soft, romantic music. Bob, who had mastered a convincing Bill McGrath imitation, called the control room, demanding to speak to DeLaney. "I got a bunch of Marine guys here for the weekend at my house in Melrose," Bob, as McGrath, told DeLaney. "Just for them, could you please play 'Semper Fidelis'?'"

Delaney reminded him, "This is *Music for Dreaming*."

"But they want to hear 'Semper Fidelis,'" Bob repeated. "Get it on fast."

DeLaney dutifully complied, and suddenly, in the middle of *Music for Dreaming*, on came "Semper Fidelis." Before it ran the full three minutes, Bob said, McGrath got to DeLaney. "He was always listening."

WHDH's eighth-floor setup allowed staffers to see directly across Arlington Street, right into the rooms of the neighboring Statler Hotel. We saw "many activities that were worthy of note," Bob said, recalling an episode with a group of hotel conventioneers directly opposite, on the same floor of the hotel. Spotting some of the WHDH secretaries, the group scribbled a sign, "We're from *Life* magazine. What's your phone number? We're in room 817." Ray then called room service at the Statler, informing them that he was with the *Life* group, and ordered eight steaks, medium rare, to be sent to 817. A succession of calls ensued, including Ray phoning the kitchen, supposedly from room 817, asking, "Where's our eight steaks?" Next, imitating the chef, he called the room, explaining that the waiter was on his way up and dropped three of the steaks, but assured them that they were still perfectly good. Confused, the *Life* man said, "We didn't order any steaks."

"A little later," Bob said, "we see the guys going to the door and a waiter is there with eight steaks. . . . We did an hour and a half with those guys."

Many guests on that side of the Statler, seeing that Paine's Furniture store closed at six at night, left their shades up, never realizing that a radio station was directly opposite, maybe only a hundred feet away. Those few individuals working WHDH late shifts, on nights after Jim Britt and Tom Hussey returned from calling the ballgame, passed around Tom's powerful binoculars—that is, once *he* finished ogling—to check out what Bob called the "unusual, personal, pigeon-eye-views."

By now the story is familiar: A Boston jock, just discharged from the service, discovers that he and his ex-GI newsman share a unique sense of humor and form a comedy team. Only, in 1959, the Boston disc jockey was George Carlin, the newsman was Jack Burns, and the station was WEZE.

As a Boston teenager at Brookline High, Jack Burns discovered *Matinee* and spread the word. "I would go around to every kid and just say, 'You've got to hear these guys, Bob and Ray,'" he recalled. "So we had, like, a Bob and Ray fan club in Brookline."

They were, Burns said, the "motivating factor for my interest in comedy." It was an interest that would ultimately lead Burns to Second City and, with fellow member Avery Schreiber, the creation of their classic Irish bigot taxicab routines, dozens of variety-show guest appearances, and their own ABC television series.

Bob and Ray made "the ordinary and the mundane hilarious," Burns said. "It was the simplicity of it that I loved. . . . I would fall apart at the age of twelve, thirteen, or fourteen. . . . They were the hippest, I thought—before the word 'hip' was around—they were hip."

During Burns and Carlin's late-'50s and early-'60s radio stints in Boston, Fort Worth, and L.A., Bob and Ray-influenced bits were inevitable. "We didn't steal directly," Burns said, but, citing a sportscaster piece the two often performed, he felt it probably had a "reminiscence of Steve Bosco 'rounding third and being thrown out at home.'"

It was at roughly the same age that Jonathan Schwartz, visiting Boston with his father, Broadway composer Arthur Schwartz, sat in their room at the Ritz-Carlton, scanning the dial for the Red Sox station. "I was always with, or searching for, a radio," said Jonathan, "and I discovered Bob and Ray. Even at that age, I knew they were telling me the truth. . . . It made a twelve-year-old boy understand them, and laugh with them." That twelve-year-old boy would one day become a broadcasting fixture himself, even if, at the time, he was the only one who knew it.

While Jack Burns's Bob and Ray fan club was confined to Brookline High, the longtime *Los Angeles Times* Arts editor and critic, Charles Champlin, then a student at Harvard, later wrote of a "curious paralysis" that came over the college each afternoon when *Matinee* was on. "Otherwise sensible upperclassmen rushed to their radios. . . . No one took one o'clock classes." There were even attempts by the students, Champlin noted, to sound like the team's various characters. "It was all very silly stuff, parodying radio at its most sincerely fatuous. The voices were wonderful, and Bob and Ray manifestly such pleasant and unassertive performers."

❦

Programming WHDH, Bill McGrath trusted his intuition, at least when it reflected WNEW. Therefore, it was inevitable that, in 1950, he expanded B&R's air-time, adding a new daily show, *Breakfast with Bob and Ray*, from six-thirty to nine o'clock in the morning. A two-man morning team, of course, was right out of Bernice Judis's WNEW playbook. As Ray once remarked, their on-air time "kept spreading, like a fungus." It was nearly impossible to find time to throw together some material when the Somerset Hotel, eager to repeat the previous year's success, again booked the duo, this time for two weeks. One rehearsal, at Bob's home in Cohasset, had to be scrapped when Ray's allergy to cats suddenly flared up. Bob and Jane had two, one of which had just had a litter of four or five. Finally, a watery-eyed Ray, sneezing his brains out, jumped in his Packard and fled back to Lexington.

The engagement sold out both weeks. One of those unable to attend was the leader of Brookline High's Bob and Ray fan club, Jack Burns. "I was too young," he said, recalling the spring night he waited outside on Commonwealth Avenue, hoping to get their autographs. "But I didn't have a paper or a pen, so they spoke to me," he recounted. "They said, 'We'll give you a verbal autograph. I'm Bob and I'm Ray—thanks for standing out here.' And I thought—'wow!'"

···

As WHDH continued to command an ever-larger market share under McGrath's stewardship, at the networks, the terrain was shifting. CBS chairman William S. Paley had become increasingly frustrated at trailing his more established rival, NBC, which attracted the bigger entertainment names, particularly the comedy stars and the higher ratings that went with them. In late 1948, however, Paley's tax gurus proposed the concept of his network purchasing top performers' programs as "properties" or "packages," in effect, turning the performers into their own corporations and allowing them to pocket a substantial tax cut at the 25 percent capital-gains rate. The upper bracket for earnings over seventy thousand dollars was then a gouging 77 percent.

Almost immediately, Freeman Gosden and Charles Correll, creators and stars of *Amos 'n' Andy*, bolted from NBC after nineteen years. Then, in Paley's biggest coup, on January 2, 1949, Jack Benny, a sixteen-year NBC Sunday-night radio institution, defected to CBS. The announcement "shook the industry," Paley observed in his 1979 memoir. In the 1949–50 season, Bing Crosby, George Burns & Gracie Allen, Red Skelton, and Edgar Bergen & Charlie McCarthy all jumped ship to CBS, further jarring the networks' ecosystem.

To a great extent, the "Paley raids," as they came to be known, reflected the two network chairmen's respective personas. NBC's General David Sarnoff harbored a disdain for the show-business aspect of broadcasting. According to his biographer, Kenneth Bilby, Sarnoff confided to an associate, "A business built on a few comedians isn't a business worth being in." Paley's programming instincts mirrored his own taste. He liked popular entertainers, reported his biographer, Sally Bedell Smith. To Paley, David Sarnoff was "a hardware man in a software business."

The NBC defections had an immediate affect on listening habits. Fred Allen, who, with Bob Hope, remained at the network, said, "My blood pressure was getting higher than the show's ratings, and it was a question of which one of us would survive."

In the spring of 1951, yet another network talent raid would be pulled off, this one with Elliott and Goulding as the principals. With each then pulling down $135 on a good week at WHDH, plus fifty cents a run on every commercial, the financial dynamics would be drastically different. As the two plotted their stealthy departure from Boston, a 77 percent tax bracket was the last thing on their minds.

4

PULLING A FAST ONE

John Moses, a stocky, jovial, forty-four-year-old agent and manager with the powerful GAC (General Artists Corporation) talent agency in New York, knew everybody, including every head waiter in town. Like his father, he at one time had been a theatrical producer with a handful of productions to his credit, including the 1945 play *Kiss Them for Me*, which introduced Judy Holliday to Broadway audiences. When on his regular rounds, Moses invariably hit the fourth floor of the RCA Building—"30 Rock"— headquarters for NBC programming brass.

"John was always wandering around," said Grant Tinker, former chairman and CEO of the network and co-founder of MTM Enterprises, a TV production company responsible for some of the most successful comedies and dramas of the 1970s and '80s. But in 1951, Grant Tinker was a twenty-six-year-old management trainee assigned to NBC Radio. As such, John Moses was not exactly a stranger to him. "He was always looking to sell something or pick up a piece of information or whatever," Tinker said. "So we all kind of knew him pretty well. . . . I don't want to say he was scrambling, but he had to make it on his own, and did."

While checking his traps at the network, a must-stop was the fourth-floor corner office of vice-president Charles C. "Bud" Barry, who had just rejoined the company a year earlier. First hired in 1941 as Eastern program manager of NBC Blue, he had witnessed his network wrenched away from General David Sarnoff's RCA electronics empire by Lifesavers tycoon Edward J. Noble, to become simply "The Blue Network." It then evolved into ABC Radio in 1945. Thirty-nine-year-old Bud Barry was a blustery Boston Irishman with a hearty, if somewhat vulgar, manner. "You'd probably want him on your side in a street fight," Tinker said. "He was tough. . . . A guy who was not looking for a fight but certainly wouldn't run from one."

The condition in which Barry found NBC's radio division upon his return would not have soothed his temperament any. By the end of the 1949–50 season, CBS boasted twelve of the fifteen top-rated shows. Surveying the carnage, he was in no position to be cavalier about recommendations of fresh, inventive—and, oh yeah, inexpensive—comedy talent, particularly when touted by a trusted source such as John Moses. The two were "very palsey," Bob said. "Things in those days were often done on friendship." Somebody, according to Bob, had either told Moses to look up Bob and Ray, or he had heard a recording of their pinch-hit performance for Morey Amsterdam. "I wouldn't strictly call it an NBC audition," Bob added, referring to the recording, "although it might have been used in selling us to the network a year later."

Whatever Barry's reaction upon hearing it, there would be no equivocation. Bud Barry was hardly one to sit back and be reflective, Grant Tinker said. He was "an aggressive and go-straight-ahead guy." Moses discovered them, Tinker continued, "before anybody higher, Bud Barry or anybody else. . . . John engineered that." But it was Barry who pulled the trigger.

In April of 1951, Moses's secret negotiations with NBC required a couple of clandestine Boston meetings with the team, whose current contract did not expire until the end of June. "We weren't comfortable having him around the station," Elliott said. "We thought we were pulling a fast one."

In one covert encounter on a Saturday afternoon—a day strategically selected because fewer station personnel would be around—the three huddled in what became their favorite Boston safe house, the Statler bar, speculating about the kind of money NBC might have in mind. Moses said, "About six or seven hundred a week."

"Apiece?!" Ray asked, incredulous.

"Yes," Moses said.

"We couldn't believe it," Bob recalled. "We used to say if we could make two hundred a week for three weeks, we'd be on easy street. That was before we heard the six or seven hundred dollars."

Bob Elliott loved his shiny, black 1950 Studebaker with the red upholstery and new, distinctive, Raymond Loewy-designed bullet-nosed swept-back front. On Friday night, April 28, 1951, driving home with Jane after a day's shift at the station, followed by an evening B&R appearance before a group of Harvard undergrads in Cambridge, the steady, lullaby-like purr of the Studie's engine began conspiring with Elliott's increasingly heavy eyelids. It was after midnight when he turned onto a narrow, six-mile shortcut from 3A to Cohasset that snaked its way from Hingham. Exhausted, Elliott fell asleep and ran into a huge oak tree, five miles from home. Jane's ribs, left arm, and leg were broken; her husband's left leg was fractured in two places. Both were unconscious. When a resident at a nearby house called the police, they claimed that they had already taken care of that accident. In fact, there had been another wreck at the same tree earlier that night.

"I recall us being moved into an ambulance," Bob said of the ride to South Shore Hospital in Hingham. "I drifted in and out of consciousness throughout the trip." On Sunday, Jane's personal physician had her transferred to Massachusetts General in Boston, where her complicated fractures would receive specialized treatment. Bob remained in an eight-bed ward in South Shore for a week, and was encased in plaster from ankle to thigh until the middle of summer.

In no time, word of the accident got out. The Hearst tabloid, the *Record*, with a circulation of around five-hundred thousand, featured a front-page picture of Elliot's mangled Studebaker wrapped around the tree, and the caption: "Local Radio Star Injured in Crash."

Handling both the morning and afternoon shows solo, Ray treated the accident lightly, selecting a garrulous, nine-year-old girl from a group of visiting Wenham school children to replace Bob as his *Matinee* "co-star for the day." The next day, after visiting Jane at Mass General, Ray commented on her wonderful spirit and pledged to check on Bob's car, which, he reported, was "running a fever."

Visiting South Shore on May 2, Goulding brought his partner a present—a copy of *Variety* that had just hit the stands, folded to an article announcing that "Bob and Ray, [a] pair of Boston disk jockeys," would be moving to NBC. Now McGrath would know for sure. Even if he did not read it himself, someone would be sure to tell him, Elliott said. "That got me out a lot sooner than I would have."

Moses had finally set the NBC deal, which called for a Monday through Friday, fifteen-minute *Bob and Ray Show* at five-forty-five in the afternoon, plus an hour-long Saturday-night program at nine-thirty, to be called *Inside Bob and Ray*. They had thirteen weeks, firm. Meanwhile, fulfilling their WHDH contract, the two continued their regular schedule, but kept the news completely secret. "We thought we'd pulled off quite a coup," Bob said.

◆◆〜

Having lived in New York, Bob was at home in the city before he arrived. "Ray," he said, "had a lot more common sense than I did. He was very careful about not breaking ties."

In spite of only a thirteen-week guarantee, for both, sheer exhilaration exceeded any apprehension. But neither had been present a few months earlier at the NBC Radio convention at White Sulphur Springs, West Virginia. *Billboard* reported that frightened affiliates "blew their tops" when Bud Barry, admitting that TV had temporarily grabbed the spotlight, declared that "this phase would pass" and that network radio had a long life before it, provided that "broadcasters don't throw in the sponge."

"We were very naïve," Liz Goulding said, recalling that her husband "seemed to take everything in stride. He wasn't a worrier outwardly. If it was internal, it didn't come across to his family."

Bud Barry, eager to smooth the transition for his new team, arranged for a dry run-through. On the Sunday before their last week at WHDH, the boys slipped down to Manhattan, and, in their new NBC studio, performed a simulated program. Elliott's main recollection of the occasion was, "I was still in the cast."

No on-air reference to leaving was made until their final WHDH broadcast on Saturday, June 30. "Well, this series of *Matinee with Bob and Ray* has come to halt," Ray announced through mock tears and sniffles and Bill Green's hokey "Hearts and Flowers" piano accompaniment. "Of course, you've heard us say this so many times, you're not going to believe us now."

"Oh, you'll believe it," responded Bob, "when you hear someone else on Monday."

Then, after signing off over their theme, "Collegiate," the Boston years came to a close.

"We just left," Bob remembered. "We did the show that Saturday and were gone."

In fact, they would be back on in Boston the following Monday, only on NBC affiliate WBZ.

5

GAME CHANGERS

The humidity was at least bearable though the midtown temperature was near eighty. Scurrying down Sixth Avenue to Rockefeller Center for their network debut, the two were not difficult to spot: the big guy, setting the pace with a determined stride, and the little guy hobbling with him despite the ankle-to-thigh plaster cast. But who would *want* to spot them? Bob and Ray were completely anonymous. John Moses had found the team a two-bedroom sublet to share. It was not exactly the Plaza, but it was close. It was directly behind the Plaza on West Fifty-Eighth Street. The wives, meanwhile, remained in Cohasset and Lexington.

Radio mavens since childhood, Elliott and Goulding were now at its epicenter. On Monday, July 2, 1951, New York City was the capital of all entertainment and booming postwar affluence. *Guys and Dolls* and *Gentlemen Prefer Blondes* lit up Broadway. Ella Fitzgerald was headlining at Café Society in Sheridan Square. Three major league baseball teams flourished along with seven daily newspapers, each with their own gossip columnists fighting for every crumb. The New York Giants were opening a series at the Polo Grounds against the Phillies amid concerns about their twenty-year-old rookie, Willie Mays, hitless in three straight games. The *Post's* Earl Wilson was reporting that George Shearing's Birdland opening stretched into the street; Hy Gardner in the *Trib* brought the news that Xavier Cugat's fiancée and vocalist, Abbe Lane, had her ears pierced to "accommodate" Cugie's gift diamond earrings. The corporate headquarters of all broadcast networks and advertising agencies were nestled within a few dozen square midtown blocks. If you were in the media, this was where you wanted to be—and stay.

In NBC's Studio 3E, a sense of unease pervaded the crowded control room. Programmers were not in the habit of allowing talent to go on the network without a script, especially in the case of two young interlopers from Boston. A floor or two above the control room was the client's booth, where a show's sponsor usually sits. It was empty.

In the dull beige, roughly twenty-five-by-forty-foot studio, a trio of NBC staff musicians, headed by organist Paul Taubman, greeted the boys. With dark hair, a chevron mustache, and a courtly manner, Taubman gave off a slightly Latin aura that belied his Winnipeg, Canada, roots. An extraordinarily talented keyboard man, he was also the proprietor of Manhattan's elegant Penthouse Club, where he entertained nightly on both piano and organ. The nightspot's working fireplace, candlelit tables, and spectacular view of the park nicely diverted any lingering stigma of its history as a speakeasy, a fact B&R would never hesitate to remind Taubman of on the air.

Backing Taubman was jocular pianist and Lena Horne accompanist, Sanford Gold, and a tall, sandy-haired, soft-spoken twenty-nine-year-old guitar virtuoso, Johnny Smith, both already heralded names in the New York jazz stratosphere. Now, every afternoon, they would throw themselves into musical bridges for *John J. Agony* and *Mr. Trace* bits.

For the first time Bob and Ray would be working with a director, forty-eight-year-old professional Scotsman, Kenneth MacGregor, fresh from Henry Morgan's NBC series. MacGregor had a penchant for pomposity, plaid ties, and, noted Elliott, letting "people buy him coffee." *Honi soit qui mal y pense* (Evil be to him who evil thinks) seemed to be his favorite expression, Elliott said. "I didn't know what the hell it meant."

An old network hand dating back to the 1930s when he was at the helm of *The Maxwell House Show Boat* and *When a Girl Marries*, MacGregor was strictly of the script-and-stopwatch school. Upon meeting the team, he was appalled. "You're going to ad-lib this?" he asked. "How am I going to direct?" A compromise of sorts was reached: Before each broadcast, a large blackboard listing that day's program elements was rolled in and positioned in clear view of Bob and Ray, the musicians, and the control room. This gave MacGregor a sense of chronological order, but of exactly what, he could not be sure. Ultimately, his main duty became timing, making sure the show got off the air at exactly 5:59:25 p.m.

"There was nothing to direct," Elliott said. "The sound guys, Agnew Horine or Sam Monroe, would come to us earlier in the day. We would say, 'We'll need some car effects, we'll need this and that,' and they would have it. Ken didn't even check. He had a good deal and he enjoyed it."

With the hot breath of television already breathing down the neck of network radio, *The Bob and Ray Show* premiered live at exactly five-forty-five in the afternoon with Ray announcing: "From Radio City in New York, Bob and Ray take pleasure in presenting The National Broadcasting Company . . ."

"And before you go any further, fellas," interrupted Arthur Sturdley (Bob, in his Godfrey mode), let me wish you an awful lot of luck here at NBC. . . . I've waited a long time to see this." Following their new theme song, "Mention My Name in Sheboygan," the first bit, for the benefit of listeners "used to hearing daytime dramatic shows at this time," was a fictional soap opera's final episode, tying up all loose ends ("David has *not* been murdered—Pike missed him completely!") so *The Bob and Ray Show* might start.

Those tuning in that first Monday caught two young men in the act of tampering with broadcasting's status quo. By network radio's comedy conventions of the day, Bob and Ray were game-changers. Without a studio audience present, it fell to the listener to determine what was funny. Each was being let in on one big private joke between these two new, often overlapping voices, which suddenly could become three, four, and five voices, all bouncing off of one another from every direction. It was like entering a house of mirrors for the ears. You had to pay attention. The satirical bits came and went throughout each program. You either *got* them, or you didn't. Explanations were not provided—ever. B&R listeners never heard the words: "And now we present our version of . . ." Nor was there even a sense of the two striving to be funny. Compared to the WHDH years, they were now less amped-up. Their jabs landed slyly. Neither was a cutup, nor a joke teller. They were pleasant, but not effusive. Their total lack of spurious affability and slickness set the two apart from the very institution they were making fun of, yet were still a part of. This authenticity also had the effect of legitimizing their characters. All were rooted in their own reality; it just was not necessarily *our* reality.

Critical response was mostly favorable. The *Herald Tribune*'s John Crosby praised their "deadpan, deadly satire." *Variety* called the two, "The brightest pair of young comics to hit the webs in some time."

That first summer, B&R's routines and characters essentially picked up right where they had left off in Boston. Special introductions or clarifications for the uninitiated, which included the entire country, were unnecessary. Tweaking was minimal. Instead of Mary McGoon's annual swim out to the Boston Lighthouse and back, it was to Bedloe Island in New York Harbor, with Tex, as usual, paddling ahead to clear the grapefruit halves. *Arthur Sturdley's No Talent Hunt, Dr. O. K.*, and the other sendups continued, as did mock commercials for invented sponsors like the A-B-C Alphabet Soup Corporation ("Each and every can contains sufficient letters to write a five-hundred-word composition on the life and times of Benjamin Franklin . . ."), and La Belle France baby food, for toddlers with discriminating taste ("Babies cry for La Belle France strained bouillabaisse à la Marseillaise").

In no time, their pictures were in *Newsweek*. The team would later grab the prestigious Peabody Award for radio comedy in their first year on the network.

"They always seemed to me as though they were a little uncomfortable with their prominence," Grant Tinker said. "They didn't seem ready for it. They hadn't planned it. . . . I don't know that they knew what they had."

However comforting the reviews, the two were not about to suddenly sell their houses and uproot the families for New York. Housekeeping in their third-floor sublet consisted of living out of suitcases and eating in restaurants. To the best of Bob's memory, they may have made coffee a couple of times. On Saturday nights, one or both raced for the Northeast Airlines Boston shuttle and an abbreviated weekend at home.

Their wives, too, did their share of commuting. "It was a riot," Liz said, recalling her first trip to the New York quarters. "Bob's cast was sitting there in the corner of the room. It was such a shock to see the thing." The thing had just come off. They could not leave the window open, she said, because "the soot came in so thick they couldn't breathe. It was hotter than all get-out."

On the eve of their first Saturday night *Inside Bob and Ray* broadcast, the boys huddled around the radio to check out the other team, Gene

Rayburn and Dee Finch. (Finch had replaced Jack Lescoulie in mid-1947). The WNEW morning duo had just started moonlighting as a CBS Friday-night summer replacement for Edward R. Murrow's *Hear it Now*. Both teams now had hour-long network shots on back-to-back nights. "We listened to it," Elliott said. "Our show was better, we thought, with no malice involved."

Guest star Peggy Lee, taking part in a dramatic spoof and belting out two numbers backed by Taubman and company, helped get *Inside Bob and Ray* off to a solid start. By the end of the summer, former Paul Whiteman alto saxist Alvy West and his band supplanted Taubman on *Inside*, springing him to return to his more lucrative Saturday-night gig at The Penthouse Club.

Peggy Lee paid a return visit a few weeks later and other notable guests appeared, including Les Paul & Mary Ford, and Billy Gilbert. But without the budget of a sponsored program, attracting A-list names was a killer. The hapless task fell to beleaguered NBC programming executive Leslie Harris, who gamely put the squeeze on agents and publicists. One *Inside* guest star, the French actress Denise Darcel, in town to promote her latest movie, *Westward the Women*, had clearly never heard of Bob and Ray. Though "cooperative and a trouper," Elliott said, "she didn't know where she was or what she was doing." Ultimately, a regular girl-singer role was awarded to slender, dark-haired Nancy Evans, formerly with Wayne King's band, *The Breakfast Club*, and *The Camel Caravan*.

Inside Bob and Ray was the first time the pair had their own announcer, in the person of Jack Costello. The Minnesotan's B&R credentials were impeccable: On staff at NBC since 1936, Jack Costello had been the announcer on *Just Plain Bill* and *Mr. Keen, Tracer of Lost Persons*, both perennial Elliott and Goulding punching bags. On *Inside*, he embraced his role as the ego-driven announcer out to overshadow the very program he was introducing. It came naturally to him. Fellow NBC announcer Peter Roberts said of Costello: "If you didn't know who he was, he told you who he was." Unassuming and studious looking, Jack Costello, in the words of Roberts, was "a politician in escrow."

It served him perfectly on *Inside Bob and Ray*. His openings, crediting Bob and Ray's voice characterizations to their "ambidextrous adenoids," dripped with contempt ("I have introduced King George, Bernard Baruch, George Bernard Shaw, and three presidents. That I should be reduced to announce the following program . . ."), as did his weekly sign-offs ("For those simply waiting around for the next program, this is Jack Costello applying the brakes to this transcribed twaddle . . ."). Having read interminable, boring network announcements, Costello now relished poking fun at them: ("A special political broadcast originally scheduled to replace the program originally canceled for this time, has been canceled so that we may present the program originally scheduled starring Bob Elliott and Ray Goulding.")

"They overlooked nothing and no one in their humorous attacks," *Variety*'s man reported on *Inside*'s July 7th debut. Victims included the highly mockable Phillip Morris—"Compare your brand with ours"—commercials of the day. ("I prefer yours. They're milder, *much* milder!") The review also pointed out that the sketches "displayed sharp wit and ingratiating spontaneity," but added, "madcap hilarity and biting satire . . . don't hold up in a sixty-minute concentration."

With a daily quarter-hour, plus the Saturday-night hour series, there was still network concern with all the ad-libbing. "You've got to have writers," Bud Barry finally told them.

"Many critics echoed the same sentiment," Elliott said.

Barry's first choice was a fellow New Englander and former NBC Blue colleague, Raymond Knight, a broadcasting trailblazer of the 1930s. When it came to satire, before Bob and Ray, and before Henry Morgan and the legendary Fred Allen, even before Stoopnagle and Budd, there had been Ray Knight's long-running *The Cuckoo Hour*.

In his effervescent character as Ambrose J. Weems, Knight presided over a collection of crazies, chief among them Mrs. George T. Pennyfeather and her Personal Service for Perturbed People. Besides starring in the show, Knight also created, directed, and wrote it, as he did many others, including *Wheatenaville*, *The Joke's on You*, and *A House in the Country*. For a time, he was also the comedy counterweight with *The Clicquot Club Eskimos*. All were listening musts for Bob and Ray in their early teens.

Knight was prolific, scripting over fifty series in addition to writing for the theater. His play, *Strings*, won the Drama League's Best One-Act award, and his revue, *Not in the Guide Book,* was the genesis of the 1935 Dietz and Schwartz Broadway hit, *At Home Abroad,* which starred Beatrice Lillie and ran for seven months. However, his 1938 comedy, *Run Sheep Run,* with William Bendix, lasted for twelve—performances, that is.

Performing his own *Cuckoo Hour* scripts, Knight was a ringmaster of intersecting wordplays, malapropisms, and puns. However, his antic on-air persona clearly did not parallel Bob and Ray's still-blossoming deadpan. But, in Barry's mind, it was a perfect fit. Like the boys, Knight was not a refugee from vaudeville. When it came to lampooning radio, Ray Knight had been the architect. "Bud Barry saw it," said Elliott, who, as a kid, had attended Knight's shows with his parents. "It was the greatest coincidence for me. I was really impressed and couldn't wait to meet him."

But Bob would have to wait. Knight, then entrenched in Salem, Massachusetts, with a wife and two young daughters, was unable to start immediately. Another writer, Art Henley, who, with his thin mustache resembled Willie Sutton, jumped into the breach. It was a few weeks after B&R's national debut when Ray Knight was finally back at the same network he had broken in with as a continuity writer in January 1928. "I couldn't start as a pageboy," he once said, "none of the uniforms fit me."

The hulking, affable, fifty-two-year-old Knight was over six-feet tall, with thinning hair, horned rimmed glasses, and a dapper mustache. "He always wore a flower in his buttonhole," Bob said. "I never saw him without that. It would wilt toward the end of the day." He quickly accommodated himself to the Bob and Ray sensibility, even further calibrating and defining it. In addition to introducing new segments, he added his spin to some of their old Boston standbys. Knight expanded on things he knew they liked, said Elliott, who also had the feeling whenever he wrote a Mary McGoon spot, "He was thinking [of] Mrs. Pennyfeather, which is the same thing, done years before."

Knight added more symmetry and a sense of structure to both B&R's sketches and the overall program. His ear for the inanities of advertising-speak became evident in various commercial parodies. ("The Flash Loan and Collection service enables you to borrow money with the left hand and repay it with the right in practically one simultaneous motion.") Another was for Grit, the paste that makes one's hands look dirty "for that honest, working-man's appearance. Lily-white hands and clean fingernails show the world that you live on an inherited income and not by the sweat of your brow."

An especially popular spoof was for an enigmatic little item called Woodlo, the "new wonder product." Listeners never knew its use. This was the ultimate Madison Avenue satire—a commercial in search of a product. ("Remember, Woodlo not only can, but it does. And it's immunized.") Ray Knight "had been agency oriented all his life," Elliott said, "so he knew it inside and out."

To this point, Bob and Ray's success had sprung from a shared, spontaneous chemistry that the two never felt compelled to define, assuming they even could. It clearly did not appear on the periodic table of elements. While they may not have known what it was, they instinctively knew what it was *not*—a point now driven home with the introduction of prepared material.

Art Henley was a talented writer of some big programs, including *The Kate Smith Show* and *We the People*, the latter a regular target of B&R mockery. However, one of his first *Inside* pieces sent up an early warning flag. "I was doing Harry Truman impressions in those days," Elliott said, "and he would bring in a thing about 'Harvey S. Fooman.' And that was not *Bob and Ray*. And that was a tip-off—just the one name."

At the start of 1952, Tony Webster, a former University of Missouri journalism major who had been working for Henry Morgan, followed Henley, setting in motion a writer carousel. With the celebrated exception of Milton Berle, major comedians were fairly principled about not stealing one another's material, and none was more so than the brilliant Sid Caesar, whose *Your Show of Shows* then anchored NBC's Saturday-night TV lineup. But, by that spring, according to Caesar, he had become impressed with Webster's "very funny material for the Bob and Ray radio show," and so found a way around the principle: Instead of the material, he stole Tony Webster.

"He was one of the great wits," remembered Webster's *Your Show of Shows* colleague Carl Reiner. "When we would all be struggling for punch lines, he would just toss them off," Reiner said. ". . . As a matter of fact, he was the only Christian in the room, so he had a different take on things. . . . He was also acerbic. We loved that. One of his big phrases was, 'Ah, your ass!' He would keep saying, 'Ah, your ass!'"

Webster's replacement on *Inside Bob and Ray* was Billy Friedberg, a former Broadway press agent and cousin to the lyricist Lorenz Hart. Friedberg actually doubled, also continuing with Nat Hiken on Martha Raye's weeks as a rotating headliner of NBC's *All-Star Revue*. A few years later he would become Hiken's head writer on *The Phil Silvers Show*—the Sgt. Bilko series. Of all of Friedberg's considerable talents, perhaps his greatest was his knack for selecting collaborators. In addition to the esteemed Nat Hiken, for a two-year stretch in the '50s he also wrote Max Liebman "spectaculars" with an emerging comedy writer twelve years his junior, named Neil Simon.

Brooklyn native Jack Roche, who had most recently written sketches for the Broadway revue, *Tickets, Please!*, followed Friedberg. Roche had earned his stripes working for Ed Gardner, the mercurial star and co-creator of *Duffy's Tavern*. Gardner was notorious for hiring and firing (and under-paying) writers, especially, as once remarked by former *Duffy* staff member, Larry Gelbart, when "under the influence, which is where he spent eighty to ninety proof of the time."

Bob and Ray threw themselves into the writers' scripts, which some-times tilted more toward conventional, punch-line rhythms than quirky satire. "We had the feeling," Bob said, "that we had to do their kind of stuff if we were going to appeal to the crowds that the networks wanted to attract. It was a semi-compromise—an accommodation." In time, their feeling would change. Occasionally, Ray Knight would come up with a premise "that was a little bit off the way our minds worked," Bob continued, "and he would fight for a thing that he thought—and *was*—funny. . . . We got to like him so much personally that we probably gave him the benefit of the doubt most of the time."

If ever there was any resentment on Knight's part, having once been a top NBC star now suddenly a writer for two network upstarts, Bob and Ray never saw it. "He was always gracious," Bob said. Although he had heard that Knight once remarked to a friend, "They're doing everything I did twenty years ago."

Having managed the sizeable leap from local radio to the network, NBC now determined the time was right for the pair's next challenge: a return to local radio. The New York flagship, WNBC, eager to counter its stodgy network image with a lighter, more local appeal, had just abducted a new program manager from, of course, WNEW, none other than Bill McGrath's old mentor, Ted Cott.

Next came filling the high-visibility morning block. Increasingly at the time—and for decades to come—the prevailing currency for local morning radio was comedy—something nobody had ever accused WNBC's current wake-up man, conductor and pianist Skitch Henderson of. Cott did not have to search far for a replacement. With two series from the same building on the network already, it was all he could do to avoid tripping over Bob and Ray in the halls. Their new two-and-a-half-hour early-morning show debuted August 27, 1951. They were now at 30 Rock twelve hours a day, fifteen on Saturdays.

In the Golden Age of local AM radio, the country's number-one market was a battlefield of clever morning personalities. The high-voltage Ted Brown, on WMGM, and Godfrey's WCBS replacement, Jack Sterling (whose show featured a live band), both had head starts dating back to 1949. But they, and everybody else, struggled to overtake WNEW's Rayburn and Finch, who, since 1947, had repulsed all challengers.

WNBC's new Bob and Ray program, sporting a bouncy theme by vocalist Buddy Greco ("Start your day with Bob and Ray before you head for your job / And if you don't start your day with Bob and Ray, start it, with Ray and Bob . . ."), introduced New Yorkers to *Mary Backstayge, Noble Wife*, a jab at the then-still-surviving *Mary Noble, Backstage Wife*, a network day-timer since 1935. B&R's multi-character version, essentially *The Life and Loves of Linda Lovely* with footlights, including the same intertwining, hilariously preposterous and proliferating plots and crises, from chronic amnesia to a baffling propensity for being shanghaied to mysterious, cannibal-inhabited islands, would endure almost as long and become one of their signature set pieces. The Lovelies and the Backstayges were artfully cross-pollinated versions of the same core characters—the same, but distinct, voices and attitudes, only with different (and sometimes not so different) names. Over the decades, any inconsistencies with a few of the characters are easily explained: Bob and Ray were not about detailed record keeping.

The early-morning program also marked the debut of "Sandwich Surprise," in which an imaginary sandwich was removed from a selected WNBC engineer or newsman's lunch bag. The sandwich's ingredients, including all condiments, were then described in exacting detail, with considerable attention given to whether the bread was cut evenly or diagonally, whether the crusts were or were not removed, and whether it was wrapped in plain or waxed paper. In following years, additional pomp and pageantry would be added when the event would be moved to "the swank Bob and Ray Gourmet Club," with the ceremonial arrival of the sandwich—typically belonging to an obscure or marginal celebrity—introduced by a regal trumpet fanfare and, to polite applause, transported into the room upon a fringed, crushed-velvet pillow by a page wearing purple knickerbockers. Then, with Lester Lanin's black-tie music playing softly in the background, the sandwich would be placed on a pedestal for guests wishing to come forward for a closer inspection. The bit contained all the B&R essentials: ridiculous premise, delightful imagery, and—not to be minimized—an easy time-filler, which, by definition, made it satirical. At a certain level, broadcasting is all about filling time.

The basic Sandwich Surprise model was always the same, only the name of the celebrity and contents of the sandwich changed. Similarly, many of the team's staples—such as Charles the Poet and The Webley Webster Players' "book reviews" (always dramatizing a totally incongruous scene aboard a pirate ship, with Ray's seething, easily provoked captain pummeling Bob's harmless, cockney cabin boy), worked on the same utilitarian principle. The routines could be summoned on the spot and stretched or cut short as time demanded.

Inevitably, with a disc-jockey format, B&R were visited by song pluggers, two favorites being Charlie Goldberg and Jack Spatz, both of whom were adept at softening them up with the latest jokes from Tin Pan Alley while pushing their latest records. When it came to pulling the music, an enterprising young man named Bill Gammie made up each morning's play list. In his do-all role, Bill Gammie unwittingly evolved into a real-life model for their character Wilbur Connally, the "young squirt who works for us."

However, unlike Gammie, who was a loyal, conscientious foot soldier, Goulding's Wilbur Connally was a clueless flunky who never exhibited even the slightest deference toward his two bosses. Shouting, "Here's your mail, Bob and Ray," he would sling it tied to a rock through the control room window, to the sound of shattering glass.

As the lead-in to *Tex and Jinx* (Tex McCrary and Jinx Falkenburg), WNBC's long-running husband and wife breakfast show broadcast from the couple's sumptuous Long Island estate, Bob and Ray, too, had breakfast on the air every morning—juice, coffee and hot dogs—delivered by one of their sponsors, Nedick's.

News was a big item, recalled Peter Roberts, one of their morning newsmen and also a familiar voice on Hearst Movietone newsreels. Provoked one morning by B&R into breaking up during one of his newscasts, Roberts was confronted by news director Bill Brooks. After listing the names of all the great NBC news voices, and citing the company's strict code of on-air behavior, he asked Roberts for an explanation. "I said I had none," Roberts recounted. "I mumbled how sorry I was, and left."

The tormenting of Peter Roberts had only just begun.

Prior to an *Inside Bob and Ray* show at 30 Rock, a last minute note session with Ken MacGregor was just breaking up. Everyone set out for Studio 3E. "I took the shortcut fire stairs to the third floor," Elliott recalled, "and emerged, almost colliding with one of the most beautiful, brunette, twenty-somethings that I'd ever seen. 'I'm looking for *The Bob and Ray Show*' she said. 'I'm Ray Knight's wife.'" Not being able to think of anything funny, as befitting a network comedian, I introduced myself and said, 'Let me show you in myself.'" He then opened the door, adding, "I used to be an usher, Mrs. Knight."

When the thirteen-week option on the team's contract was exercised, the boys felt reasonably certain they would be staying in New York, despite the fact that George Perkins, WHDH's new—but misinformed—program director, was answering listeners' inquiries about their return to Boston with form letters stating that Bob and Ray were expected back in the fall.

Elliott sublet a penthouse on East Fifty-Second Street, with an expansive, seldom-used terrace. "At this point," he said, "my marriage had been deteriorating over the past couple of years, although Jane did make a trip to New York and inspected the premises, giving her approval. Her visits became fewer and fewer."

After scouting houses and schools on Long Island's North Shore, Ray and Liz, expecting a new baby in October, rented a ranch-style home in Sands Point. A gala house-warming party included Bob, Ray's brothers Phil and Joe and their families, and his sister Ann, in addition to Bill Gammie, and, recalled Bob, Ken MacGregor, who managed to make a meal out of the hors d'oeuvres.

Ray had determined early on that living in the city was not for him. "He never wanted to fraternize with anybody in the business," Bob said. "I didn't go out of my way to, but being in the city, I was able to do a little more. . . . I don't think he was as socially minded as I apparently was at the time." There were occasional drinks with John Moses, Bob added, but "I probably had more with him than Ray did."

Over the years, some of Bob's closest friends were professional artists. Ray was most at home with old friends from Lowell, and his family. "He was kind of private," Tom Goulding said. "He liked family, and family, and then maybe the family."

When dealing with the press, both could be cryptic and vague. Ray was especially tight-lipped. During an interview, he could change the subject abruptly by injecting a non-sequitur question at the interviewer. "I mean, he'd really come in from left field with something," Bob said. When years later the noted *New Yorker* journalist Whitney Balliett was preparing an affectionate twelve-page piece on the two, he first interviewed Bob in the city. He then went about setting up a Long Island visit for a similar conversation with Ray, who "was kind of put out," according to his partner. "Ray said, 'Jesus, how close is this guy going to get to us?' . . . I mean, here's a guy doing a profile for the *New Yorker*. . . . That didn't sit well with him."

In such interviews, each had perfected his own stock answers. They mostly concealed their process and craft, like many performers, intuitively sensing that knowledge of how the machinery works would not necessarily make the audience enjoy it any more.

Both had been raised on Fred Allen, Laurel & Hardy, and Robert Benchley. Benchley, in particular, had made a huge impression. "I read everything he ever wrote," Ray told Dick Cavett in 1968. "I really loved his work." Yet, growing up, he added, comedy "never entered my mind. . . . I never set out to be a comedian." Under "occupation" on his income-tax return, he once threatened to write "pomposity puncturer" because, he pointed out, "That's what it said in *Newsweek*." On Bob's tax returns, he always entered "announcer," or "actor," never "comedian."

"With most comedians," said Chris Elliott, "their alter ego is their comedian ego, or their comedian personality. And the other side is who they really are. I don't think that's the way it was with them at all. . . . They weren't pretending to be something they weren't."

B&R did not run with the Jack Carters, Buddy Hacketts, or Shecky Greenes, though they admired them all. They did not have seats at the comics' roundtable at the storied Friar's Club, or Lindy's, or their Seventh-Avenue double-A franchises, Hanson's drug store and the B&G Coffee Shop; nor were their signed photos part of the celebrity mosaic at the Stage and Carnegie delicatessens, or their names on any sandwiches. None of it was calculated; it was just who they were. After signing off each day, both were out the door while their closing theme was still playing.

With her husband tethered at NBC for so many hours a day, Liz returned to Ray's family in Lowell for the birth of their daughter, Barbara, on Sunday, October 14, 1951. The very next evening, another adorable lady made her debut: a redhead named Lucy Ricardo. Overnight, *I Love Lucy* would become TV's first smash hit. With the coaxial cable having just reached the West Coast, the new medium had shifted into high gear and was desperately searching for talent. Radio would be the first place it would look.

6

AMATEUR NIGHT IN WEST NEWTON

T elevision was already acting provocatively," Fred Allen noted in 1949, "trying to get radio to pucker up for the kiss of death." By 1951, to finance their fledgling TV operations, the networks were reaching into the less and less deep pockets of their radio divisions. But as TV's audience rose, radio's dropped proportionately as, inevitably, did radio ad rates. By subsidizing television's birth, radio was hastening its own death.

It was in the middle of these countervailing forces that Elliott and Goulding found themselves that October. John Moses and Bud Barry now contemplated adding to the boys' fifteen-and-a-half hours a week of airtime by introducing their understated style to television. The question of exactly how it would translate to the new medium was set aside for the moment, as was the fact that Bob and Ray had absolutely no background in TV. But then, in 1951, nobody did. All Barry and Moses knew was that comedy was then king. Milton Berle had been the first out of the gate, followed six months later by Sid Caesar, and on October 5, 1951, the first appearance by "The Honeymooners," on Jackie Gleason's *Cavalcade of Stars.* Barry's television intentions struck at the heart of the B&R extrovert/ introvert dynamic. They had "trepidations," Bob said. But as TV clearly represented the future, they felt—or at least were convinced—they should try it. Besides, they had heard all the stories of vaudeville's dying days, and how many performers chose to wait until the "talkies blew over."

As neither had ever appeared on the new medium, Barry realized that he should at least see what Bob and Ray would look like on TV. He hurriedly arranged for them to appear on *Date in Manhattan,* a morning show hosted by the venerable Ed Herlihy on the network's local outlet, WNBT. The director was twenty-five-year-old Dwight Hemion, eighteen Emmy Awards still in his future. Whatever it was Bob and Ray did on *Date in Manhattan* that October morning, it apparently did not discourage Bud Barry.

A kinescoped pilot for *The Bob and Ray Show* was then produced, and the network liked what it saw. The only question was where to put the team on NBC's schedule. The answer suddenly appeared when *Life* magazine and Procter & Gamble dropped their partial sponsorship of another popular team, *Kukla, Fran and Ollie.*

Network brass knew that replacing "KFO," as they referred to it, had to be delicately finessed, hardly a page in Bud Barry's playbook. The delightful "Kuklapolitan Players" and their revered creator, Burr Tillstrom, had been fixtures in the nightly seven o'clock-to-seven-thirty slot since 1948. Nevertheless, it was decided to cut back *Kukla, Fran and Ollie* to a quarter-hour, with a new *Bob and Ray Show* taking over at seven-fifteen.

Predictably, Tillstrom was not happy. And it did not help matters any when he inadvertently learned of the decision in a phone conversation with the manager of the network's Milwaukee affiliate, who referred to a company memo identifying the new show only as having "better audience appeal." The press pounced. *Variety* headlined its story: "Bob & Ray As Kukla TV Mates." Now, not only was Tillstrom steamed, but B&R— skittish about television to begin with—hardly relished being cast as heavies evicting a couple of adorable puppets. So much for NBC's delicate finessing.

A *Bob and Ray Show* TV staff was quickly assembled, headed by producer Pete Barnum, an avuncular, Santa Claus-sized man with thinning reddish hair. Arriving every day from his home in Chappaqua, Barnum was a comical sight crammed into his tiny MG convertible. The director was Doug Rodgers, with a theater background as both an actor and director going for him, as well as leading-man good looks. The obvious choice for musical effects was Paul Taubman, who also continued with the radio series.

On radio, Elliott and Goulding were "just naturally funny guys," Grant Tinker said. ". . . Kind of like Topsy, they became *Bob and Ray*. It sprang of itself. It just happened. Nobody planned it." On radio, inhabiting their off-balanced world required only a suspension of disbelief, with the audience, in effect, becoming willing accomplices and their own casting directors, a degree of engagement impossible with television.

"Trying to portray these characters as people already imagined them was difficult," Liz said, "because everybody had their own idea." And that included Bob and Ray themselves. Both had pictured their imaginary cast in their minds for years, images that would now be shattered. Each of their regular features presented its own set of obstacles, but none greater than their signature spoof, *The Life and Loves of Linda Lovely.*

"We had a lot of anxiety," Bob said. "Ray was going to do Linda Lovely somehow," he remembered. "And then we said, 'We've got to have a real character—a real person.'" Ultimately, the compromise was to outsource the title role to an actress, but not have her speak. Linda would only be a visible presence as the other characters talked about and around her.

After interviews with several actresses, Pete Barnum settled on the young, pretty, poker-faced daughter of an Episcopal missionary with fourteen years of service in China. The actress, who had originally trained to be a concert singer, was Audrey Meadows. At the time she was fresh from two years on the road in *High Button Shoes.*

"We said, 'Can you ride a horse?' She said, 'Yeah,'" Bob recounted. "'Dance? Sing?' She [told us she] could do most anything. Later she told us an actress always says she can do anything they ask her. We were still naïve for years about a lot of things."

Recalling the interview in her autobiography, Meadows wrote:

> Being born a nervous wreck and with being out of work adding to my nervousness, I went into my nonstop spiel, babbling along, cascades of words, words, words. . . . Bob hesitatingly raised a hand. I paused to inhale. "Do you think you could start on Monday?" he asked. . . . "You'll play a character called Linda Lovely—and it will be easy for you."
>
> "Oh, how is that?"
>
> "Well, Linda Lovely never speaks."

On Monday, November 26, 1951, NBC took out a half-page bold-print ad in the *New York Times*, announcing that night's debut of their new team: "Great Big Brand New Evening Series . . . TV Premiere Tonight!" Only, the "new team" was Vivian Blaine and Pinky Lee. Their new fifteen-minute program, *Those Two*, was debuting at seven-thirty that evening. At the bottom of the blurb, almost as an afterthought, in much smaller typeface, the ad stated: "Tonight, 7:15 Bob & Ray, the comedy-satire guys' TV debut."

That evening, the *Kukla, Fran and Ollie* audience had no difficulty discerning Burr Tillstrom's state of mind. Mocking his new, enforced-trimmed format, throughout the show Ollie ordered his fellow Kuklapolitans to talk at a rapid-fire pace in order to preserve precious time. Thus was the lead-in to Bob and Ray's TV premiere.

Easing their way into television, the boys opened their first show with their recognizable voices only, hiding their faces behind beekeeper netting. This was followed by a parody of the then-popular *Lights Out* program, featuring Bob and Ray as two disembodied heads levitating over two candles—in the spooky style of that program's host, Frank Gallop. Next, Ray as Mary McGoon offered a recipe for frozen ginger-ale salad, which, among other ingredients, called for the cubing of a marshmallow. Unlike the Linda Lovely solution, surrendering the Mary McGoon role to an actress was never considered. Without Ray Goulding's patented falsetto, the character would clearly not be the same. Yet having him appear in full Milton Berle-style drag would be so over the top that it would just not be Bob and Ray.

The solution was to shoot Mary's segments as if looking through the frame of a picture window (a gobo, in TV parlance) into her "experimental kitchen," with Mary—Ray in a dress—visible only from the top of her apron to her waist. As Mary went about her cooking, Doug Rodgers then cut to a close-up of just her hands—unmistakably Ray's—as she prepared frankfurters for Valentine's Day, or demonstrated how to keep meatballs hot after they reach the table by knitting a meatball cozy out of spaghetti.

True to the plan, in the first *Linda Lovely* installment, Audrey Meadows had no dialog. That entire first week, Linda was only referred to as she stuck to stage business, such as feeding an exotic rubber plant, unaware it was really a deadly nightshade. Sometimes she sat knitting between Bob and Ray on the couch, forcing Ray (as David Lovely) and Bob (as Uncle Eugene) to lean forward or backward to talk around her.

Inevitably, this device proved unwieldy, besides being a waste of Audrey's talent. "We kicked the problem around," Bob said, "even had her saying just 'yes,' or 'no' in response to our dialog, but we needed more input."

By the middle of the second week, it was decided to have Meadows speak. "Audrey fell into the whole bit beautifully," said Liz. "And after she was able to use her voice, it was a funny voice, too."

Audrey found improvising comedy demanding, requiring "every skill you could bring into play," she wrote in her memoir. "Bob and Ray were subtle gamesters in a sport in which, if you had to ask the rules, you weren't up to the competition."

The nightly *Linda Lovely* segment started with a "premise or general outline," Audrey explained. "You had to dance through the minefield of their banter." Though there were some isolated lines of dialog indicated, it was basically catch as catch can.

"We were really in the same boat, all three of us," Bob said. "Many times we relied on Audrey to pick up on something we said. Other times she would throw out something and we would react. . . . The more remote the lead-in, the better Audrey's non-sequitur answer fit. She was very good."

On-camera opening narrations by announcer Bob Denton, with his sober, businesslike visage but wry delivery, served to fill time while, off-camera, Elliott, Goulding, and Meadows scrambled to make costume changes. Frequently, Denton would be forced to ramble on with lengthy plot summaries of the previous *Linda Lovely* installment. ("Just after kindly old Dr. John had warned Linda that any excitement or sudden shock would be harmful to David Lovely's recovery from the strange malady, peanut fever, Fielding Lovely, David's long-lost, black-sheep, no-account brother, called to demand eighteen-thousand dollars ransom money for Uncle Eugene's safe release.")

A shoestring budget, cramped studio, and the limitations of a live show demanded simple sets and a minimum of ambitious physical or visual components. A make-believe contest, in which viewers were invited to "own one of the Great Lakes," simply featured the boys standing behind a table on which rested five different-sized glass fishbowls. In the bowls were live goldfish, swimming in "water flown in from each of the Great Lakes, courtesy of Sturdley Airlines."

Many of Ray Knight's radio routines were easily adapted for television. There were the Bob and Ray Do-it-Yourself Kits, such as the Boomer Political Kit with its list of "explosive" issues, one being, "Why is it that

President Truman has his own personal airplane when little boys and girls have to walk to school?"

Hard-sell pitches ("Our loss is your gain!"), on behalf of the Bob and Ray Overstocked Surplus Warehouse, dealt with inventories of dubious merchandise. One offered war-surplus items sent back from Cuba, including 322 pairs of canvas leggings which were used only once—going *up* (not down) San Juan Hill, together with twenty-four cases of canned corned beef, clearly stamped San Juan Hill, 1898. ("If you do not find this corned beef all you had hoped it would be, just leave word with the executor of your estate to return the unopened cans to us.") Another advertised an Easter season supply of chocolate rabbits that "through the carelessness of one of our alert, uniformed, attendants . . . were stored next to steam pipes," resulting in their being offered as "edible, all-chocolate *wobblies*." Other than the addition of a prop or two, most pieces required hardly any interpolating for television, such as a pitch for Forbush simulated anchovies ("the anchovies which look like anchovies, smell like anchovies, but do not taste like anchovies"), or Forbush's Carefree Dinnerware ("'Carefree' means, of course, slightly chipped, cracked, or broken").

Scenic designer Lou Sanman either procured or had built any bizarre prop called for, from a man-eating mulberry bush to the ingredients for Mary McGoon's pabulum popsicles. He had a "same-wavelength sense of the ridiculous," Elliott noted. His permanent "home base" set included a mounted elk's head, prizefight bell, and a *Whistler's Mother* print, showing her head facing backward.

Without musical numbers or commercials, there was no time to change scenery. As a result, Bob, Ray, Audrey, or announcer Bob Denton had to be on camera every second. So, at Pete Barnum's suggestion, an all-purpose production area was designed, with four large, side-by-side panels on which were painted various backdrops—a living room with drapes and striped wallpaper, a city sidewalk, and so forth. Bob, Ray, or Audrey, as if pulling down window shades, would then, on-camera, lower the appropriate backdrop to change the scene at the beginning of a sketch. The set had no practical doors. All entrances and exits were from the side. It was television while the foundation was still being poured, and—for then or now—the rarest of animals, a sketch show without a studio audience. But because the comedy was not dependent on jokes, it did not matter—not that the crew ever suppressed their laughter, nor did people working late who regularly huddled in the sound-lock between the hallway and the studio to catch a few minutes of the program before going home.

Just as on radio, the boys projected barely heightened on-air personas. They were easy company. They did not pander to or force themselves on the audience, nor did they come across as professional nice guys, or traffic in show-biz schmaltz. They effectively distinguished themselves by appearing normal. That there was no definable on-air character of "Bob Elliott" or "Ray Goulding" merely reflected how they perceived themselves: sort of celebrity surrogates, *in* show business, but not *of* it.

"It's sort of a subtle distinction," Chris Elliott said. "Obviously that separated them from the throng. . . . It was sort of like visiting with two uncles that make you laugh all the time when they're together." On the air, the two were counterbalanced: a big guy with dark hair and a mustache; the other, shorter, and with lighter hair. Both could play straight or be funny and do any number of voices and accents. The lure was the relationship and interaction; you wanted to learn their secret handshake.

"Ray had a great knowledge of what made him funny," Bob said. "He had a funny appearance, and it caused all kinds of arguments with Moses the day he shaved his mustache off. We had established the image of Ray with a mustache, and I can remember the big furor it created. . . . I always agreed the mustache made him funnier."

"All our stationery and everything had Ray with the mustache," said his sister Ann, who had just started as the team's secretary. "I walked into the office that day and I knew something was different. . . . He was shaving and realized, 'Oh, my God! I took half of it off!' So then he took the other half off."

"We had a sunlamp in the bathroom," explained Liz, "and he was looking at it instead of looking where he should have, and just did it. And once he had done part of it, he had to do the rest. He hadn't planned it. It was an early-morning thing, out of the blue. . . . NBC made him wear a fake one afterwards."

Having to adapt to cameras, props, blocking, and cue cards was tantamount to basic training on the front lines. "They were unpolished performers," Grant Tinker said, recalling the boys' early TV series. "They were naturally funny together and their material was inventive and fresh. But they came to it without any stage experience. . . . It was almost like they were funny in spite of themselves."

"I remember them drawing chalk marks on the floor for where they were supposed to stand," Liz said. "And they were kidding about, 'We can't look down and see where we're supposed to stand.'"

"We weren't being obstinate," Bob said, "but we were used to sitting and naturally getting up, and we figured a camera would follow us."

Coby Ruskin, who moved over from NBC's *All-Star Revue* in January as producer and director, rarely marked the floors for performers. Ruskin told *Life* magazine that he "merely just reminds Bob and Ray to occasionally face the camera."

At fourteen minutes and thirty seconds, each program moved at an unforgiving pace. Wardrobe changes were made on the run. That first week, an Arthur Godfrey take-off found Bob fumbling with the uncooperative buttons on his Hawaiian shirt for much of the sketch. "One night," Bob said, "we got into a bit and it was going very well and after about thirty-seconds, the floor director remembered one of us should be wearing a coat and he just simply threw it over the camera into this live scene we were doing. He got a big laugh from the group gathered in the doorway. There were never any recriminations. Everybody was part of the show."

Sometimes the program would end early and the two would be forced to fill the extra time by reading bogus fan mail. ("I like your show very much, Bob and Ray. Please tell me the name of it and what network you're on.") Signing off after one particularly ragged show, Ray cried out, "Thanks for not throwing anything!"

"Actually," Ray told *Encore* four decades later, "when you look back at those early shows, it was pretty primitive. We just thought of it as radio with a camera on."

But Liz recalled her husband being "appalled" at how really naïve he and Bob were. She said Ray felt some of the older shows were "very unprofessional."

"We were kids," Bob agreed. "They're embarrassing. . . . But from a mindset of when it was in the life of TV, that really was inventing television. . . . We knew we were on what would be the biggest thing since movies, but we didn't know it was 'the Golden Age,' or whatever we were."

"One of the most delightful programs on the air," wrote the *New York Times*' Jack Gould of *The Bob and Ray Show*'s TV premiere. Unfortunately, he was referring to *Kukla, Fran and Ollie*, whose airtime the team had inherited. "Bob and Ray tried hard, to be sure," Gould acknowledged, but called their efforts "incredibly inept . . . monstrously unfunny" and "enough to rattle a viewer's teeth," in contrast to Tillstrom's puppets with their "warm and engaging personalities." While John Crosby in the *Herald Tribune* was over-whelmingly positive, referring to the team's "special essence" and "exquisite parodies," he also noted that "they take some getting used to, especially on television. Come right down to it, Bob and Ray will have to get a little used to television." "Kukla, Fran and Ollie trimmed from a half-hour," began the lead sentence of *Variety*'s critique, which went on to suggest that Elliott and Goulding were victims of "jitters" and "unfamiliarity with a new me-dium." Jack O'Brien, in the *Journal-American*, wrote that Elliott resembled "a scared Buster Keaton," and Goulding, a "convicted Thomas Dewey."

NBC VP Bud Barry had his own opinion: "It looks like 'Amateur Night' in West Newton!" he announced, words that would forever rever-berate in Elliott and Goulding's psyches. The phrase would find its way into the team's routines for decades, frequently in reaction to the *Mary Backstayge* troupe's numerous opening-night debacles.

In total shock, Barry huddled with his lieutenants, Mitch Benson and Leslie Harris, and—as was his style—took immediate action. His quick fix was to hire a tutor to advise his new team on the art of humor. Inexplicably, his choice was not a television expert, but a retired radio pioneer from the crystal-set era named Phillips Carlin. On staff before there even was an NBC, Carlin was primarily a sportscaster. He had long been associated with the legendary Graham McNamee, with whom he broadcast three World Series in the 1920s, plus college football games and heavyweight champion-ship fights. If Phillips Carlin had any comedy credentials, they completely escaped Elliott and Goulding. It seems that Carlin, who at one point in the early '40s was the Blue network's vice-president of programming over Barry, was long owed a favor. It was the "friendship angle," Elliott recalled. "They threw him a bone."

After their local, morning-radio stint on Tuesdays, Bob and Ray, following orders, dutifully reported to the same booth at Cromwell's drugstore on Sixth Avenue. There, over breakfast, they patiently endured Carlin's critiques. "We used to dread that morning," Elliott said. "He would come in with specific notes. . . . And he would tell us what we did wrong on this bit or that bit. . . I seem to remember he always wore an overcoat and an old-fashioned sports announcer's type snap-brim fedora, which he always kept on. . . . He was a pleasant enough guy, but square as all get out."

During one breakfast, Bob remembered, Carlin referred to a previous night's sketch, one that had called for Audrey Meadows—supposedly unnoticed by the team—to make an entrance on roller skates. Carlin pointed out, "You had the girl come in on roller skates and you didn't mention it."

"He didn't get it," Bob said. "He couldn't figure out why she came skating through. . . . It was such a chore for us."

Ray would come home from those sessions holding his head, Liz said. "Maybe," he told her, "Bob and I should wear clown suits."

"They couldn't stand it," Ann agreed. She recalled that she was specifically instructed that should Carlin ever telephone, she was to say that Bob and Ray "weren't there." She added, "They never would call [him] back if they could avoid it." On one occasion Carlin finally told the two, "You have a very stupid secretary. She never gives you my messages."

"Eventually we tried foisting the breakfast meetings off on Ray Knight," Bob said. "But Carlin didn't like that. He took the assignment very seriously."

In addition to Carlin, Pete Barnum invited stand-up comic Jackie Miles, an equally incongruous choice (albeit for different reasons), to attend the show's rehearsals and then impart his advice.

An alumnus of the Catskill resorts, the skinny, downtrodden Miles, with his soft, shaky-voiced delivery, was an excellent monologist and a particular favorite of fellow comedians. His material usually centered on hard-luck losers at the track and in life. One of his classic lines concerned a sad sack cashing his one-cent relief check. "How do you want it?" asked the teller, "heads or tails?" In persona, style and material, Miles was the complete antithesis of Bob and Ray. They were satirists. He was a storyteller.

The first meeting took place in the mezzanine of NBC's cavernous Center Theater. During the rehearsal for that evening's show, Miles stayed by himself and watched intently. When it was over, as B&R waited, he went off in a corner and huddled with Moses and Barnum. "Afterwards," Elliott recalled, "John said, 'Well, he didn't have much to offer—nothing!'" It was the first and last such meeting. To Miles' credit, he, too, apparently recognized the folly of melding their divergent styles.

On February 5, 1952, the show was cut to just Tuesdays and Thursdays (alternating with Gertrude Berg's *The Goldbergs*). Of course, for most TV performers, a half-hour a week was plenty, but there was no mistaking it was the first time Elliott and Goulding's magic carpet ride encountered turbulence. Until then, they had always been adding air-time.

That winter, *Mary Backstayge, Noble Wife*, with Audrey in the title role, made its TV debut, but not until the continuing *Linda Lovely* plot was resolved. In one tidy episode, all of the characters were conveniently killed off.

One evening, a bit required Audrey to scream. Not sure she could pull it off, she suggested her sister, Jayne, who had performed a frightening scream nightly in summer stock. During one of the play's rehearsals, Jayne Meadows recounted, after letting loose with her scream, a woman passing by the theater ran inside to see if someone was in danger. With Bob and Ray, Jayne released her voice-over piercing scream at a microphone next to a monitor to be in sync with her on-camera sister.

Jayne was no stranger to B&R's TV studio. On occasion she would run Audrey's dinner over to her from the apartment the two shared on West Fifty-Third Street. "We were like twins," Jayne said, "very close." She had also known John Moses, having appeared on Broadway in 1945 with Judy Holliday and Richard Widmark in *Kiss Them for Me*, which Moses co-produced.

To promote their new team, NBC also assigned the boys to their TV coverage of the 1952 Easter Parade. From their "vantage point" at 49th and Fifth, dressed in formal striped pants and three-quarter-length coats, Bob and Ray were called upon by co-hosts Dennis James and Faye Emerson for their on-the-spot observations, which, invariably, involved everything except the parade. The network also arranged B&R appearances on NBC Radio's *The Jane Pickens Show*, and *The Big Show* with Tallulah Bankhead.

Occasionally, after the TV program, the boys would have a drink with Moses, usually at the English Grill in Rockefeller Center. "One evening,"

Elliott related, "Henry Morgan stopped by our table. We mentioned what we'd been discussing with John—that with morning radio, the network strip, and the TV show, we were now putting in nearly eighteen hours a week. Henry's response was, 'Fuck you. I'm out of work!'"

After eight months, the quarter-hour radio series introduced a new component: actual commercials. Colgate-Palmolive became the team's first network sponsor, provided they move to the eleven-thirty morning time slot, broadcast before a studio audience, and tailor their material specifically to housewives. They wisely agreed.

New dramatic spoofs ensued, like *Murder for Housewives*, during which women could "stay home quietly washing breakfast dishes every morning and hear crimes committed before noon." A frequently repeated new bit was *The Bob and Ray Teenage Clinic*, with Chester (Bob) and Hester (Ray) dramatizing answers to fictional "listeners'" questions ("What do you tell a precocious, good-looking boy of fourteen who can't live on an allowance of $375 a week?").

In fact, catering to the female listener was largely an illusion. At their core, most of the bits were factory-installed *Bob and Ray*. Most would have been no less amusing to a targeted all-male audience, such as the "ivory grower" (Ray) unable to keep up with the demand for piano keys and billiard balls because his wife, a "very neat housekeeper," only lets him raise one elephant at a time in their small apartment in Queens. The same held true for bogus offers from The Bob and Ray Overstocked Surplus Warehouse, including a St. Patrick's Day special for "two thousand simulated shamrocks that—owing to our colorblind buyer—turned out to be orange."

With Colgate bankrolling the show, the writing budget increased, if only slightly, and a tall, thirty-nine-year-old Yale grad named Fred S. Pearson II was added. Pearson had grown up on the South Shore of Long Island, the son and grandson of engineering financiers. His grandfather, after whom he was named, and grandmother had gone down with the *Lusitania* in 1915. Pearson shared a cubicle with Knight, just down the hall from B&R, whose second-floor office overlooked Radio City Music

Hall. On warm summer evenings, as Grant Tinker pointed out, the windows of the Rockettes' dressing room, directly across Fiftieth Street, would be left open. "It was a fringe benefit," he noted. "Better than most of the shows we were broadcasting."

From the start, Knight and Pearson had two things in common: Both could stay sober long enough to turn out a fifteen-minute script, and neither wanted on-air credit. In Knight's case, it had to do with ex-wives. He had "alimony problems," Bob said. "He didn't want to let anyone know where he was." With Pearson, it had to do with vanity. As a former editor at G. P. Putnam's Sons, and having just made a splash with his humorous book, *Fractured French*, and its sequel, *Compound Fractured French*, both receiving high praise from the *Saturday Review of Literature*, he cringed at being linked to *The Bob and Ray Show*. He "looked down on it," Elliott said. "With a book like *Fractured French* . . . He probably said, 'I don't want to be associated with *this!*'"

Still, Elliott and Goulding liked him. The warm and disarming Pearson happened to have a terrible stammer. It was hard not to pull for him, especially during production meetings when it took him longer to pitch a Chester and Hester premise than the actual finished sketch when performed on the air.

The Colgate-Palmolive-Peet Company, as it was then called, oversaw its shows with occasional tugs on the reins to ensure that there were no conflicts with their products. *The Bob and Ray Show* hawked Ajax, Vel, and Colgate chlorophyll toothpaste. Each morning at eleven o'clock, the firm's ad agency, William Esty & Co., dispatched senior account executive Bill Templeton to 30 Rock for a B&R read-through of the entire twelve-page script. During one particular week, a young female assistant named Betty McCabe was filling in for Bill at the meetings. In collusion with the boys and Ken MacGregor, Knight, and Pearson slipped in some dummy dialog prior to Betty's arrival in Studio 6A's control room.

With everyone managing to keep a straight face, Bob and Ray did not read much beyond: "Come down from your *Ivory* tower! The *Tide's* in. It *Duz* us good to *Cheer* for *Joy*, and run down to the *Surf* and enjoy *Lifebuoy* . . ." before Betty was up like a shot and on the phone to the agency.

Happily, the boys never had any run-ins with the advertiser's dictatorial chief executive officer, Edward Little, notorious for his lack of show-business savvy. During his company's sponsorship of *The Colgate Comedy Hour*, Little had asked NBC vice-president Pat Weaver, "Who is this Abbott N. Costello you keep talking about?"

～

With the TV series on hiatus, and Stan Freeman, witty café pianist and Blue Angel mainstay, temporarily stepping into the WNBC early-morning spot, John Moses persuaded NBC and Colgate that his clients deserved some time off in Miami Beach. However, the suits insisted on one little proviso: The two network obligations, the daily Colgate quarter-hour, and weekly *Inside Bob & Ray*, had to continue as part of the "vacation."

A busman's holiday of daily remote broadcasts was clearly not what they had bargained for; nevertheless, Elliott and Goulding chose to look at the positive side. After all, it was three weeks in Miami Beach. What could possibly go wrong?

Moses hastily arranged to originate the shows in front of tourist audiences at the Tatem Surf Club, a six-story, seventy-room oceanfront hotel at 4343 Collins Avenue, first opened during the 1938 winter season by Tatem Wofford, the scion of a wealthy Florida family.

Unassuming looking and on the slim side, therefore affably—if not hilariously—nicknamed "Chubby," Wofford had started working at age nineteen in his parents' first hotel, the Wofford, at 24th and Collins. His family built the place in 1924 in plenty of time for the 125-mile-an-hour hurricane of 1926 that killed 113 people.

By the spring of 1952—his parents now long departed—Wofford was a man desperate for favorable publicity. The 1950–51 Kefauver Senate Committee investigation into organized crime had just established that known "gangsters" and "racketeers" used the Wofford Hotel as their headquarters to control syndicate-linked "racing wire services and bookmaking establishments for a number of years." An attempt at damage control—changing the name from Wofford Hotel to Wofford Beach Hotel—had not exactly done the trick.

His family holdings now confined to the Tatem Surf Club, Wofford jumped at the opportunity to help salvage his name in the reflected glow of *The Bob and Ray Show* and promote the hotel as a fun place to spend some time—and money.

After only a couple of shows, Goulding received a call from Fred Goldman, a close friend dating back to their Lowell High days. "I can't believe you guys are there," Goldman told Ray, surprised and amused at the choice of the Tatem Surf Club as the team's Miami Beach broadcast site. Goldman went on to explain that he and his family had recently been turned away from the very same hotel because they were Jewish.

As Ray and his partner quickly discovered, the Surf Club was one of the last "restricted" hotels on Miami Beach, and Tatem Wofford was, as Bob put it, a "bigot of the first order. . . . So anti-Semitic—outspoken!" In 1949, a Miami city ordinance made it unlawful to display discriminatory notices in places of public accommodation. Though the "Restricted Clientele" signs disappeared, a few hotels, in their own ways, continued to let Jews know they were not welcome.

Ray never talked about his religion, Liz said, but "he lived it." Having been raised on stories of Lowell's Catholics being discriminated against—including his own father for wearing a black armband when the pope died—had left an indelible impression. He had no tolerance for any kind of social injustice, and in high school had been quick to come to Fred Goldman's defense when his friend encountered prejudice from some Catholic students.

The atmosphere quickly became tense. Goulding conferred with Elliott, and then they both conferred with Moses, comfortably established at the Roney-Plaza. "John was as flustered as anybody else," Elliott said. It had been Moses, after all—who was Jewish—who had lined up the Surf Club.

"That," said Liz, the irony not escaping her, "was the funny part of it—unbelievable!"

Obviously, reminding anyone familiar with the Tatem Surf Club that Bob and Ray were the hotel's big attraction would certainly not enhance their image, or that of NBC or Colgate-Palmolive. Everyone's fun on the beach was suddenly overrun by crisis management. It was "sticky," said Elliott, always in command of *le mot juste*.

A volley of telephone calls between Miami and New York ensued. Though privy to the arrangements, NBC's Bud Barry and Mitch Benson had been consumed by far more urgent priorities—such as seeing that their radio network still had a pulse—than poring over Elliott and Goulding's vacation itineraries.

In his own defense, Wofford was not about to point out that he had always graciously rolled out the welcome mat for Jewish underworld boss Meyer Lansky. In the end, there was little choice. The broadcasts were promptly yanked out of the Tatem Surf Club and into the studios of NBC's Miami affiliate, WIOD, thus eliminating any promotional pitches for the hotel. As part of the agreement, however, each show contained a passing reference to Wofford himself, a quick, throwaway non sequitur. All parties were not exactly thrilled. A drab studio was clearly not the most exotic locale for the program's Miami Beach stay. But the decision spared lawsuits and any controversial fallout. Moses, evidently not the most thorough travel agent, did, however, like most good agents and managers, have a knack for smoothing things out.

Though deprived of a studio audience, the shows went off well enough. To this day, fond memories of a fishing trip on the yacht *Busy Bee* out of Haulover Beach Marina are still evoked by the seven-foot sailfish mounted on Elliott's office wall above a certificate, dated May 18, 1952, attesting to his two-and-a-half-hour struggle to land the thing. Thanks to Wofford, it was Bob's second-most memorable event of the trip, and also the last of his travels with Jane. In the months following, the situation between the two "worsened," Bob said. "The marriage—begun when I was barely twenty—was grinding to an end." From the start, he said, none of their parents had applauded the merger.

One Man's Family was a soap opera begging to be lampooned. Its characters performed with virtual "Kick me" signs on their backs. For years, Bob and Ray happily complied. But their version, *One Feller's Family*, would be missing in action when the team's TV series resumed July 5th as a weekly, Saturday-night, half-hour summer fill-in for—yes, *the* original—*One Man's Family*. Since *Family*'s devoted, longtime sponsor, Miles Laboratories' Alka-Seltzer, was also picking up the tab on the boys' show, they wisely figured Alka-Seltzer brass would appreciate one less headache to cure.

RIGHT: Bob, at fourteen or fifteen, perusing *Radio Stars of Today*, "probably," he suggested, "looking for a picture of Ransom Sherman or Myron Wallace" (later to become Mike Wallace).

BOTTOM: Bob, at nineteen, hosting *Depot Dialogues* at Boston's North Station. Following the sneak attack on Pearl Harbor and consequent fear of lurking undercover enemy agents, such *Man on the Street* programs were soon moved to more easily controlled indoor venues.

Captain Ray Goulding with his nine-year-old nephew, Bill Miles, at Liz's grandparents' home in Attica, Ohio, 1945.

Bob (left) with Fitz (William Fitzsimmons) at the Battle of the Bulge in December 1944.

"It got plenty scary."

At the WHDH studio organ prior to a *Matinee with Bob and Ray* broadcast.
"It wasn't always funny, but it was something."

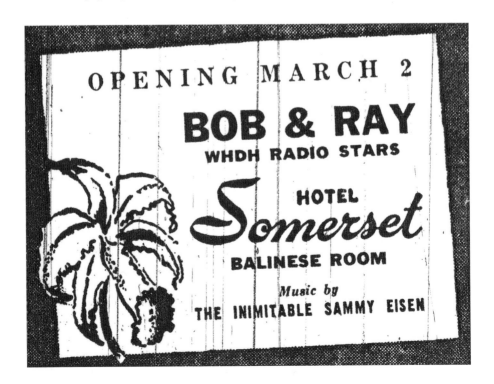

In Studio 3E for their July 2, 1951, NBC network debut. Not visible is Bob's ankle-to-thigh cast.

Ray Knight working on tomorrow's *Bob and Ray Show* script. He usually wrote in longhand at home and brought it to the studio to be typed.

"They're doing everything I did twenty years ago."

Hiding their faces behind beekeeper's netting to ease the transition from radio during the opening seconds of *The Bob and Ray Show*'s TV premiere, November 26, 1951.

With Audrey Meadows on the NBC TV series.

"You had to dance through the minefield of their banter."

TOP: More dubious merchandise from the Bob and Ray Overstocked Surplus Warehouse.

"Forbush 'Carefree' Dinnerware—the plates the nation eats off of."

RIGHT: Rehearsing with Cloris Leachman at NBC in 1952.

"You never knew what they were going to do next."

Top: A run-through at an empty Aqueduct racetrack, July 20, 1953, during a season in which NBC had no television studio available for their show.

Left: Unforeseen political forces in Washington helped launch the WINS morning series.

"Bob and Ray started the ball rolling, for New Yorkers, at least, who wanted to rail against McCarthy."

Replacing Audrey Meadows, then on Broadway with Phil Silvers in *Top Banana*, was a former Miss Chicago of 1946, Cloris Leachman. "I just remember it was the hottest summer in my history in New York City," said Leachman, whose apartment, she added, had no air conditioning. "Oh, my God! I'd lie there with a wet towel over me and I couldn't sleep at all. . . . So all summer long I was absolutely cuckoo tired. And I'd go down there to do the show and I had no ability not to laugh. Being so tired, I couldn't control it. And they would start this sketch and I would just start laughing at them. Helpless! Helpless! . . . You just beg for mercy."

Now, with a half-hour in prime time, many of the sketches by Knight and Billy Friedberg were longer and more venturous. Some even contained musical numbers with special lyrics and choreography, featuring vocals by Elliott, Goulding, and Leachman, all backed by Alvy West's band. One, Leachman recalled, was a lampoon of the nightly weather forecast performed as an over-produced variety show-style production number. "We did a version of 'Singing in the Rain' . . . me and Bob and Ray in our raincoats," she said. "It's funny business—just being silly. I'm good at that."

In alternating entrances and exits, Cloris Leachman raced between dual *Mary Backstayge* roles, playing both Harry's devoted, innocent wife, Mary, and his scheming leading lady, Jessica Culpepper. Reflecting on the experience, Leachman evoked the image of "Tom Sawyer painting the fence. He drew people to him," she said. "I think that's what they did. They'd just get busy at something and you just stepped right into it. . . . You never knew what they were going to do next. We were live television; I didn't have any scary bones about it."

Grey Lockwood, then also at the helm of *The All-Star Revue*'s Jimmy Durante and Martha Raye shows, split the directing duties with Coby Ruskin. Lockwood, too, did not know what they were going to do next, which made plotting camera shots in advance impossible. Instead, Lockwood said, he covered *Mary Backstayge* sketches like a sporting event. "As long as they stayed at least two feet from the back wall, to avoid lighting problems, and didn't move too far downstage—because I couldn't shoot off the set—I could cover everything. . . . I would just keep a medium two-shot, basically from their waists to just above their heads. Coming from radio, they weren't action people."

From week to week, *Buzz Burton's Sports Final* (Elliott, in what would later be his Biff Burns voice) addressed controversial sports topics, such as the wisdom of admitting bowling into the Olympic Games. Among the special mock offers was the Bob and Ray Shipwreck Kit ("Have you ever seriously worried about being set adrift in the open sea?"), which included a supply of beautiful bottles, each one "containing a message written by some of the world's greatest authors."

"They imitated real people incredibly well—that ordinary quality," Lockwood said. "It was that combination of everyman's speech and everyman's sound. . . . there was no 'theater' about anything they did."

Lockwood considered the series a plum assignment. There was none other like it, he said. "I would be rehearsing a Martha Raye show and get a call that Bob and Ray need a director for next week. I'd interrupt the rehearsal and take the call to get the job. . . . They were comfortable to be around; nothing was a big deal."

As with much of early television, Bob and Ray's shows were a natural extension of their radio work, leaving the viewer, as *Variety* put it, with "more to listen to than to watch." While noting the "pointed and sharp" sketches, and developing "staunch Bob and Ray cult," the review of the summer series premiere also observed that the "Herculean chores" of their insane radio and TV schedule "unfortunately displays the effect that such a drain can have on their creative spirit."

With the arrival of the fall season, NBC tinkered with the format to fill a fifteen-minute hole on Tuesday nights at ten-thirty, between Herb Shriner's *Two for the Money* and Bob Considine's ten-forty-five news commentary. The plan was to inject Bob and Ray into a fictional nightclub setting, a tired concept even in 1952.

The new program, *Club Embassy*—for P. Lorillard's Embassy cigarettes—exhibited all the characteristics of a lovechild conceived from a chance encounter between a network sales rep and an ad agency account exec. It was all about selling cigarettes. The show's hostess was Embassy spokeswoman Julia Meade, who, puffing away, regularly urged viewers to "inhale to your heart's content." B&R's sketches were performed in front of appreciative "guests," in reality, paid extras seated at ringside tables inside NBC's Studio 6B. The contrived surroundings were at cross-purposes with the material, which, of course, had to be played to the camera. It was, after all, a television program. Equally incongruous was the presence each week of violin virtuoso Florian Zabach, whose selections included such chestnuts as "Hot Canary," "Fiddle Faddle," and "The Whistler and His Dog," all with inevitable solos ending with a close-up of him winking at the camera.

Whoever came up with the *Club Embassy* format did the duo "dirt," *Variety* reported, adding that, the comics "distinguished themselves on the premiere despite the show, certainly not because of it."

An opening-night target was Richard Nixon's famous "Checkers" speech—it was the final month of the '52 Eisenhower/Stevenson campaign—with Ray interviewing Bob as a scoutmaster who had been dipping into the funds. ("Scathingly funny," wrote *Variety*'s reviewer.) Other topical bits during the run included a sendup of the Tuesday-night CBS competition, *Danger*, and *See It Now and Then* with Edward R. Sturdley and Horace W. Hostile, a play on Edward R. Murrow's *See It Now*, which was produced by Fred W. Friendly. After twice screening a kinescope of the latter bit, Friendly—the future president of CBS News—sent the boys a letter, stating that he and Murrow found the sketch "a completely refreshing experience. . . . Speaking for Edward R. Sturdley and Horace W. Hostile, we were delighted." A parody of Fred Waring and his Pennsylvanians—Fred Sturdley and his New Mexicans—prompted a similarly wry response from the orchestra leader's office.

Thanks to Lorillard's juicy checkbook, *Club Embassy*, in contrast to the team's original nightly TV series, reflected more of an extravagant, big-budget variety show look, paradoxically undermining its very premise. The more ambitious the sketches and production values, the less indigenous to a nightspot they appeared. One week, Bob and Ray did their version of a politician's whistle-stop tour. The candidate in question is seen hanging from a rope below a hovering helicopter as he visits, first, a farmer milking his cow, and then, a skyscraper construction worker catching hot rivets in a bucket. This was all accomplished with background flats and rolled-in film clips. The following week, the team's *High Noon* sendup called for various rear-projection screen images—a sheriff's office, a western street, and a saloon—together with constant dissolves to a close-up of a clock as the minute hand creeps inexorably closer to twelve—all conventional video effects, SOP for television, not nightclubs.

Ray Knight and Jack Roche, on double-duty from the two network radio series, shared the writing chores, and were joined—on one occasion only—by Danny and Neil Simon. The series followed on the heels of Audrey Meadows's debut with Jackie Gleason in his "Honeymooners" sketches, replacing Pert Kelton in the role of Alice Kramden. However, she still managed to rejoin Bob and Ray Tuesday evenings, juggling both shows for the rest of the year. As *Club Embassy*'s October 7th premiere approached, Meadows's Gleason show reviews were still coming in, including one from the *World-Telegram*'s Harriet Van Horne, who wrote, "I shall never forget how funny Miss Meadows was on *The Bob and Ray Show*. But I liked Pert Kelton's gravel-voiced Alice much better. It was earthier."

As it happened, *Embassy*'s producer, Joe Cates—pioneering TV figure, Broadway producer, father of Phoebe, and brother of TV director Gil—had just defected from the Gleason show, *Cavalcade of Stars*, on the DuMont network. "I had a migraine headache every Friday night before the show," Cates told Gleason's biographer William A. Henry III, recalling his two seasons with the comedian. "And it didn't go away until I threw up. When I left *Cavalcade*, the headache went away, too." If *Club Embassy* triggered its return, Cates kept it to himself.

Early in *Embassy*'s run, NBC's vice-president in charge of television, Pat Weaver—father of Sigourney—called on the team to infuse some comedy into his brand-new *Today* show. The program was broadcast every morning from a street-level studio, essentially part of the RCA Exhibition Hall. Large windows facing onto West Forty-Ninth Street enabled tourists and passersby to stop and ogle. During the team's early-morning radio show, the service elevator would be held and, during a news break, take them downstairs, where they would race outside to the window. *Today* host Dave Garroway would then switch to Bob, who would interview Ray as one of the gawkers. The *Today* appearances continued for a while, every Monday and Thursday.

One morning, a call came through to the control room from network president Niles Trammell, angrily wanting to know about "those two idiots outside. Doesn't the one guy know that he's talking to the same guy every day?"

With *Club Embassy*, the *Today* appearances, and their two network radio series, B&R's hardest gig was the early-morning block. In the less than a year and a half that the team had been broadcasting in the mornings, Rayburn and Finch still remained in the penthouse.

General manager Ted Cott again reflexively looked to WNEW. Instead of lifting another idea or two, this time he went directly after the station's on-air talent, waving a tantalizing contract at Rayburn and Finch to come over to WNBC. As Cott also headed the network's local-television outlet, WNBT, his offer also provided for future TV projects. First accounts had the deal a *fait accompli*. But then Dee Finch decided to put his money—a reported five hundred thousand dollars for five years in a WNEW counter offer—on radio, and remain at the station. Rayburn, eager to jump into television, as well as continue in radio, left for WNBC.

Monday, November 17, 1952, *The Bob and Ray Show* was replaced by its former competition, Gene Rayburn, now performing as a single, in direct competition with his ex. It was a brazen move on Cott's part, but business as usual for the New York morning radio wars. Bernice Judis was not happy, as evidenced by WNEW's new "copycat"-themed jingle aimed at those "adopting" her on-air personalities and programming concepts. They "might just as well have rewritten the jingle to read 'copy-Cott,'" Cott told a reporter, "since obviously they mean me."

Finch broke in a new partner, Gene Klavan, from Baltimore, via Washington and Philadelphia. They, too, debuted on Monday, November 17th, now doing business as Klavan and Finch. One more round of musical chairs was still to come. When Bob and Ray listeners swamped WNBC with complaints, particularly about missing their morning installments of *Mary Backstayge*, Cott prevailed upon the boys to record new daily episodes, which ran twice each morning under the banner: "Gene Rayburn presents *Mary Backstayge, Noble Wife*."

With *Club Embassy*'s December 30th broadcast, it was decided to spotlight music rather than comedy. Bob, Ray, and Audrey were succeeded by vocalist Mindy Carson, who was later replaced by Connie Russell, before

NBC finally closed the doors for good on "television's smart, new *Club Embassy*," as the program proclaimed itself.

~

Traffic was light as Bob's cab raced down to East Nineteenth Street. Moments before, he had gotten a desperate call from Ray Knight's wife, Lee, stating that her husband had passed out in the vestibule of their apartment building. When Bob and the cabbie arrived, Knight was "completely out," Bob said, but they were able to get him into his apartment.

Bud Barry had known about Knight's drinking problem, as had Ken MacGregor. "Slowly it became evident to us," Bob said. "He would do a day's script, turn it in and disappear for a couple of hours. He'd be downstairs at Hurley's. . . . He had one bout in a dry-out place upstate in late '52. And then he came back and we kept him on, and he got worse over time."

Ray Knight died in Columbus Hospital, February 12, 1953, his fifty-fourth birthday, leaving his wife and two young daughters, Colony and Shannon, and a mound of debts. "Everyone was concerned about Lee," Liz said. "It was a shock. I guess he had been ill for maybe a month. But I didn't know it was that serious."

"It was really the end of a major cycle of radio history," Bob said, "which we may not have realized at the time. We felt the great loss of his presence, and his contributions. I felt it very personally, and Ray did, too, and so did people like MacGregor, who had known him so much longer."

The Knights' oldest daughter, today Collie Elliott Santangelo, a children's book author and illustrator, was left with just a couple of memories of him. In what may be the best of these, she said, she was four-and-a-half or five, and her father had just returned home, wearing his heavy overcoat and brimmed hat. He just stood there, grinning. "All of a sudden I realized there was a kitten poking out of his breast pocket, and one out of the other pocket. He had brought back two kittens for me and Shannon. That is a very strong memory." There was a considerable difference in Lee and Ray's ages, Collie said, noting that if Knight—having been born in 1899— were alive in 2011, he would be almost 113. "I like to say," she laughed, that "my biological father was born two hundred years ago."

7

NOMADS WITH EARPHONES

By nature, Bob and Ray were cautious when not on sure ground, trapped between ambition and insecurity. They were not dynamic, Elliott said. Despite all the success, "We lacked confidence a lot of the time."

In spite of their apprehensions, the two were not immune to influential forces at GAC, who, in their desire to increase their young comedy clients' exposure—not to mention commissions—instinctively turned to a two-man act's natural haunt: nightclubs. Immediately, the boys had foreseen one conceivable hurdle: They did not have a club act. But Art Weems, the slim, sandy-haired head of GAC's nightclub stable—and brother of famed bandleader Ted—was not about to let that stand in his way, especially after hearing John Moses rave about the boys' two SRO engagements at the Somerset in Boston. So what if Moses never actually saw the act?

Nevertheless, playing it safe, Weems decided on a trial run at a midtown spot, concluding—for reasons known only to him—that Elliott and Goulding first had to break in the act in New York City, before being booked in, say, Altoona.

Fortuitously, the GAC stars had been in alignment. A major client, Peggy Lee, who had done a couple of guest-shots on *Inside Bob and Ray*, was soon to headline at La Vie en Rose. It did not take much to sell her on sharing the bill for one night, given that Lee's personal agent and Weems's boss, Tom Rockwell, also happened to be the president of GAC. As for the club's always nattily turned-out owner and operator, Monte Proser, there would be no resistance. Always covetous of GAC's impressive talent roster, Proser knew when to do a favor.

The chic, intimate East Fifty-Fourth Street club—with its plush, red interiors—was primarily known for name singers of the day, such as Mel Torme and Joni James. This only added to B&R's anxiety. Suddenly, their deadpan approach was about to be thrust into the uninviting domain of the traditional straight man/stooge template of nightclub and saloon comedy teams. As the two waited offstage they could see Peggy Lee in the middle of her playful version of "Hard-Hearted Hannah," during which she brandished a prop gun. The audience's laughter lifted their spirits, but only for a moment.

With Eddie Fisher sitting ringside, along with the inevitable cabal of GAC suits, and introduced by Lee, Bob and Ray performed an updated version of their Somerset act. They lampooned some popular shows of the era, including their *Dr. O.K.*, *John J. Agony*, and the *Gillette Cavalcade of Sports*, the latter with Bob sporting bandaged razor nicks all over his face, and Ray as a grizzled baseball vet harboring total contempt for the game's younger players. But, again, the biggest laugh-getter was the old Somerset standby, Ray blowing smoke rings as the man behind the Camel billboard, this time at "Times Square." The response was exhilarating. The GAC suits were thrilled, none more so than John Moses. Now, when promoting the team's club act, he would actually know what he was talking about.

Bob and Ray's nightclub career, such as it was—success in Boston, and then New York—was clearly ascending. Where next? Miami? Las Vegas? Hollywood? The answer was swift in coming: Buffalo. The pair was booked to headline for one week, two shows a night, at the Town Casino.

If Buffalo was a strange choice, an even greater one followed. Inexplicably, Weems talked the team into scrapping their entire act. The comfortable Somerset bits—now La Vie en Rose-tested—were suddenly history. Weems prevailed upon a writer (a GAC client, of course, the name now long forgotten) specializing in cabaret acts to supply the pair with shticky, zinger-laced stand-up routines, even including hokey vocal arrangements. "I remember it now as being completely foreign," Elliott said of the material. "It was like a bad dream." Moses tried to be supportive, but he was under Weems—"the instigator," Elliott called him—who could be formidable, especially when confronting two naïve, young, Boston radio guys not given to making waves.

The morning of the March 16th opening dawned with reports of a snowstorm due to hit that evening. The club's newspaper ads also set off alarms. Hyping the St. Patrick's Day-eve kickoff, the blurbs proclaimed: "Bob and

Ray—those laugh-happy sons of old Erin!" An afternoon rehearsal of the newly conceived musical score with Moe Balsam, a "bandleader out of a thirties movie," in Bob's words, left them feeling even more unsettled.

Predictably, the snowstorm arrived; the audience did not. In contrast to the cozy La Vie en Rose, the Town Casino was a cavernous edifice of tufted-fabric walls draped with dramatic burgundy swags, and its cabaret tables surrounded by tiered rows of semi-circular booths. Greeted by sparse applause, B&R could spot only a few scattered patrons among a sea of empty white tablecloths. "There was only an ashtray on them," Bob said, and "no people sitting at them. All you could see was white." Ray thought he was "suffering from snow blindness," he remarked afterwards. "We plowed through whatever it was we had," Bob said. "They didn't dig it at all. . . . I can't remember what we did. It's such a bad experience that I've apparently blanked it out."

Following the first show, the two quickly sought refuge in Moses's nearby hotel suite, where they happened to be joined by Oscar Levant, a friend of the agent who was appearing locally a day or so later. Levant did his best to be encouraging. At that point, given the events of the day and evening, looking to the acid-tongued Levant for cheering up did not strike anyone as surreal. "It's such a funny picture," Elliott said, "but then we were devastated. . . . We were crying to John, 'Jesus, we can't do a week of this!'"

For Levant's benefit, they then started to repeat the material. "It wasn't *Bob and Ray*," Elliott went on. "It was just awful." After five minutes, Levant cut them off. "Go back to the stuff you know," he advised. His reasoning, though hardly inspiring, was hard to argue with: "It can't be worse," he told them.

Incredibly, the second show was packed. Plugs during their previous week's NBC Colgate shows had apparently paid off. But midway through their first bit, it became painfully evident that the excited throng had not come to see them, but rather the other headliner on the bill, Billy Ward and the Dominoes, a premier R&B group of the day. Screaming fans, particularly females, could hardly wait to shriek and faint at the passionate voice of lead singer Clyde McPhatter, whose sensual "Sixty-Minute Man" was a monster hit. This was not a crowd that had ventured out in a snowstorm to see Steve Bosco routines and Arthur Godfrey impressions.

"Nobody knew who we were," Bob said. "It wasn't our kind of crowd. It wasn't for the whole week, but we managed. . . . We got through it."

Closing night, the two gifted Moe Balsam with a pair of cufflinks, only to discover that the custom was cash. Then, after being ushered into the club's dreary basement office by "two bruisers," Elliott recounted, the manager was "very hesitant when he gave us the check. . . . I mean, this was real mobsterville. . . . He wasn't happy with what we had done. He *was* happy with Billy Ward and Dominoes. . . . GAC gave up pursuing night-clubs at that point. That wasn't our field, and we knew it."

The boys were on the first train back to New York.

••~

By the spring of 1953, NBC had turned Elliott and Goulding into nomads. At one time or another, they had shows at every hour of the day and night. Having dropping *Inside Bob and Ray* and the late-morning Colgate series, they were given a thirty-nine week WNBC fifteen-minute six-thirty evening strip, a Friday night summer game show, *Pick and Play with Bob & Ray*, and an across-the-board network midnight-to-one-in-the morning slot. During the latter, they frequently kibitzed with Paul Taubman and soundman Agnew Horine. More precisely, "Taubman" and "Horine" were Goulding-voiced incarnations of the real-life staffers, thus sparing NBC having to cough up AFTRA fees. Trolling their 30 Rock "studio audience," B&R routinely interviewed each other portraying various night owls with nowhere better to be after midnight than a radio studio. "Little gems of pointlessness," was how John Crosby described the segments.

The team's TV series returned April 27, 1953, on yet another new time and day, Monday nights at seven-thirty, with *Variety* declaring them NBC's "peripatetic property." Everybody should be happy, the journal reported, "That is, until the order is issued to move again." The review of the premiere noted that their "humor is sharp and bright. The pace is fast and the material is zany."

Since the program was only fifteen minutes, once a week, Bob and Ray hoped Audrey Meadows, by then concluding her first season with Jackie

Gleason, could again join them. However, Gleason's manager, "Bullets" Durgom, protective of his client's rich CBS contract, resisted. Words became heated and "an impasse was reached," recounted Meadows in her 1994 memoir.

> Jackie was summoned to rule from on high.
>
> "Why do you want to do this, Aud?" he asked.
>
> "Because when I needed a job, they took me on when they didn't have to," I said. "Now they need me."
>
> "That's the best reason I know," said Jackie. "I'll be watching the show if it doesn't run into the cocktail hour. Leave Alice here. Go be Audrey."

While the Monday-night series *did* have Audrey Meadows, it is more noteworthy for what it did *not* have—a band, a sponsor, or even its own studio. NBC's entire Monday-night prime-time lineup was comprised of live, New York-based shows, including the ninety-minute *Robert Montgomery Presents*. Having sponsors, they all had priority on available studio space. The lack-of-facilities headache hit home with one B&R viewer in particular, Bob's former Feagin classmate Jack Carter, whose own NBC *Saturday Night Revue* variety hour was extradited to Chicago. "We would always be in the smallest studio, or in one corner of the biggest studio," said the boys' director Grey Lockwood. "We were always running from one little theater to another."

The June 29th show, from NBC's newly equipped Colonial Theater at 62d and Broadway, was an early experimental broadcast to test RCA's new compatible-color system. Reflecting on the occasion years later, Ray recalled the chief concern of NBC VP Barry Wood, precipitating "a big discussion on whether red or blue was funnier. Work on that for a while." A few weeks later, the show was moved to the International Theater at Columbus Circle. On several Mondays, NBC could not dig up *any* studio. That summer, using pickup crews, the network was forced to originate *The Bob and Ray Show* at scattered sites around the city, such as the July 20th broadcast from Aqueduct racetrack.

One week, the boys were given a choice: Either broadcast from the Weehawken ferry, or from Philadelphia. The July 27th show was performed live from the ferry slip on the Manhattan side.

Announcer Dick Dudley explained at the opening of the August 3rd program that Bob and Ray are in their "vacation spot in uptown New York . . . drinking in the fresh, outdoor air, cooking meals in the open, cavorting on real grass; in short, getting back to nature." The two were then introduced coming out of a pup tent in deep right field at the Polo Grounds. The entire quarter-hour emanated from the New York Giants' fabled ballpark on the Upper West Side.

The live remotes demanded that all material be tailored to accommodate the limitations at the various sites, thus eliminating conventional sets. All backgrounds and visual effects consisted of whatever was available at the particular locale. On the Monday the two were forced to broadcast from Cromwell's—the site of their enforced Phillips Carlin-tutored comedy classroom—the show opened on an extreme close-up of one of the drugstore's napkin dispensers. Over the opening theme, "Sheboygan," a hand reached in and, one-by-one, slowly pulled out six individual paper napkins, each with its own separate title written on it: Bob Elliott . . . and Ray Goulding . . . present . . . The National Broadcasting company . . . which presents . . . *The Bob and Ray Show.*

The pair was then discovered sitting in an air-conditioned booth, vowing to never again endure a muggy, hot, miserable Fourth of July, with the inevitable crowded roads and beaches.

> *Bob:* November first, we've discovered, is invariably a clear, cool, pleasant day—ideal for Fourth of July celebrating.
> *Ray:* If this idea appeals to you, and you'd like to back us in the campaign to move the Fourth of July . . .

Then, *Biff Burns' Sports Extra* found Bob interviewing Ray as a retired, ex-flyweight champion about his new career, creating special fragrances for men. ("He-man aromas . . . 'T-Shirt,' 'Bull Pen' and 'First Baseman's Mitt.'") The entire bit was played at the store's perfume counter.

This was followed by a routine specifically staged for the drugstore: an installment of *Mr. Trace, Keener Than Most Persons,* in "The Missing Ivory Cigar-Holder Murder Clue." A Cromwell's phone booth provided the setting for the sketch's pivotal scene, with Bob as "the surly old investigator," Mr. Trace.

MR. TRACE

(ON PHONE)

You say you think someone is trying to kill you, Mr. Willoughby? Pshaw. . . . But why would anyone want to murder you? . . . What gives you that idea? . . . Oh? You're wrestling with the murderer right now? . . . Well, I . . . What's that? . . . A shot! . . . Mr. Willoughby? . . . Mr. Willoughby? . . . And now a body falling to the floor! (CLICKS PHONE) This sounds serious. I must contact my assistant Mike Delancy. *(DIALS)* . . . Hello, Mike? . . . Get over to the expensive penthouse apartment of wealthy Jason Willoughby right away. I think he's been murdered. . . . Get all the facts you can and meet me at Cromwell's Drugstore in Radio City in half an hour. Goodbye.

When Delancy (Ray) arrives, the resolution of "The Missing Ivory Cigar-Holder Murder Clue" takes place, fittingly, at the drugstore's cigar counter. The murder and all the "action" is off-camera, or, as in radio, in the audience's imagination.

In ad-libbed segments, Grey Lockwood often had no clue as to when to fade out on a scene. "I never knew what the end was," he admitted. "I would often just go with the organist." Paul Taubman was an "absolute genius," according to Lockwood. "He could play anything. I never told him anything! . . . He understood them."

As for finishing a show on time, Lockwood also found himself in the dark. "I never knew," he said. "The P.A. would just call out how much time was left: 'Four minutes . . . three minutes . . .' And so on. We were always giving them signals: 'Cut' . . . 'speed up' . . . 'stretch.'"

Their sense of timing, honed by the radio years, served them well.

On September 28th, the network managed to free up one of their larger soundstages for the show, a big barn of a place, way up at 106th Street.

The following Monday, October 5th, Bob and Ray greeted viewers in a small basement studio that only recently had been converted from stables for Central Park carriage horses, a fact which became readily apparent on humid days. The address: Seven West Sixty-Sixth Street, the home of the American Broadcasting Company. Though the NBC midnight radio series continued for a period, they were now working for ABC every evening, from seven o'clock to seven-fifteen, preceding *John Daly and the News.* "We shifted our allegiance rapidly," Bob said.

Audrey Meadows, then starting her second season with Gleason, was succeeded by Marion Brash, a shapely, twenty-two-year-old blonde whose background had primarily been in the theater, including an arduous spell on the road in *Born Yesterday,* playing the Judy Holliday role, Billie Dawn. "It was one year of one-night stands," she said, "with a truck following a bus with all the sets and costumes. It was about as low class as you can get." Her only television experience had been a few months on *Rocky Corbett, Space Cadet.* Brash recalled very little of her Bob and Ray audition, other than that it was unconventional. "There was a puppet show in the same studio," she said, "and for some reason—I remember vaguely, very vaguely—being asked to do an improvisation with one of the puppets."

A new serial was introduced, a medical spoof, *Hospital Corners, U.S.A.* ("a story of today, based on sickness and disease, reflected in the life of a small-town country doctor"). If viewers missed *Linda Lovely* or *Mary Backstayge,* they at least felt at home with variations on the same storylines, as in a "peanut fever epidemic" brought on by the elephants when the circus hit town.

Like Cloris Leachman, Brash played two roles: Dr. Greg Norton's shrewish wife, Belle, and his sexy nurse, Eileen Dover. "Eileen Dover was a very buxom kind of nurse—bosomy," Brash explained. "In other words, you put it all together, it's 'I leaned over.'"

"In true Bob and Ray style," recalled Hank Behar, then a twenty-nine-year-old ABC lighting director, "they never alluded to her beauty or anything else. She was just another person in their world."

An American Airlines ticket agent and aspiring comedy writer, Earle Doud, was hired for the series based on a twenty-eight-page sample script. Doud would later serve hitches on the NBC *Comedy Hour* and *The Tonight Show* with Jack Paar. Most notably, however, in 1961, Earle Doud, then partnered with Bob Booker, created the Camelot-era sendup of the Kennedy White House, *The First Family,* a comedy album starring Vaughn Meader as JFK, and the follow-up LP, *The First Family, Vol. 2.*

Thanks to Doud, a lasting impression of the series for Bob and Ray was arriving at the studio in the afternoon and seeing an alligator or llama being held outside. "Every bit had a camel or something in it," Bob said.

"He was wild—absolutely wild," said Ann, who, with her husband, Bill, had accompanied the team to ABC to handle cue cards. She recalled a Doud sketch for a following day's show that required a live platypus that had to be kept overnight in water. He suggested that she take it home with her. "No, I can't!" Ann told him. "No way in hell am I taking that home! . . . Earle was a whacko, in my mind."

One Doud canine/feline-themed bit advised pet lovers to invest in the Bob and Ray Animal Trust Fund so that "in the event that something happens to you," your cat or dog would be properly looked after and someday be self-supporting. The fund provided for Bob and Ray becoming the animal's legal guardians. "We adopt your pet and his inheritance," they assured viewers.

Another Doud bit was a mock plea for viewers' assistance on behalf of previously booked guests, a band of Belgian Congo headhunters. ("Unfortunately, not being able to speak English, they arrived a month early. If any of you have an empty room in your house, you can be of service to us . . .")

Commercial lampoons were diligently mined, including the Bob and Ray Bank for Convenience-Minded Customers, featuring safe-deposit boxes built on the outside of the bank, and a Bob and Ray Home Butter-Printing kit. ("Why should a hotel have their initials in the butter and not you?") The Bob and Ray Overstocked Surplus Warehouse offered "a submarine that at one time belonged to a powerful nation." It comes equipped, they said, "with three executive officers, a surgeon, and sleeps forty-six."

"The impression I got is that there was practically no planning to the show," commented Hank Behar, who regularly observed the program in the control room, perched directly behind director Paul Burgraff. "Truth be told, all the bits didn't work, just as they didn't in radio. But their charm was that they just went on as if nothing had happened. Above all, they were supremely gentle souls."

Between the camera run-through and airtime, the boys, together with announcer Charles Woods, and occasionally Paul Burgraff, would stroll over to the Café des Artistes on 67th. The elegant cocktail lounge, an appendage to the Belle Époque-themed dining room and its country French cuisine, was a dramatic step-up from NBC's local watering hole, Hurley's, with its closet-sized kitchen that seemed to specialize in grease fires.

Hurley's was technically a bar and restaurant with the emphasis strictly on the former, said George Atkins, a writer on Jonathan Winters's old Tuesday night NBC series. "Hurley's served food, but seldom to the same person a second time."

With the last weeks of the NBC night-owl radio show overlapping their new TV series, and five hours each evening between the two, Elliott and Goulding could bank on the Café des Artistes and other midtown haunts for killing time—and a round or two of Wild Turkey, Ray's favorite. They had already discovered the East Side's Envoy and Press Box restaurants—two of Bob's favorites—for their steak-centric dining. When pressed, both agreed that Envoy was tops.

Steak, on the rare side, was Ray's passion. He and Bob discovered Peter Luger's Steak House in Brooklyn through Jack Spatz, their song-plugger friend. Later, Luger's opened a second spot in Great Neck, which Ray and Liz frequented, becoming almost like family to its manager, Carl Dickert. "A dear friend," Liz called him. "We really were quite close." In addition to her husband's love of fine food and restaurants, Liz said, "He loved to watch some of the waiters and their attitudes—some of them so officious—and get characters from them."

A frequent B&R lunch stop—for a period, "Four noons out of five," according to Bob—was Southerners Marc and Edith Ruben's Absinthe House on West Forty-Eighth Street. The place seemed to attract everybody at NBC, from Martha Raye to Dorothy Collins and the *Your Hit Parade* gang. It was also a favorite spot to take old WHDH cronies when they came to town. There, with their steaks, the boys relished the shrimp remoulade appetizers for the very first time. They even tried duplicating the dish at home. But given the results, both suspected that, for proprietary reasons, Marc and Edith had not been totally forthcoming when sharing the recipe.

8

MCCARTHYISM IN SKUNK HAVEN

With network radio on the ropes, local independents were quick to take advantage. In New York, in early 1954, a sleeping giant of a station, WINS, lured away Robert J. Leder, sales manager of WNBC, by offering him the titles of vice-president and general manager. Joining him was WNBC's music programmer, Robert S. Smith, as his new program director. Other NBC personnel jumping to WINS included a time salesman, traffic director, and head of publicity. Leder announced that he was also bringing over Bob and Ray, and their WNBC newsman, Peter Roberts, to do mornings, six-thirty to ten o'clock, Monday through Saturday, starting March 22nd. No, Leder claimed with a straight face, the eight WNBC defectors did not represent "a raid."

He was a "born persuader," Peter Roberts said of Leder, "a strange kind of wonderful guy." At the time, WINS' biggest attraction was New York Yankees baseball. Crosley Broadcasting, having determined that radio was dead, had just unloaded the station for $450,000. The new owner, J. Elroy McCaw, however, still detected a heartbeat. McCaw had been an aide to General "Hap" Arnold, chief of the U.S. Air Force in World War II. "Elroy knew where the bodies were buried," Roberts said.

McCaw, whose home was in Seattle, only slipped into New York for the sole purpose of overseeing budget-cutting measures. The bespectacled, bank clerk-appearing owner's perspective on making money started with a core principle of never spending any. For McCaw, it was imperative: he did not have any. Barely scraping together the down payment, he was left with no cash flow, according to Rick Sklar, who wrote commercials for the station before becoming its programmer. "Elroy believed there was virtually no reason to have to pay for any goods or services," Sklar noted in his memoir. He ordered station light bulbs changed to sixty watts and the program logs typed single-spaced to save paper. Besides mastering circuitous, tollbooth-avoiding routes to the airports, Sklar stated, for a period McCaw's city living expenses were solved by commercials for the Hotel Wyndham.

At one point, Elliott recalled, McCaw inexplicably had all the large studio clocks removed. When replacements were weeks late in arriving, the team was forced to announce morning time-checks off their wristwatches. "Nobody could figure it out," Bob said. "You own a radio station and you take the clocks out!"

Also newly arrived from McCaw's San Francisco property KYA was sports director Les Keiter, whose booming voice and bombastic style was all Bob and Ray needed to turn him into one of their foils ("The less Keiter, the better"). Soon, Keiter, too, became a victim of the owner's cost slashing. Reluctant to pay the exorbitant fees for high-quality broadcast circuits on New York Knicks' road games, McCaw's engineers devised a modified telephone with the handset replaced by Keiter's microphone, enabling WINS to transmit out-of-town games over a telephone line at a substantially cheaper, long-distance rate. "This was big-time sports radio done in a very amateurish way," Keiter said, recalling a "laughable" Knicks' broadcast from Philadelphia. "All of a sudden, I heard a voice interrupting my play-by-play. And that was the operator. She kept saying, 'I'm not talking about basketball, I'm the operator.' There was total confusion. . . . I would be describing: 'Guy Sparrow takes the ball into the front court,' and the operator said, 'How are you spelling Mr. Sparrow?' And I said, 'Operator, I'm in the middle of a ballgame! I can't sit here and discuss that with you. . . . Would you please get off the line until we get through with this game!' . . . It was a ludicrous situation."

When the Giants and Dodgers departed for California, the Yankees also made a move, abandoning WINS, their radio home for fourteen seasons, in favor of rival WMGM, the Dodgers' former station. To fill the baseball void, McCaw hatched a scheme to originate late-night studio play-by-play re-creations from Teletype reports of San Francisco Giants home games. But Keiter was resistant, telling his boss, "This is the Big Apple—they won't buy a re-creation here." Not true, said McCaw, who decided to soften Keiter up with a little Manhattan wining and dining. Which trendy midtown gastronomic palace did he select? Nedick's, a glorified hot dog-and-orange drink stand. The upshot: Keiter said he recreated every Giants home game for the next three years, adding that, to McCaw's credit, he did grab the Nedick's check.

If WINS was to be revitalized, McCaw knew the morning drive time was the starting point. The competition was formidable, beginning, inevitably, with WNEW and Gene Klavan and Dee Finch. The two were now entrenched, though success had not come overnight. Their initial programs, Klavan described in an unpublished memoir, had embodied "four hours of tension, manipulation and juxtaposition of two crazed improvisational performers trying to find common ground. It wasn't all bad; it was simply too much: too many characters, too fast-paced, too much flailing trying to find our roles."

"In a way, it was a step down," Peter Roberts commented about the jump from NBC to WINS. "But in another way, it was a step up."

At the network, according to Elliott, there was the prevailing sense that they could not be as "loose" as they ultimately became. "There was still the feeling that this was NBC. To start at the network and then move to WINS was a strange reversal."

Between commercials, weather forecasts, wacky station giveaways, and dropping in a steady stream of promos and slogans ("For music, news, time, and weather, keep your dial where the tens come together"), Bob and Ray were visited by their homegrown cadre of regulars. Dean Archer Armstead (Ray), the "agricultural director of Bob and Ray's Lackawanna, New York, field station," was usually accompanied by his assistant, Robin I. Pickett (Bob), who translated his colleague's barely intelligible reports on everything from planting underground blooming dahlia bulbs in the snow to perfecting a hybrid peach with fuzz on the inside. Robin was a three-tiered composite impersonation of veteran radio performer Arthur Q. Bryan's characterizations of both Elmer Fudd of Warner Bros. cartoons, and Doc Gamble of *Fibber McGee and Molly*. Others who dropped by included the simultaneously speaking McBeebee Twins, inspired by the real-life McFarland Twins, Art and George, twin sax-playing bandleaders, and Ray's Natalie Attired, who would literally "say" a song, that is, merely speak the lyrics to the pounding beat of her accompanist/drummer, Eddie (Elliott). In their own unique way, decades before rap, Natalie and Eddie were prescient.

Fortuitously, events in Washington that April helped launch the WINS series. McCarthyism was raging, and the proceedings at the Army-McCarthy hearings were folded into the plot of each morning's *Mary Backstayge* episode. Mocking Senator Joseph McCarthy was then considered quite daring. Only two months later, after praising Edward R. Murrow's acclaimed *See It Now* counterattack on McCarthyism, CBS anchor Don Hollenbeck committed suicide. He had been incessantly attacked for hewing to a perceived CBS "incipient pink line" by Jack O'Brien, the caustic Hearst-owned *New York Journal-American* columnist. It was a tense time.

Striking close to home for Bob and Ray was the case of their former TV director and close friend, Coby Ruskin, who had also found himself a victim of the McCarthy era. "I remember him telling us," Bob said, "that because of blacklisting, he and his wife had some fifty bucks between them, and that was it." They had seen a painting that they had liked very much, Bob continued, and "spent, I'll say forty-nine of the last fifty. . . . That took a lot to do, but it was also satisfying something they both felt."

Ray's personification of the Wisconsin senator was chilling, capturing every vocal tic. "B&R started the ball rolling," Roberts noted, "for New Yorkers, at least, who wanted to rail against McCarthy."

"It was an incredible few weeks of their best work, and all ad-libbed," recalled Ed Graham, then a twenty-five-year-old Young & Rubicam copywriter who often stopped by their studio and would later join them as a business partner. "Ray took Joe McCarthy and was hilarious," noted Graham, referring to Goulding's role as the hectoring commissioner Carstairs, who was trying to put the kibosh on Harry Backstayge's plans to construct a sixteen-story summer home in Skunk Haven, Long Island. "Bob not only had Joe Welch down cold, he even did Roy Cohn and Karl Mundt. . . . That anyone could or would even bother to imitate Karl Mundt amazed me. But Bob had his own thought processes. And so it went with Word Carr."

Mary Backstayge's unctuous-sounding "announcer," Word Carr, was Bob's sly imitation of vintage radio voice Ford Bond, a network presence since 1929, signing on and off dozens of NBC shows, the original *Mary Noble, Backstage Wife* among them. He was the type, Bob said, you would think of as "announcing in a tuxedo at ten-thirty in the morning." The fact that Ford Bond was long retired in the Virgin Islands was irrelevant. Elliott's Word Carr was so meticulously defined that any listener giving it even a moment's consideration would conclude it had to be an imitation of *someone*.

Bob's mind was "complicated," Graham said, referring to the Ford Bond-Word Carr connection. "In Bob's mind, giving your word was your bond, and a Ford was a car. No one but Bob, Ray, and I ever cared. And I'm not even sure Ray did, but it meant something to Bob: someone to spoof while still admiring them."

Over the *Backstayge*'s theme music, Les Baxter's "Celestial Nocturne," Bob, as Word Carr, set the scene for each day's adventure, thereby steering his partner—whose reactions he always could anticipate—into funny areas. "If not in the actual opening remarks," Peter Roberts said, "he would guide him verbally along the way. He would say, 'Yes, but . . .' and, 'What about . . .' or, 'Do you think that so-and-so . . .' He would give him a step he could take without being too obvious that they were headed off in another direction. That subtlety was there. He was very, very good at that."

In addition to the plot, both had to keep in mind each of their respective characters' topics of the moment. With all present in a scene, there were six or seven plates to keep spinning. Sometimes, when either sensed that the storyline was not progressing, they would have somebody enter with a "bombshell" to dramatically shift the direction of the narrative. Ray, in particular, was also in the habit of suddenly tossing in a ludicrous non sequitur to achieve the same effect. "With the help of characters," Bob said, "we could get out of anything."

Part of that training came from growing up listening to radio and sound effects and imagining somebody walking into a room and saying something, Chris Elliott pointed out. "The rhythm of that happening in your head instead of reading it off a script, or instead of seeing it in a film is totally different." To be able to visualize such a scene, he continued, "and keep it going without knowing where it's going to end, and making it seem like it's coming together without any effort—and maybe it *was* coming together without any effort—is definitely a gift. . . . Probably their imaginations were what fueled all that."

Added demands would be placed on those imaginations one evening when the pair anchored WINS' coverage of the circus's annual visit to Madison Square Garden. The best seats the tightfisted McCaw would spring for when it came to the boys' broadcast site were next to a utility tunnel through which the performing animals entered. All they could see, Elliott remembered, were "close-up views of the elephants' asses as they paraded around the ring."

"Marilyn Monroe sat astride a white elephant that night," recalled movie and theater critic Jeffrey Lyons, then only nine. "First time I'd ever heard of her." It would not be the last. He also recalled Bob and Ray interviewing his father, prominent Broadway columnist Leonard Lyons, afterwards. Lyons and his family had been invited to march in the opening-night procession.

"Our baby sitter," Jeffrey explained, "was a big Bob and Ray fan and introduced my younger brother Douglas and me to their humor. When moving into a West Fifty-Seventh Street apartment many years later, Jeffrey continued, he discovered that the previous occupant, Marshall Efron of PBS's *American Dream Machine* had left a box in the middle of the living room. "It was a treasure-trove of Bob and Ray tapes. . . . On our annual vacation, to Spain, I'd take about a dozen hours of B&R shows to listen to by the pool each day in Torremolinos. It became a ritual."

~

"Vic was left on our doorstep," Elliott said of the sardonic, indefatigable, twenty-five-year-old Vic Cowen, whom the team inherited at WINS. "He was a crackerjack." Cowen, raised in Queens, was the son of a florist who had lost his business during the Depression and then ended up working for the very people who had bought it from him. After high school and a few years on the CBS-page staff, he had landed in WINS' music library working on DJ Jack Lacey's programs, *Listen to Lacey* and *Lacey on the Loose*.

Initially handling music clearance and selecting the records, Cowen's *Bob and Ray Show* contributions soon expanded to include clever production effects, goofy musical selections, and recorded oddities. As the program became a prime stop on the record-promotion circuit, Cowen would corral guests such as Steve Lawrence & Eydie Gorme, and Doris Day to record additional "drop-in" material which, when inserted into the show out of context, sounded purposefully inane. "Vic had a wonderful ear," Elliott said, also noting that some of the performers caught on to his methods and ultimately became "gun shy of doing those things."

Vic Cowen was very effective in marshalling Bob and Ray's talents, Peter Roberts said. "He had suggestions for what they should do—how they could combine their talents in a more unified way. . . . His instincts were very sound, very good. Never negative—always a positive approach to things."

But from time to time Cowen's suggestions would be shot down. "Mostly it was Ray who overruled him—quietly, but overruled," Roberts said. "Bob tended to defer to Ray. . . . Ray liked to take command. Ray liked to take over. Bob was very quiet."

As Roberts did his first morning newscast, Ray was already eating breakfast, thanks to The Teheran, a Persian-Italian-American restaurant across the street. Long a *New Yorker* haunt, its owner, Hank Mazzucca, once confided to one of the magazine's staffers, "Nobody wants to eat Persian food five times a week." Mazzucca provided breakfast to B&R every morning. According to Roberts, each day's orders were plugged on air: "Eggs Benedict, waffles, French toast . . ." In truth, the breakfasts were always the same: two steaks, bread, and coffee. "It was the only item the night watchman at the restaurant could prepare," Roberts explained. "The regular staff didn't arrive until nine o'clock."

➵

Since their prank-playing days of sending unordered room service steaks to a Boston hotel suite, B&R had further sharpened their instincts for spotting easy prey. Such a man was Peter Roberts. Montreal born, Ottawa raised and Canadian tall, with horn-rimmed glasses and a rich, warm voice, Roberts was, in his own words, a "somewhat stuffed-shirt type." As the boys observed at WNBC, he was also easily provoked into fits of uncontrollable laughter at the most inopportune time—the middle of his morning newscasts.

"They used to do just everything on earth to break him up," Liz Goulding said. "I mean silly, ridiculous things."

"I was a ready victim," Roberts admitted, "because I could never contain myself from laughing . . . and they moved quickly to capitalize on it."

The Peter Roberts laugh was distinctive and infectious. Once started, it would seemingly sustain forever, dipping periodically only when he would sigh, "*Ho-ho*," followed by a woeful, "Oh, you shouldn't have!" His desperate, stoic attempts to repress the laughter—inevitably unsuccessful—made it that much funnier. "You could open any magazine," Bob Elliott explained, "and hold up any ad with big print letters, and he would laugh. It became that good."

The immediate WINS surroundings, however, provided no inspiration. "It was a pretty cruddy building," Roberts said of the station's second-floor operation on West Forty-Fourth Street. The walls were drab, the equipment dowdy, and the offices merely adequate. The editorial staff of the *New Yorker* magazine was a few floors above, he added, but "we never met up with or saw any of that group." The physical setup resembled a "V" with Bob and Ray's studio on one leg, the news studio on the other, and one common control room at the base of the "V," where the engineer sat.

One morning, the team interviewed Willis Hanks, a thirty-nine-year-old African-American New York postal clerk, about his forthcoming attempt to swim the English Channel, and for whom the boys were helping raise money for his daily Battery-to-Staten Island training sessions. Following the interview, Roberts heard a tap on the other side of the glass during his newscast. It was Bob, stretched out horizontally, kicking and flailing his arms, supposedly swimming by. It looked like "an insane example of the Australian crawl," he observed. Baffled, Roberts stopped for a second and then continued reading. Then there was another tap. It was Bob again, this time moving in the opposite direction, grinning and waving as he "swam" out of view. Roberts exploded in laughter. "This was too much," he recalled. "I was out of control." The team had used a small rolling table the height of the bottom of the window, with Ray crouched down, pushing.

It was all for fund raising, Elliott said, referring to Hanks's channel swim for which Bob and Ray had even fashioned a studio tote board. "That's the only reason I would have done that."

After a few weeks passed, Roberts assumed he was home free. But, suddenly, there was another rap on the glass. This time it was *Ray* swimming by with a silly grin. "I went sky high," Roberts recalled. "The tears were pouring out of my eyes." (Sadly, Willis Hanks's endeavor ended up being worthy of Wally Ballou coverage. After seven hours in the freezing channel, the skipper of his tiny pilot boat determined they were too far off course. Nine miles from the English coast—two miles wasted by his swimming in the wrong direction—Hanks finally had to be pulled from the water with a leg cramp. The skipper admitted that he had no idea where they were.)

One winter morning, Roberts recounted, a "shapely but dumb" model, having just publicized a Columbia film that takes place in the Arctic, was in a hurry to change back into warm clothing from her revealing bunny-fur costume. The model and the studio PR man were next due to visit the competition at WNEW. She was directed into Roberts's studio just as he started his newscast, convinced by the boys that he was blind and rehearsing reading his script in Braille. All he could do, Roberts said, was put his hands over his forehead and keep reading on, though, he admitted, "I sneaked some quick peaks. . . . She took off her bra and then stepped out of her panties and picked up another pair from her bag." That did it, he recounted. "When I saw the panties fall just to the right of my script, I just couldn't contain the laughter."

A loose duct in the station's antiquated air-conditioning system, which ran along the ceilings with suitable openings in all studios and offices, also proved to be source of torment. From behind the elevator bank, during newscasts, Ray raised himself to the duct and emitted strange, incongruous sounds combined with soft, plaintive cries of "h-e-l-l-l-l-l-p!" "I broke up completely," Roberts stated.

Finally, the team announced on-air auditions to replace Roberts because of his "lack of professionalism." A few mornings later, deep-voiced Frank Gallop, NBC's longtime announcer on the Milton Berle and Perry Como shows, actually showed up, again sending Roberts over the edge, which, in turn, started Gallop laughing.

Sometimes the boys sneaked into his studio early and attached an almost-invisible thread to some miscellaneous item on the table. During his newscast, they would start pulling on the thread. As soon he saw the thing slowly moving, Bob said, he would explode.

On such occasions, Vic Cowen made sure the engineer always hit the record button. Neatly edited together, Roberts's laughing jags were then played and replayed for years to punctuate anything even remotely inane. Contrasted to the newsman's slightly pretentious persona, the breakups seemed that much funnier. Off the air, Roberts never complained. "He would break up just talking about it," Elliott said. "It was the chemistry between Peter and us; just looking at us was enough for him."

"My life—certainly my image—changed completely," Roberts stated. "It turned into the best years of my life. B&R altered my personality."

An alert PR man named Jordan S. Ramin, brother of conductor/arranger Sid Ramin, contacted Roberts about cutting a record. A 45-rpm disc featuring his laugh backed by a Sid Ramin-arranged musical riff, "The Ho-Ho-Rock 'n' Roll," was distributed by RCA. Roberts ultimately received three royalty checks, each for less than one hundred dollars.

WINS 1010 resided at the upper half of the New York dial, nestled side by side with WMGM 1050, where B&R's competition also included the clever Ted Brown and his wife, Rhoda. Ray's brother and Ted's WMGM cohort, Phil, had introduced the three, and they were always playing stunts on each other. *Ted Brown and the Redhead* broadcast every morning from a basement studio at their Riverdale home, joined by their producer, Frank Mancini, and an engineer from the station.

"Ray got Ted's number at home through Phil," Elliott said, "and called him early one morning, pretending to be an engineer at WMGM. We're on the air but Ted and Rhoda are home, half awake."

"I get a call from 'master control,'" Brown later recounted to journalist Arnold Passman. "'Listen, we had a big storm last night and the transmitter is basically destroyed, so you won't be going on at all today; it's impossible.' And I hung up. So I tell her to go back to sleep. Then, jeez, I thought I hadn't heard a wind, nothin'. What storm? But I still believed it, right?

"About five to seven, I said, 'Jeez, somebody better tell Frank . . . he's down there. So I put my robe on, ya' know, and I'm walkin' down and I just get to the top of the stairs and they're comin' up after me.

"[I asked,] 'What are you guys doin' down there? There was a big storm last night—the transmitter blew down.' And now when I heard myself articulate it, I realized how stupid it sounded. Goddamn Bob and Ray had gotten my private number. I swear they sounded exactly like an engineer."

Another early-morning caper involved Stan Freberg. "He'd been in town and sat in with us," Bob said. "He gave us his number—but his home number—and said, 'Call anytime.' So we called him early in the morning out there. He answered and we said, 'We're up! . . . You said to call anytime.'"

"Of course, it was eight o'clock in New York and five o'clock in Pasadena," said Freberg, recalling B&R's wake-up call. "I said, 'Do you guys know what time it is?' And they said, 'Ha-ha-ha. Is that a funny guy? *'Do you know what time it is?'* Boy, what a funny man.' And I said, 'Well, it's five o'clock in Los Angeles.' And they said, 'No, it's eight o'clock in New York.' And I said, 'There's a three-hour time difference.' And Bob said, 'I never heard of that. Did you ever hear of that, Ray?' He said, 'No, I don't think so. It's eight o'clock everywhere.'"

"It just went on as long as we could keep him going," Bob said.

"So anyhow," Freberg continued, "they called me again the second day. And I went through the same thing all over again. So the third day I got up at four-thirty in the morning, made coffee, and was sitting by the phone, waiting, and they never called. So finally I called them in New York at WINS. And I said, 'I've been waiting for you guys to call.' They said, 'Yeah, we knew you'd be onto us by the third day so that's why we didn't call.'"

According to Carl Reiner, Bob and Ray made life "bearable." Reiner was referring to his commute from New Rochelle to New York while working on *Your Show of Shows* and *Caesar's Hour.* "I had them for at least forty-five minutes every day and marveled at what they did. . . . I was such a bore when I came to work. I'd say, 'Did you hear those guys today?' I was like a one-man band promoting them. . . . Everything about them was so askew and straight. If you didn't listen carefully, you would think you were listening to just boring talk. They were so low-key, but so wonderful."

Carl didn't have to sell Sid Caesar who admitted to an incurable Bob and Ray addiction, one which likely led to his discovering Tony Webster.

Once the ABC TV series went off on July 2, 1954, Elliott and Goulding's workday ended at ten o'clock in the morning. So their lunchtime presence at the Black Angus steakhouse on a late-summer day was strictly obligatory. WINS was throwing a luncheon in honor of its latest big-name attraction, Alan Freed, whose new late-night program was set to debut in early September.

Since 1951, Freed had become a late-night phenomenon, blasting fifty thousand watts of rhythm and blues over WJW Cleveland. Impressed by what he heard, McCaw offered him seventy-five thousand dollars to come to WINS. McCaw could always make up the difference through cost cutting; there were always lower-wattage light bulbs.

With invited radio and TV columnists present, only one person was yet to arrive—the guest of honor. Bob and Ray dove into more hors d'oeuvres and another round of rye and water and bourbon and water, respectively. Eventually, word was received that Freed's flight from Cleveland had been delayed by mechanical problems. "It turned out he never made it," Bob said. He added, "Ray and I both got sick on over-ripe shrimp cocktails. That's what I remember about the arrival of Alan Freed."

With *The Bob and Ray Show* and *Alan Freed's Rock and Roll Party* bookending the broadcast day, and Yankee baseball with Mel Allen in between, WINS' lineup was now totally schizophrenic

The Gouldings' purchase of a home in Plandome Manor on Long Island marked the end of friendly but ever-present needling by a politically conservative couple next door. It had started in 1952, when, aware of Ray and Liz's liberal views, the neighbors invited them over for a drink to gloat over Eisenhower's election victory. Depression-era influences had been instrumental in forming both Elliott and Goulding's politics. "Ray was an extremely liberal Democrat," Ed Graham said, "who wanted Humphrey over JFK for the 1960 nomination because of Humphrey's stand on labor issues. And also, JFK was a rich kid, whom he later embraced, warily."

Tom could not recall his dad equivocating between Humphrey and Kennedy. "We liked Humphrey," he said, but—noting the Catholic/Boston/New England connection—pointed out that "the ties to JFK were much stronger."

"Politically liberal, definitely," Liz agreed. "I'm sure Bob was, too, but not as profoundly as Ray was. . . . I think maybe Ray influenced Bob to a degree."

Having served under Eisenhower in the war, Bob did vote for him in his first term. "Then I changed," he said. ". . . I'm not a rabid political person to begin with, and nowhere near as wrapped up in it as Ray was."

While Ray was still in the Army, a Fort Knox medical corps captain, upon hearing the bulletin of President Roosevelt's death, announced that the news called for a big celebration. "Ray practically decked him," Liz said.

As the Gouldings were moving into their new split-level at 6 Luquer Road, events were also evolving in the city. Burdened by mounting responsibilities, Ray Knight's widow, Lee, was trying to piece together her life. Following her high-school graduation in Charleston, West Virginia, and a summer writing scholarship at Northwestern, Lee Pepper had come to New York with her mother, who, not exactly crazy about the move, put her in the Martha Washington Hotel for women—after carefully looking it over. She was soon joined in the city by her closest high-school friend, Barbara Gumm.

Lee was determined to be known as a New Yorker. "She did everything she could to lose her Southern accent," Collie said. "She didn't much like being reminded that she came from the South. . . . She was born Virginia Lee, and legally dropped it."

One of her mother's first jobs in New York, Collie recalled, was as an elevator operator in the Chrysler Building. "She lasted one day because—it was a manual operation in those days—she closed the door on some fellow's head. *On his head!* . . . She was so appalled, and he was probably pretty ticked off."

Lee had more success working for the Grace Downs Modeling and Air Career School. For a period, she also modeled hats for Elizabeth Arden and cosmetics for Richard Hudnut. Barbara, too, landed modeling work and would later marry prominent NBC television director Kurt Browning.

Either Ray Knight's first or second wife, according to Collie, was Lee's mother's best friend. Knowing Lee would be seeking work in New York, Collie explained, "Somehow, Mom was given the name of Ray Knight because he was a big shot." In 1943 and '44, under Bud Barry's reign, Knight was the production manager of the newly spun-off Blue (and later ABC) Network, for which he also scripted *Gibbs and Finney*, co-starring the much-adored Parker Fennelly, and wrote and performed on *The Three R's*, a daily, mid-afternoon half-hour with bandleader Joe Rines and announcer Glenn Riggs, subtitled, "An Adventure into Idiocy." It lasted three months.

Lee made an appointment to see him at the Blue's Rockefeller Center headquarters and was shown into his office. "He was bent over double," Collie said. "His back had gone out. So the first conversation she had with him was basically to the back of his head because he was totally folded over; she couldn't see his face."

As with any "meet cute" out of a Billy Wilder screenplay, the two later married, on July 12, 1946, in Boston. Knight was forty-seven; Lee, a child bride of twenty. "She was very pretty, really beautiful," said Collie, recalling her mother's participation in a beauty pageant a year earlier. During the 1944–45 season, Ray Knight directed the Ed Wynn and Alan Young shows for Young & Rubicam, both agency packages on the Blue network, whose powerful New York station, WJZ, sponsored the annual "Miss New York City" contest. A good word from Knight to the station's public-relations director, Don Rich (who, conveniently, produced the event), and, just like that, his next bride-to-be was not only one of the contestants, but also among the fifteen finalists at the August 1945 ceremony at the Ritz Theater. However, during the talent portion of the contest, the judges, including *Daily News* Broadway columnist Danton Walker, and bandleader, composer (and, more recently, the network's musical director) Paul Whiteman, determined that Lee's routine was, in her own words, too "risqué and suggestive." Not that her material didn't draw laughs, the loudest, in fact, from the show's emcee, who just happened to be Ray Knight, who also just happened to have written it. As expeditiously as Knight had gotten Lee entered into the competition, he had gotten her disqualified. The winner was Bess Myerson, who a month later would be crowned Miss America. The judges apparently found Bess's keyboard performance of Grieg's *Piano Concerto in A Minor* less offensive.

In the first week of November 1945, Knight began hosting a forty-five-minute daily WJZ wake-up show, *Good Morning, It's Knight*, at seven-fifteen. Over a year and a half later, he and Lee brought their daughter, Collie, born June 22, 1947, home—at the time, the Royalton Hotel on Forty-Fifth Street—from the hospital. A few days later, they were informed that WJZ had dropped the program. After pursuing various projects, including a spell as a TV weatherman at WPIX, Knight moved his family to his hometown, Salem, Massachusetts, where Shannon was born July 10, 1950.

"Mom was either his third or fourth wife," Collie said, adding that her impression was that ex-wives (nobody seems able to put their finger on an exact number) to whom he owed money, probably "didn't see that money, or at least not all of it. . . . Mom told me that he was occasionally several steps ahead of the sheriff."

Following Knight's death, Lee—with John Moses's help—met Ted Cott, who hired her for a position with WNBT. It was there that she learned TV production. A friend arranged for her girls to be enrolled at the Rudolph Steiner School. Collie began kindergarten, and Shannon was put into "pre-nursery," the youngest child they had ever accepted.

Throughout the next few months, Bob recounted, "Lee and I had an occasional lunch together, catching up on each other's activities: our shows, her job, how the girls were doing. We blended well; saw eye to eye on things and, more and more, enjoyed each other's company."

The same year Bob's attorney was hammering out a separation agreement with Jane's counsel. The weekend shuttles to Cohasset had already ceased. In time, Lee's position at NBC improved. Eventually, she worked as an assistant director on Herb Sheldon and Richard Willis's daytime shows, frequently with directors Ted Nathanson and Dwight Hemion.

By spring 1954, Bob and Lee were dating and had fallen deeply in love. Only a few close friends, Ray among them, were aware of their marriage intentions. Ray's initial reaction, Bob said, was "one of acceptance, if not outright enthusiasm. He knew about the ups and downs of the divorce negotiations and was sympathetic, but I did feel he had unspoken reservations about our move."

On the other hand, the prospect of their marriage was a forgone conclusion between Bob and Lee, and Collie and Shannon. Bob had become a fixture within their circle. Frequent talk by the girls of a future sibling to join them was met with assurances of, "When the time comes. When Mommy and Daddy are married."

The time did come, on June 2, 1954, a few days after the divorce decree became effective. The wedding was at DeWitt Memorial Church on Rivington Street on Manhattan's Lower East Side. Lee's longtime friend, Barbara, and her husband, Kirk Browning, were the witnesses. Also in attendance was Collie, seven, and Shannon, three. Bob was thirty-one, Lee twenty-eight, and, like her new husband, an only child.

Following the brief ceremony—performed by a minister, recalled Bob, whose "threadbare shirt-cuffs were apparent even in the dimmed lighting"—the wedding party moved to the pastor's office behind the altar. Shannon, holding Bob's hand tightly, looked up at him and asked: "Do we get the baby now?"

"I think," said Collie, "after being married to Ray Knight with all the difficulties that that involved, to be married to Dad must have been heavenly for her. . . . They've had a real marriage."

"Lee was good for Bob," Liz Goulding said. "He became more himself. She was sweet and loving. She was interested in show business and more at ease around celebrities than I was. . . . She showed me the ropes, where to shop and all. I was a Midwesterner; I'd never been to the big city; I'd never seen the ocean. We had lakes."

"A year later, he adopted us," Collie said. "And that's no easy task taking on two stepchildren. He did it without—at least to me—a discernable blink of the eye. . . . I can remember, we had to go to a judge and he asked us if we wanted this man to be our father. And we both said, 'Yes!' It was either me or Shannon . . . one of us turned to him and said, 'Can we call you Daddy now?' . . . He's a very gentle and a very generous person, in a quiet, undemonstrative way."

Now numbering four, the Elliotts moved into their new digs in Greenwich Village.

A month later, Audrey Meadows's sister, Jayne, married Steve Allen. Bob, Ray, and Steve, all ex GIs, had arrived in New York only months

118

apart, launching network shows in the wake of hit, largely extemporaneous programs in local radio (Allen at KNX in L.A.). Not that any of this was discussed over cocktails at a couple of parties the boys had recently attended at Steve's Upper East Side apartment. On such occasions, all three—something else they had in common—found small talk to be excruciating. However, Steve proved more adept at avoiding it by noodling at the piano for hours. Bob and Ray's initial guest-shot on Allen's *Tonight!* (the exclamation point was dropped a couple of years later) marked the first of thirty-four late-night appearances, spanning the program's Allen, Paar, and Carson eras. On their November 19, 1954, debut with Steve, *Tonight!* was only in its second month, essentially an extension of Allen's year-old local late-night spot for B&R's former boss, Ted Cott. The most significant changes involved expanding the program to one o'clock in the morning, and moving it to the network's Hudson Theater, which was "especially selected," Steve explained, "because it sleeps eight hundred people."

•••

Olive Pit, Stanley Steamer, Virginia Hamm, Jack Rabbitt, and April Showers—not new Bob and Ray characters, but real people—shared the stage with the boys when they returned to prime-time television, Monday nights on ABC. This time, the vehicle was a panel show, *The Name's the Same*, one of a flock from the Goodson and Todman production house. Then in its fourth year, *The Name's the Same* had lagged behind the firm's bigger successes, *What's My Line?*, *Beat the Clock*, and *I've Got a Secret*. Robert Q. Lewis had been the moderator for most of the show's run, but on April 11, 1955, Bob and Ray, introduced as sponsor Ralston Purina's "original Checkerboard Squares," took over from its most recent host, Dennis James.

The game's gimmick centered on panelists Walter Slezak, Joan Alexander, Roger Price, and Audrey Meadows trying to guess each contestant's name, which was the same as an object, action, or famous person. The second week, one of the contestants with a famous name was Goulding's nine-year-old son, Ray, Jr. There were also weekly guest stars, representing the spectrum from Rhonda Fleming to Jack E. Leonard, all, of course, with a movie or upcoming appearance in need of a plug. One week, Van Johnson, advising B&R on how to change their hair styles, tried various wigs on each. Another week, the two performed a radio rendition of *Mr. Trace*, with guest star Spike Jones as their crazed sound effects man.

In developing their programs, Goodson and Todman maintained a full-time staff of dummy panelists and contestants at their midtown offices, where B&R were sequestered for hours, moderating practice games under the tutelage of Mark Goodson himself.

On the air, the two dropped in some of their trusted bits, including a demonstration of the Bob and Ray One-Tree Hammock, but from the start, the two immediately sensed that their catalog was not a snug fit within the program's rigid format. The routines felt marginalized. Their main role was introducing and interviewing the contestants and administering the game, functions they had always poked fun at with any number of variations of their *Ladies Grab Your Seats* sketches, with unctuous emcee, the "loveable Larry Lovebreath." Now, the joke was somehow on them. Squeezed behind their tiny moderator's desk with the contestant between them, they had to play everything straight. It was "an awkward thing," Bob said. "We didn't have our whole heart and soul in it."

Twin moderators on a panel show that barely required one was perhaps not the smartest casting. But then, what did Goodson and Todman know about two-man teams? Following the June 13th broadcast, Clifton Fadiman slipped into the host's chair. By the end of summer, the series was off the air.

Bob and Ray's longest running television success—a nine-year run—was still ahead.

9

THE BERT AND HARRY CAMPAIGN

In late 1954, Ed Graham, a writer on Young & Rubicam's General Electric account, was convinced that commercials could sell a product and be entertaining at the same time. To prove his point, he chose what he felt was Y&R's worst advertising of that day, a campaign for their regional beer client, Piels, one of the many smaller breweries that were forced to battle for market share a tier below the major national brands. The then-current Piels spots, an innocuous jingle and hard-sell pitch ("Piels contains less NFS, non-fermented sugar!") had been in place for years.

Graham, a Dartmouth graduate, was very brash, recalled Jack Sidebotham, the talented art director on the Piels account. "He would say outrageous things," Sidebotham said. "He was truly a crazy person. And for those of us who loved him, he was wonderful. And for those of us who were offended, he wasn't such a great guy. But we were good pals—I enjoyed his idiosyncrasies."

Graham had been thinking of a way to meet Bob and Ray and had pitched them at Y&R every time a project came up. When Piels purchased a two-and-a-half-hour variety special, *Welcoming New Year's Eve to New York*, on the local CBS outlet, he once again said, "How about Bob and Ray?" The program, on December 31, 1954, was emceed by Bud Collyer and featured various comedy and musical guests, including Orson Bean and jazz great Teddy Wilson. At midnight, Robert Trout at Times Square greeted 1955 from the rooftop of the Astor Hotel. Bob and Ray performed four bits, but the Piels spots were left to The Honey Dreamers quintet and announcer Jimmy Blaine, all unaware that a new campaign was in the works. It was at this point that Ed Graham started hanging around B&R's WINS studio.

When it was decided to look for a new Piels concept, a lot of people at the agency submitted ideas, Sidebotham said. "Ed's idea came with Bob and Ray. He was, as we all were, big admirers." Graham came up with the concept of the Piels Brothers—half-pint, bullying Bert and lanky, befuddled Harry—animated owners and pitchmen for the brewery. (The actual firm had been founded in 1883, in Brooklyn, by the Piel brothers, Wilhelm, Gottfried, and Michael.)

"Harry was the quiet, shy guy," Sidebotham said, "and Bert the bumptious wise-apple." In fact, Harry's slender build bore a striking similarity to his visual creator, Jack Sidebotham, dubbed "the human bobby pin" by a Y&R colleague. Graham even developed full biographies for each: Harry was a 1921 all-Metropolitan forward on Brooklyn's Samuel J. Tilden High School basketball team (undefeated). Bert, at one point, was a Graham-Paige Motor Car distributor. "The Piel brothers were totally Ed's imagination," Sidebotham said.

But it was an impossible sell within the shop. Conventional wisdom in the black-and-white TV era held that beer was best sold with close-ups of it being tantalizingly poured into tall Pilsner glasses. "For the suits of the day," Sidebotham said, "it seemed not dignified enough for a big brewery to be selling the beer with these joker characters."

Elliott remembered a Y&R higher-up, after looking at Sidebotham's storyboards, proclaiming, "If that sells beer, I'll quit!"

At the time, the hard sell dominated Madison Avenue. TV campaigns were designed around a combination of repetitive, undocumented product claims and assaulting visuals. For years, Anacin's promise of painful headache relief was accompanied by images of a pounding hammer in the head. Today, it would be laughable. In 1955, it was just boring. The Doyle Dane Bernbach agency's innovative "think small" series for the Volkswagen Beetle was still years away.

Agency-account execs' resistance to humor was rooted in a fear of the client, that "cloudy person who has to listen," as Ray described him in a 1961 interview about the Piels campaign. "They are afraid that they would have to scrape him off the ceiling."

Agency jobs were tenuous, Sidebotham said. "If an account was lost, then there would be heads chopped."

When the Bert and Harry campaign was first shown to Piels, they did not like it, Ed Graham said. "They just stared at it and said they were happy with what they have." So George Gribbin, a "wonderful creative director," noted Graham, did something that was typical of Y&R at that time. "He went to the brewery and said, 'I think you're making a mistake and I'd like a chance to see if I'm right. I know you guys like this "non-fermented sugar" stuff. Let it continue in major markets. But give me two test markets and let's see how they do.'"

Piels' advertising and sales managers agreed.

But one more obstacle remained: When Ed Graham wrote the scripts, he had heard Bob and Ray's voices in his mind; the concept embodied them. "The idea for the campaign and Bob and Ray were one and the same," Sidebotham continued. But the Y&R production people were reticent. There was pressure from the senior staff to hire other actors. "People are always wanting to get their fingers in the pie when something pretty nice is going on," he said. "I remember Tony Randall was one of the first we had to audition. The people who were doing that had no concept of the concept. Tony Randall is a wonderful actor, but . . ."

When casting commercials, voice-over auditions for animated characters are just as competitive as for on-camera actors. Forty teams read for Bert and Harry, including the iconic Mel Blanc playing both roles. "We went back more than once," Elliott said. "It narrowed down, I think, to us, and Ed was persistent—I mean, Ed was adamant." Ultimately, after hearing their final audition, according to Graham, Bob and Ray were unanimously selected.

Bert and Harry debuted in New York as radio spots in August of 1955, and on television, first in two test markets, Harrisburg, Pennsylvania, and Binghamton, New York. "They skyrocketed," Graham said. "They were going to run the test for six months. By December, they decided, 'Screw it—we'll just go on the air with the whole thing.' But it was George Gribbin who did it." In December, Bert and Harry appeared in all Piels markets, radio and TV, in twenty- and sixty-second commercials. UPA Pictures, originators of the Mr. Magoo cartoons, produced the first series of spots in their graphically innovative flat style, based on Sidebotham's designs.

The radio commercials were a "mild success," Ed Graham noted. "But with the same soundtracks and Jack Sidebotham's visuals, suddenly everybody was talking about them. . . . Jack had a natural warmth about him that he communicated in his work. Even an angry Bert became loveable when Jack drew him." Bumbling their way through the blurbs, the endearing Bert (Ray) and Harry (Bob) mocked themselves and traditional advertising speak ("Throat wise, it's delicious."), frequently addressing the audience as "consumers" and not above reminding them that "these commercials cost us a fortune."

As entertaining as the spots were, Bert was hard sell, Bob pointed out, referring to the cantankerous brother's blustery pitches ("Piels tastes best of all because it's driest of all!"). "Coming from a little short, fat guy," Bob said, "it was the reverse of what we're used to. So agreeable and acceptable—and that was part of Ed's psychology. . . . We give him full credit for Bert and Harry."

One viewer, recalled Graham, did not find Bert's hard sell so agreeable and acceptable. Complaining to the head of the brewery, a woman wrote that Harry and Bert (as they were initially billed) were hatemongers, citing their dialog: "Friends of Harry and Bert, arise as one. March to your local tavern and demand that they carry Piels on tap. If they do not, then congregate elsewhere." The woman had heard "Friends of Harry and Bert" as "Friends of Aryan birth." "All the commercials were pulled," Graham said, "and re-recorded as Bert and Harry. The edits jumped out and always annoyed me."

Bert and Harry were an immediate success, visually and verbally, Elliott said. "Passers in the street would recognize us, and instead of Bob and Ray, they would yell, 'Hey, Bert and Harry, how are things going?!' Sometimes we took offense when it first began, but then we pretty well accepted that there were four of us."

The campaign became so popular that the brewery, inundated with requests, published the commercials' scheduled broadcast times and stations in Manhattan newspapers. One Piels promotion had Bert and Harry giving away an actual island, with Bob and Ray on hand in the Bahamas to make the official presentation to the winner. The spots themselves captured first place at the Cannes Film Festival. By 1956, sales were up by 21 percent, according to the *Daily News*, which, referring to Bob and Ray, stated: "Manifestly, the two of them were put on this earth to do Bert and Harry Piel."

The spots even poked fun at their own success. In one, a studio tour guide (Bob) interrupts, informing his group, "This is Bert and Harry's studio. They do beer commercials which claim to be funny. The shrimpy guy on the left acts very obnoxious and the big dumb guy gets very mixed up. Most of their gags are wearing thin now."

When sales later failed to keep pace with Bert and Harry's increasing popularity, the brothers struck back. In one spot, Bert scolds viewers, "Some of you—and you know who you are—were laughing at our commercials and not buying our beer. The free ride is over! We have a new theme: 'I'm laughing with Piels in my hand.' What's fair is fair."

Every year the team had an obligatory golf date with the president of Piels, Henry J. Muessen, and his second in command, Tom Hawkes. One would pick Elliott as his partner; the other, Goulding. Muessen and Hawkes, unlike B&R, were fairly accomplished golfers. On these occasions, the executives became the performers. For eighteen holes, Bob said, "they graciously pretended to know like we knew what they were doing. We were real duffs. . . . We always looked forward to getting back and having a drink and dinner, which meant that day was over."

On the heels of the successful Piels campaign, which ran for six years plus a couple of revivals, Graham left Y&R for B&R, joining the team to establish their own company, creating national and regional campaigns for other major advertisers. The world of balance sheets and profit margins would prove daunting.

It was a bitterly cold winter day, but the site was ideal. After all, the man was famous for having come from Salem, Massachusetts. What more appropriate setting could there be for the scattering of Ray Knight's ashes than the park surrounding Salem's picturesque harbor? The Elliotts had not exactly looked forward to this solemn occasion; in fact, they had put it off for a couple of years. But that weekend's visit to Bob's mother's home in nearby Somerville had made the timing propitious.

Bob and Lee walked out to a carefully selected spit of land at the water's edge, and from a bag removed the urn—basically, a metal container larger than a coffee can. But when Bob went to open it, the top was too tightly sealed; it would not budge. Given the contents, pounding, wrenching, and prying were out of the question. With no tools in their rental car, the two drove back into town. Fearing a hardware-store explanation would surely invite unwanted questions, Bob simply ran into a deli, bought a beer can opener, and the two returned to the spot. "It was the only thing I could think of," he said.

But just a few holes with the opener, it turned out, did not do the job either. Because the remains contained fragments of bone, the whole top had to come off. With fingers freezing, Bob proceeded to puncture side-by-side holes around the entire circumference of the container. "It took quite a while," he said, "like ten or fifteen minutes. . . . We looked around. I guess it's illegal. We felt very furtive in doing it."

With much effort, he and Lee finally managed to scatter Knight's ashes, the stiff wind blowing them only slightly off course. "He would have laughed," Bob added warmly. "Ray Knight got a bang out of situations like that. And we figured he *was* laughing, if such a thing were possible."

◆◆◆

As Elliott perused the *Racing Form* that Friday morning, one horse caught his attention. Shannon Sound had the ring of a winner. Not only was Shannon the name of his and Lee's youngest daughter, the odds were fifteen to one. As any horse bettor knows, he thought to himself, a coincidence this good could not be overlooked. For a time, Bob was in the habit of dashing off to either Aqueduct or Belmont Park after the morning show. Other days he placed bets with the WINS switchboard operator whose boyfriend was a bookie. As he was about to make the transaction that Friday, May 13, 1955, Lee called to announce she was starting labor.

Elliott hurried downtown for the birth of their daughter Amy at St. Vincent's Hospital. Shannon Sound won that day, paying fifty dollars for a two-dollar bet. "I never regretted missing the wager," he said. "Nor did I ever let her forget she made me miss it! Amy was the biggest payoff I could have hoped for."

The following week, Sunday, May 22, 1955, was a benchmark date in the slow decline of network radio: Jack Benny's final broadcast. Inexorably, larger and larger shares of the audience—not to mention advertisers—continued to defect to television. At NBC, Pat Weaver could measure the success of his television network by the corresponding collapse of his radio network. Nielsen figures indicated that radio listening declined sharply at night. However, daytime numbers, on weekends in particular, were significantly higher. An adman at heart, Weaver believed in numbers. To rescue NBC Radio, he focused on weekends when there were more listeners in cars.

His drastic fix was called *Monitor*, not a program but a "continuous service," spanning forty hours, from eight o'clock Saturday mornings to Sundays at midnight. *Monitor* had a completely scripted, tightly produced magazine-of-the-air format of news, sports, comedy, music, and live pickups of special events and band remotes. When asked at a press conference to describe his radical new project in two words, Weaver came up with: "kaleidoscopic phantasmagoria." Once on the air, this was refined to the simpler—and endlessly repeated—slogan: "Going places and doing things."

Weaver's silver bullet for NBC Radio would run for nineteen years, and include humorous segments from Ernie Kovacs, Nichols and May, George Gobel, and others. But in its early-impact years, no comedy names were more closely identified with *Monitor*'s success than Bob and Ray. Their vignettes appeared fifteen to twenty times a weekend. Even that was not enough for some listeners. Groucho Marx spent an entire 1956 *Monitor* interview complaining to NBC's Shirley Thomas about the timing of Bob and Ray's bits. "The one thing that disturbs me," Groucho said, "is that they're not on long enough. . . . I'd like to see them up there for twenty minutes. . . . I think they're wonderful—a superlative I rarely use."

Monitor's home base was an electronic fishbowl called "Radio Central." Its old name, Studio 5B, was deemed too mundane sounding. In fact, it was 30 Rock's old fifth-floor master control given a complete facelift. Each of *Monitor*'s two-man anchor teams, called "communicators," sat at an immense control console facing a producer, board and turntable engineers, and twin, capsule-like announcer's booths on either side. There was lots of glass, clocks, and TV monitors. NBC press releases boasted that broadcasters had, at their instant command, open, two-way circuits to twelve individual overseas and domestic pickup points at any one time. Whether or not anything important was happening at any of these places was another matter.

Radio Central was a key stop on the NBC studio tour. Emerging from the fifth-floor elevator, guests could observe the broadcast through the glass with a perfect, unobstructed view of the backsides of Ben Grauer and Frank Gallop, or whoever the twosome happened to be. "Visitors would rap on the window," said Peter Roberts, who with Hugh Downs anchored the noon-to-three o'clock Saturday block. "You'd turn and smile and wave back at them. It was a little overpowering at first—vanity takes over."

The NBC tours were a premise in waiting for Bob and Ray. From their booth in Radio Central, either as Wally Ballou or himself, Bob interviewed Ray as various members of a passing tour. The bogus tour interviews were "sure-fire," Bob said, explaining that sometimes he would have an idea ("Here's a gentleman wearing a Hula-Hoop . . ."); other times, Ray would come up with a character on the spot, once playing the tour guide himself. To fight the boredom of ten or twelve tours a day, he explained, he swings his group into the NBC accounting department and rummages through the files. "Incidentally," he asked Bob, "do you realize that you two together don't make as much as your engineer?"

Another indigenous premise centered on *Monitor*'s distinctive, identifying audio trademark, the high- and low-frequency oscillating "beeper" sound that opened and closed every half hour. With the assist of a slight echo effect, Bob and Ray would descend many floors below Radio Central to a subterranean vault for a fictitious visit with Gore, Elliott's entombed, Boris Karloff-sounding "keeper of the beeper." The two also poked fun at the frequently employed *Monitor* device of having a host ask live interview questions to a celebrity guest's previously taped answers. Bob and Ray's "interviews" invariably ended in an incomprehensible jumble of totally out-of-sequence questions and answers, and the squeal of rewinding tape as the engineer frantically searched for the corresponding reply. A variation on this was "newsman" Gabe Preston (Ray) phoning from Washington to pre-record his commentary for later broadcast, only to give up in frustration after endless fluffs, false starts, and the sound of more rewinding tape. One B&R *Monitor* segment about "planting redwood seedlings along a driveway and happily anticipating shade trees three hundred years hence," even managed to breach *Good Housekeeping*'s safeguards and pop up on the magazine's otherwise-common-sense pages.

When actual glitches occurred, über-producer Mike Zeamer relied on the team to cover. "Mike would stick his head in the door and say we're going to need a minute and a half at the end of something," Bob said. "That's why we were hired." For B&R, it added up to working seven-day weeks with crossword puzzle-filled Saturdays and Sundays, tethered to their small announcer booth. It also meant declining many weekend invitations, including, for Bob, his fifteenth Winchester High School reunion, which fell on the same day as *Monitor*'s debut broadcast.

The first hour of that June 12th premiere was simulcast on NBC Television and featured a "tour interview" with Goulding as a visitor unable to comprehend why anybody would televise a radio show. The *New York Times*' Jack Gould picked up on this point, writing, "The two media got tangled up in a "hodge-podge." Pat Weaver "started something" yesterday on NBC, Gould stated. "Just what it is, however, he may be the only man to know for a while." This time Bob and Ray escaped Gould, unscathed. He was more focused on Miss Monitor's provocative weather report—calling it "an irresistible invitation to an unforgettable evening."

At five-foot-seven, with cascading red hair, Tedi Thurman, a Midville, Georgia, native, was a fashion-magazine cover-girl discovery of Mike Zeamer. Twice an hour, over a background of lush romantic music and introduced as "Miss Monitor," Tedi presented the current temperature readings around the country. She was an instant hit. Her voice, Elliott noted, was on the deep and sultry side and made even more so with her distinctive pronunciation of what she referred to as the "temper-toor."

"In Atlanta, the temper-toor is seventy-one, fair." Then there would be a pause. "Cleveland, fifty-four, cloudy." She would leave a beat between readings, as if expecting some listener, for whatever reason, to be jotting down the figure. "It reminded us," Bob recalled, "of our fish report days of a few years before." After her list of temperature readings, Miss Monitor would often conclude her reports with, ". . . and me? I'm thirty-six, twenty-six, thirty-six."

Tedi shared the same announce booth with B&R, and, after her stints, the three would often chat. She had a "pleasant, slightly offbeat personality," Bob said, and once referred to hush puppies as one of her favorite dishes to prepare. "We feigned disbelief that there was such a thing, or that they were the Southern delicacy she claimed. The next weekend, she arrived at the studio with a batch, hot from the fryer. . . . They were great!"

Bob and Ray did not have to stick out the live *Monitor* appearances too long before convincing NBC to let them pre-record their vignettes. Many fun, weekday-taping sessions ensued, with Zeamer directing at first, then Arnie Peyser. Thus ended their seven-day workweek, and with it, Tedi Thurman's home-cooked hush puppies.

Establishing their commercial and animation operation, Goulding-Elliott-Graham Productions, Inc. (informally referred to as "GEG," as rhymes with "leg"), Ed Graham found space on the twenty-fifth floor of the art deco Graybar Building at 43rd and Lexington, on the eastern edge of Grand Central Terminal. A contractor who had worked on Graham's future mother-in-law's East Side apartment was hired to turn the place into a production company. After the WINS show one morning, Bob and Ray went over to see how it was coming along. "The guy had laid the thing out," Bob said, "so there were two offices. One for Ray, and one for me, overlooking Grand Central; we both had a huge window. But Ray's office was just a little bit wider and a little bit deeper than mine. . . . I think, probably Ed said, 'Ray is the bigger of the two guys using them.'" The offices were only separated by an eight-foot partition that did not come close to reaching the thirteen-foot ceiling. "You could throw paper airplanes over the top of it," Bob said.

When completed, a beautiful photograph of Lee and a framed cover of a vintage *Time* magazine featuring the first-ever review of radio adorned the pale-green walls of Bob's office. Prominent on Ray's office wall—salvaged from somewhere and quintessentially Ray Goulding—was a framed map designating "Major Land Uses in the United States." Just off their and Ed's adjoining three offices was a large room converted into a recording studio, complete with two vintage, waist-high Ampex model 201 tape machines—serial numbers six and forty-four—purchased secondhand when Arthur Godfrey's office was upgraded.

The demand for offbeat, animated advertising concepts was second only to the demand for clients, and, without the latter, there was no need for the former. Initially, some business came in the door on Bert and Harry's coattails. As with the Piels template, the starting point on a new campaign was the creation of a central continuing character to provide continuity between the company and the product. But there is no Central Casting for engaging animated characters. For that, Goulding, Elliott, and Graham were in debt to a circle of unsuspecting acquaintances and colleagues, both past and present, whose various personality traits and idiosyncrasies were appropriated and exaggerated—usually without their knowledge. They would find somebody, said art director Mike Smollin, another Y&R émigré, who "had a characteristic that we could pull on."

The characters would then be placed in a setting comically indigenous to the product. Long, tedious hours were spent around a conference table, spitballing various notions. "We used to call them 'bleed sessions,'" Bob said, "where we'd sit with Ed . . . and just try to find an idea or hook or something."

The general policy was to keep copy points to the barest minimum, Ray explained in a GEG-industry presentation, relying "on the humor device to get and hold attention for the sell." One entire sixty-second spot in a campaign for General Motors Guardian Maintenance consisted of reciting a list of over twenty names of "GM customers" who had failed to bring in their vehicles for recommended service. ("Those who haven't know who they are . . . Bring your car in now . . . and avoid the embarrassment of being reminded on the air.")

Nationwide Insurance, seeking to dispel the discomfort associated with the somber subject of life insurance, employed GEG for a series of whimsical radio dramatizations contrasting prospective life-insurance candidates with their respective occupations. ("Mornings I test mushrooms at the super-market. Afternoons I repair high-tension power lines, and I moonlight as a target in a hatchet-throwing act.")

GEG's San Francisco market radio campaign for Calso Water was on the air for ten years. Other clients included Millbrook Bread, Alcoa Aluminum, Papermate pens, Cumuloft Carpets, Glidden Paints, and Interwoven Socks ("Are you missing important things your friends saw while you were bending over to pull up your socks?").

Occasionally, a character for a campaign was drafted from the B&R stock company's deep bench. Their "old-time radio announcer" Kent Lyle Birdley (Elliott), in one spot, recommended GE bulbs and fluorescents to a tongue-depressor plant comptroller (Goulding), who, because of poor lighting, had issued a $960 check to the office boy and a forty-three-dollar check to the company president. ("An efficiency expert was brought in and said, 'Turn on the lights!' And they were already on.")

Imaginative Andersen's Soup visual characterizations of Robert "Pea Soup" Andersen (Bob) and his two chefs, Hap-pea and Pea-wee (B&R's McBeebee Twins voices), were the creation of Mike Smollin. Hap-pea and Pea-wee operated a Rube Goldberg-like "pea-sorter with an automatic reject feature" that detected and discarded defective peas. Smollin's touch contributed to another Cannes Film Festival award for the Andersen's spot. "It just sort of rolled off the drawing board, if you will," Smollin said modestly. To this day, guests at the soup company's California restaurant have their photographs taken in life-size wooden cutouts of the characters.

One client, IBM, arranged a tour for the team of their corporate head-quarters at 57th and Madison, recalled Tom Goulding. Demonstrating one of the company's then-revolutionary computers, an IBM executive punched in the name "Ray Goulding." Instantly a data-filled profile of Tom's privacy-wary father was produced. "When he came home," said Tom, "he was livid: 'They had so much information. They even knew where I lived!'"

Jack Sidebotham remained at Y&R but freelanced at GEG, a practice not uncommon in the agency world, he said. "None of us were ever paid enough that we could live on our salaries." One of GEG's earliest successes featured Jack's rendering of the prim Emily Tipp, animated pitchwoman for Tip-Top bread, resulting in the brand having the best sales year in its history. Margaret Hamilton provided Emily's voice, with Carl Reiner voicing all the other roles.

Bob, Ray, and Ed had decided it would be wise to produce some campaigns without B&R's voices, thus expanding the potential marketplace. Animated commercials for Milkbone dog biscuits featuring Carl Reiner's slightly professorial voice as Champion Spot, a handsome looking, Mike Smollin-designed mutt with a spot and a Milkbone sash across his chest, ran for five or six years. "I really enjoyed those sessions," Reiner said. "Ed would give you leeway to just have fun." Broadway comedienne (and Reiner's *Caesar's Hour* wife), Shirl Conway, lent her voice to the animated, multi-diamond-wearing Sheila Kenway, who used liquid Soilex to clean her Rolls-Royce's whitewalls.

One presentation that never made it on-air was a demo for Chase and Sanborn coffee. They wanted "a Bert and Harry sensibility," Ed recalled, and GEG did not want to repeat themselves. "Instead, we hired two young kids, named Jerry Stiller and Anne Meara (parents of Ben Stiller), and did some live spots. They were terrific, and would have been a huge success. But the agency had their hearts set on a Piels Brothers imitation."

At the time, B&R, along with Stan Freberg's West Coast operation, pretty much had the field of humorous commercials to themselves. The trio did not necessarily perceive themselves as rivals. As Ray would later tell *Television Magazine*, "When we hear that a prospective client is going to have a commercial done somewhere else, say . . . by Stan Freberg, we know it is going to be good, and it doesn't bother us. We think, there's an expert and Stan does good work and that's going to help the whole industry of humorous commercials."

"Bob and Ray and I didn't pay any attention to what account executives had to say," Freberg pointed out. "We just did what we wanted to do." The reluctance to let go of the hard sell was, as he put it, simply because agencies were "in love with [mock-announcer's voice], 'Say, Mother, next time washday rolls around . . .' But the success of Freberg and Bob and Ray changed everybody's mind about humor." It was, Stan said, Bob and Ray's work for Piels beer, and his for Great American Soups and Sunsweet prunes, that "enabled us to stay alive. And then Madison Avenue began to pay attention to us."

For some time, Pat Weaver had wanted to expand NBC Television's seven-forty-five in the evening, fifteen-minute *Camel News Caravan* to twenty-five minutes. To fill the remaining five minutes of the half-hour, Weaver turned to Bob and Ray, feeling their humor was uniquely compatible with his news-and-information programs. Years earlier on *Today*, their bits had lifted some of the comedy load from the sagging shoulders of chimpanzee J. Fred Muggs. Weaver put up the money for five, five-minute pilot episodes of a B&R soap, *The Kertencalls*, an animated version of *Mary Backstayge*, involving "fleebus," the mysterious disease that causes its victims to walk as if they were sitting down.

Unfortunately, in the middle of production, NBC chairman, General David Sarnoff, hatched an idea of his own: to replace Weaver with his son, Robert Sarnoff. Any Pat Weaver project at the network would now likely be DOA. Still, efforts were made to sell *The Kertencalls* elsewhere, but it was "hopeless," according to Graham. "No one was interested in five-minute shows." Some years later, the same story, with Mike Smollin's illustrations, was sold as a book, *Linda Lovely and the Fleebus*, to Dodd, Mead & Company. Smollin's charming illustrations later appeared in numerous publications, children's books in particular, dozens involving the *Sesame Street* characters.

In spite of *The Kertencalls* setback, and a *Lawrence Fechtenberger, Interstellar Officer Candidate* project featuring an animated Lawrence, Jet Ordway (both Goulding) and the sneering Mug Mellish (Elliott), which met a similar fate, GEG continued pursuing other pilot opportunities. A particularly ambitious undertaking was *Bob and Ray's Hollywood Classics*, a series of movie-genre satires based on Smollin's storyboards. Two animated half-hour prototypes, *Test Dive Buddies* and *Kid Gloves*, were produced, as were sound tracks for an additional ten, all plotted but ad-libbed by the boys under GEG's Kennedy Films banner. Graham's favorite, a pirate-picture takeoff called *Three Sheets Windward*, featured the cantankerous Captain Wolf Larson opposing forces with Captain Claude, leader of a gay pirate ship. "It was great," Graham commented, "except for the small negative that we never sold it—or *Test Dive Buddies*, or *Pigskin Partners*, or *Kid Gloves*, or any of them. Really too bad."

As ad accounts grew, multiple subsidiaries were formed. Every step of animation was a corporation. It was Ed Graham's belief that, if GEG owned it all, they could put out a better, more individualized product. Ed was the president of each corporation; Bob and Ray were officers. A couple of animation companies, each with its own set of artists, were set up, one several floors below suite 2545, another on West Forty-Fourth Street. An animation camera company was established for cell photography, plus an ink-and-paint operation at Times Square. All were vulnerable to the inevitable slow periods. The animators, inkers, and painters were unionized, Graham explained, so they were used to quick layoffs. Still, the firm hated to run the risk of losing the good ones, particularly if work seemed just around the corner. "At the peak, we probably had fifty to sixty employees," he said. "When times were flush, we loved it. We quaked when things were slow."

"Oh, my God," Bob said. "We had fourteen checkbooks to sign every payday!"

The rock of the place was a tall, smart, exceedingly warm twenty-seven-year-old named Ruth Kennedy, who came over from Y&R in the first wave with Graham. Her GEG job description, she claimed, was being "the only gal."

"She was our housemother," Graham said, "absolutely the best." With the group's increasing reputation for offbeat concepts, 2545 suddenly became a destination for any self-promoter with half an idea, including, Kennedy said, a circus freak and a group seeking backing on a Silly Putty venture.

As to what was truly viable, outsiders had their ideas, and B&R had theirs. As performers, they perceived themselves as "two regular guys," Elliott said, "riding herd on a flock of off-center characters." In the office, he continued, "we adopted a third-person attitude toward ourselves and our characters, and maintained a careful proprietorship over it all. 'Bob and Ray wouldn't say that,' or 'Bob and Ray don't think that way,' became convenient and effective shorthand in dealings with agents, managers, ad people, and interviewers."

Ultimately, one afternoon a week was set aside to screen out crackpots. The guys called it "Nut Day," according to Kennedy, but not everyone was wacky; some were very reasonable. One, Jonathan Winters, was both. Another who dropped by was "Crazy Ernie," as Kennedy called Ernie Pintoff, who in Graham's opinion, animated the best of GEG's Tip-Top bread spots. One day, a young Jim Henson and his wife came by with a collection of their puppets. "I thought they were good," Graham remembered, "but I never liked puppets and neither did B&R. Jim found work shortly afterwards."

Sometime later, one of Henson's TV guest-shots featured his puppets assuming the roles of a couple of Elliott and Goulding's characters pantomiming to a recorded Bob and Ray routine. "Stupidly," Elliott said, "we got a cease-and-desist order, rather than see it was a wonderful promotion for us."

The "we" in this instance included a trusted B&R accomplice, their close friend and attorney, Stan Schewel, whose warm, easygoing Virginia overtones existed side by side with an abrupt, lawyer-like command of the language, especially when drafting a letter. As Ray once put it, "Stan could make a thank you note sound like a threat."

In GEG's first year, Graham invited his former Y&R colleague Jack Sidebotham to be best man at his wedding, and Bob and Ray to be ushers. Held at St. Bartholomew's on Park Avenue, it was a very formal affair, with men in the official party in full-morning dress, including waistcoats, gray gloves, striped trousers, and tails. Throughout, Bob said, Ray "grumbled," but "Ed was our partner; we felt we should do it." Afterward, the reception was at the St. Regis Hotel, with limos lined up to transport everyone up to Fifty-Fifth Street, and then over to Fifth Avenue. But soon the limos became "fewer and fewer," Bob said. "It got down to a tossup of who gets the last one, Bob and Ray or somebody else. The wedding planner picked other people. And that pissed Ray off. So we said, 'We'll walk up. Forget the car!' And we walked up Park Avenue in full tails. He was real ticked."

Marching up Park Avenue, the two—one fuming, the other only looking straight ahead—looked as ludicrous as they felt.

Bob and Ray's one similarity with other great teams was their dissimilarity with each other. They were "two very different guys," Graham pointed out. "And when you get into comedy teams, you pretty much have to have opposites. . . . Like most of Ray's characters, he was buffeted by his emotions."

Ray's characters—the likes of Webley L. (for Llewellyn) Webster, Steve Bosco, Charles the Poet, and a parade of delusional lost souls—tended to be more outspoken and hyperbolic. "Ray was funnier," Bob said. "The more dependably funny, I think."

When a "guest" with a ridiculous occupation or hobby was interviewed, Ray almost always played the part. By "believing" him, Bob's deadpan, level-headed interrogation—in effect, pushing against the premise—functioned as a ground wire, ratifying the absurdity and further advancing it.

When the mikes were turned off, Jack Sidebotham found Elliott and Goulding ironically true to the Piels brothers' characters Ed Graham had created for them. "Harry [was] very deferential—genuinely a gentleman. A gentlemanly guy, Bob was. And Ray was genuinely bumptious and very outspoken about things and stuff," Sidebotham said.

"Bombastic," was the word Ruth Kennedy applied to Ray. As for his partner's shyness, she recalled a day the staff was ordering lunch at a midtown Polynesian restaurant. When the waiter came to Bob, Ruth said, he "merely pointed to an item on the menu to avoid saying pooh-pooh platter."

Graham, who was present at the lunch, said it was definitely not a case of Elliott simply putting everyone on. "Bob was a guy who was not going to be smart-alecky in public. He was a very quiet, reserved guy. . . . A very enigmatic guy." Contrastingly, Ray, said Graham, would "read the riot act, and also could be terribly charming. . . . Ray was a guy who kept stuff bottled up and then exploded. But he never exploded at Bob that I'm aware of."

"No, he really didn't," Bob agreed. "He could blow up in front of me if we were alone. But it wasn't *at* me. . . . There were flare-ups . . . I always had a feeling he did a lot of it for effect. I know he did. . . . I think he did have kind of a fence around himself, or, at least, people got that kind of an impression."

It was Graham's contention that Ray's alter ego was his ever-present on-air character, Captain Wolf Larson, the scurviest, most unpredictably tempered pirate to ever sail out of the Dry Tortugas. On the deck of his imaginary ship, the *Rita B*, or on a tropical island, the port-addled Captain Larson was subject to hilarious personality swings each time he was bopped on the head by a swinging yardarm spar or a falling coconut, sending him into alternating fits of seething rage and smarmy affability. Graham found

Ray very easy to talk to, but there was the sense, he said, that "Captain Larson was always lurking somewhere nearby."

Ray's blowups did not occur often, Graham continued. "These were sort of periodic moments. . . . Then he would stew and you would just steer clear of him. Bob would remember that he had to go get his shoes shined somewhere or something, and people would just drift away." Yet Graham never knew Ray to explode when a job was at stake. "Given his idiosyncrasies," he said, "Ray was a very, very professional guy."

Still, he could be suddenly set off right before a taping session, creating a pall over the studio. "Those were kind of tight moments," Bob said. " . . . I think I knew him well enough so that I could almost look at something and figure out how he would take it. . . . He could fly off the handle very easily if something appeared to him as ridiculous or unjust. And he, in my opinion, often overdid it for effect or the final outcome."

Graham had his own analysis: "It was Captain Larson getting hit on the head by a coconut." But, referring to the "nice" Ray, Graham stressed that "there was no more charming guy to spend some time with."

10

ESCAPE ARTISTS

The Mutual Broadcasting System could hardly dazzle advertisers with a roster of glamorous names. After *Queen for a Day*'s Jack Bailey, its star register plummeted precipitously. But it offered something else: stations, over five hundred of them—more than twice as many as CBS, the second closest.

For two decades, Mutual was popular with children for its late-afternoon action-adventure serials. By 1955, with the after-school crowd lured away by the same shows then available on television, radio adventure serials were suddenly on the critical list. At five o'clock on Monday afternoon, October 3rd, Bob and Ray put them out of their misery for good.

Kiddies tuning in for favorites *Sergeant Preston of the Yukon* and *Wild Bill Hickok*, were surprised—or frightened—to hear the gravely voiced Leona Anderson, the "World's Most Horrible Singer," croaking, "Bob, Bob, Bob and Ray, Ray, Ray . . ." the opening theme for their new fifty-minute show, *Stand-By with Bob and Ray* (in New York, opposite the first hour of Phil Goulding's record show on WMGM). The boys had their own action-adventure inventory, including such spoofs as the angst-ridden *Matt Neffer, Boy Spot Welder* and (sponsored by "chocolate cookies with white stuff in between them"), *Lawrence Fechtenberger, Interstellar Officer Candidate* who during the Mutual run, using a first baseman's mitt, managed to catch a satellite orbiting the earth a few feet off the ground, and built a man-sized robot that cried like a baby.

These and other B&R perennials, such as *Ladies Grab Your Seats* and *Jack Headstrong, All-American American* ("Quiet, Billy! There's no time for that now!"), were performed with virtually no preparation. Bob or Ray might suggest a notion or narrative for that day's episode. If particular effects were required, soundmen were alerted. There were no scripts, no outlines, and no notes—nothing on paper.

How did they do it? "It's not a mystery if you have somebody who is on the exact same page as you," said Carl Reiner, citing his "Two-Thousand-Year-Old-Man" routines with Mel Brooks. "If you paste him against the wall with an impossible question, he rises to the occasion. My purpose is: get a comic genius mind in panic, and you've got something really good. In panic, they'll save themselves with brilliance." It is akin to marriage, Reiner observed. "You know what's going to come out . . . if you ask them a certain question." Refining his point, he added, "You *don't* know what's going to come out. You know *something* is going to come out."

Bob and Ray's bits and their protocols had been marinating for a decade and were now assimilated and in the pair's collective memory bank. In contrast to the WHDH days, the two had become escape artists. In the middle of an *Aunt Penny*, or a *Mr. Trace*, there was no Elliott and Goulding; they seamlessly disappeared into the bits. Because they had created their nuanced characters, they believed in them and could speak through each one's prism. Rehearsing was as pointless as reviewing the alphabet before an eye-chart exam. Instead, during records or commercials, the two were lost in crossword puzzles or doodling. There was no need to talk. They had been together so long that they could finish each other's silences.

"There was no part of my day that was as joy-filled as when Bob and Ray came on the air," said actor, satirist, and author Harry Shearer, who was in his early teens when he first discovered the team on Mutual. "There was something about the relationship between the two of them that connected with me, even as a child," he said. "The way they worked off of each other I just found mesmerizing, fascinating, and endlessly appealing." One felt that relationship in every performance, he said, without them ever making a big deal out of it, or putting that in front of the material and making the show about them. "It didn't seem as if they led with their egos," Shearer said. ". . . They weren't there to tell you about themselves, they were there to tell you about the world that they observed. But you still had this profound sense of that relationship. . . . It was a very direct influence on me."

As a child of radio, Shearer had been introduced by his parents to the comedy mainstream of Bob Hope, Bergen & McCarthy, and Jack Benny, entertainers, as he put it, who "stood on a stage and were funny to an audience." Bob and Ray represented a "new departure" Shearer continued. "People working, more than anything else, to entertain themselves and each other, and the audience was in on it. It had a different performance style. . . . It was at the same time more intimate and more grand because it could create any environment. . . . That you could create all these little worlds in what I imagined, as time went on, was an increasingly tiny radio studio for them, was also mesmerizing for me."

Bob and Ray were considered to be "gentle," Shearer pointed out, partly because of their "underplaying," and partly because, as broadcasters, they "were working in the medium they were making fun of." They had to be just "subversive enough" yet not a "brash and blatant assault" on the institution they inhabited. They kind of got to the "back side, or under side of what makes this stuff tick," he said. "And, in that sense, I thought it was profoundly irreverent."

The team's infectious camaraderie hastened a desire on the part of some listeners to perceive the two as inseparable, both on and off the air. Not so, they often pointed out. "We're together all the working day," Ray once told the *Tonight Show* audience. "And then I go one way, and he goes another."

"Looking at it from the outside," Shearer commented, "it could have been a key to the longevity of their working relationship. They went off to their separate corners, and to their own lives."

A few miles northwest of Harry Shearer's home in L.A.'s West Adams district, another radio at 144 South Mapleton Drive was also faithfully tuned to Mutual each afternoon. Recognizing Elliott on a Manhattan bus almost twenty years later, Judy Garland's biographer, Gerold Frank said, "You know, you're in my book." If Frank was selfishly thinking in terms of royalties, it worked. In no time Elliott picked up a copy of *Judy*.

Garland listened to the radio "passionately," Frank wrote. "She had one in her bathroom and Sid [Luft, her husband], when he was home, could hear her laughing there, especially when the very popular *Bob and Ray* program was on. This was her very private period."

At Mutual, as with WINS, there was not the sense of being under the thumbs of network VPs that existed at NBC. Mutual brass had enough on their minds just trying to keep the lights on. Thus, much of the craziness of the local morning show was easily transported, thanks in large measure to Vic Cowen, who, with his amassed collection of voice tracks, accompanied B&R to the network. Now, Cowen's wacky sound and musical effects and spoken-word curios—lifted off of everything from old Eddie Lawrence and Buddy Hackett albums to recorded foreign-language lessons—were sprung on the entire country. There were bizarre train sounds from Reginald Gardiner, double-talk from Al Kelly, sneezing jags and hiccups from old Spike Jones 78s, all dropped in at the most ludicrously auspicious moment. "He was intuitive," Elliott said of Cowen, who now enjoyed the credit of director. "He could smell a bit coming where he knew exactly what should go in. . . . He had a wall of these things."

Next to Cowen in the booth was engineer Ronnie Harper, who, in the middle of an ad-lib bit, innately knew what effect Cowen wanted and would instantly cue it up. "It was sleight of hand," Bob said. "There was a wonderful three-way thing." This was still in the days before cartridges and cassettes—everything was on discs. In the presence of Ronnie Harper, a resident of Massapequa, Long Island, one was always only minutes away from hearing the word "fucking," said Bob. He was a virtuoso at inserting it into the middle of sentences, words, even syllables. B&R frequently recalled him complaining about his daily commute on the train from "Massa-fucking-pequa."

Completing a troika of imaginative technicians were Al Schaffer and Barney Beck alternating on sound effects. If not watched, soundmen "devoured us," Bob said, adding that Schaeffer was "heavy" on the effects. We often had to "keep a little brake on him." Schaeffer and Beck also incorporated their effects into performing audience warm-ups and entertaining at V.A. hospitals.

Combined with *Monitor*, Bob and Ray were now on the air nationally seven days a week. The local WINS show also continued six days a week. By dropping the costly action-adventure programs in favor of Bob and Ray, Mutual saved a nice chunk of money, none of which appeared to be plowed into promoting their two afternoon stars. It was up to the audience to find the boys. Little by little they did.

In April 1956, Mutual's VP of sales, Henry Trenner, announced "the biggest time sale in network radio in the last five years," a McKesson and Robbins Pharmaceutical Company, forty-five-minute Monday through Friday sponsorship of B&R, with the program re-titled, *Your Druggist Presents The Bob and Ray Show*. Then, in late November, Mutual added an additional eleven-fifteen in the morning B&R quarter-hour as a lead-in to *Queen for a Day*.

Announcer George Putnam, a ubiquitous voice on both newsreels and the networks of the 1940s and '50s, was hired to read the McKesson spots. It was not always easy. Like Peter Roberts, Putnam (not to be confused with the West Coast newscaster of the same name) was easily stirred to laughter and, as with Peter Roberts, at the most inappropriate times—for him, that is. As the McKesson pitches concerned intimate, personal-care products, Putnam was constantly calling listeners' attention to "those unattractive excess pounds," "embarrassing perspiration odors," and "unsightly pimples." The more intimate the copy, the easier B&R could provoke his outbursts. In contrast to Roberts's more sustained convulsions, Putnam's were like a thunder clap, instantaneous but short-lived, lacking the former's excruciating efforts at maintaining his composure.

Seventy-one-year-old Leona Anderson's rasping, off-key tones, covering a range of two full notes, was an antidote to the swinging, melodic DJ theme songs of the era ("Let's all hobnob, with Ray and Bob . . ."). B&R had first discovered Leona on Steve Allen's *Tonight* show. She had also inflicted her numbers on Ernie Kovacs and Jack Paar's audiences. Sweet, frail-thin, and always wearing a hat, Leona would occasionally stop by to plug her album, *Music to Suffer By*, selections of which—"Limburger Lover" and "Rats in My Room"—would be played, or, on occasion, be woven into a sketch, such as "The Disc Jockey Murder Clue" episode of *Mr. Trace, Keener Than Most Persons*.

Reviewing her album, *Los Angeles Times*' critic Philip K. Scheuer wrote, "I took a copy home, suffered through 'I Love Paris,' 'Chloe,' and 'Indian Love Call' and quit." *The San Francisco Chronicle* reported that Miss Andersen belts out ballads "in a husky voice that only skirts the melody."

"I sing standard songs which cannot be ruined," Leona said. "I don't sing very off-key—just enough." A resident of the Waldorf, Leona's long, if intermittent, career stretched back to roles in a few Broadway musicals. She was the kid sister of "Broncho Billy" Anderson, America's first cowboy star, who later put her in some silent films. At one time Leona had been a serious opera hopeful, and, with her brother footing the bill, had studied voice in London. But she never made it. "So," she said, "I decided that if I couldn't be the best, I'd be the worst."

⌇

Monitor's producers, writers, and production units were scattered throughout 30 Rock's seventy stories. In 1955, thirty-year-old Tom Koch, a continuity writer for the Sunday-evening segment, shared space with NBC's premier TV anchorman John Cameron Swayze's news writers, a proud clique that considered themselves a few cuts above radio people. "They had no use for us; felt we were white trash or something," Koch said.

Raised in Broad Ripple, Indiana (he claimed it sounded more colorful than Indianapolis), the laconic, self-effacing Koch (pronounced "Cook") previously wrote for *Welcome Travelers*, a Chicago-based, reality-TV show that reveled in the woeful stories of victims of misfortune. Every afternoon, pathetic souls recruited by program scouts combing the city's train and bus terminals, related desperate tales of seeking critical medical treatment, wrenching family separations, and being taken by get-rich scams, only to be left stranded and destitute. Then, for their troubles, host Tommy Bartlett invariably presented them with a totally impractical gift. "They would give cancer victims a nine-by-twelve rug to solve their problems," Koch said.

Cranking out streams of patter for hosts Dave Garroway and Don Russell's three-hour *Monitor* block involved linking dozens of disparate elements of the broadcast marathon. It was "maddening," Koch said in his Lee Marvin sound-alike voice, a "killer job; over one hundred pages a week." By October, he had had it. "I finally just kind of cracked under the pressure," he recalled, "and took a leave of absence and moved in with my wife's family in St. Louis." More precisely, his wife's parents lived in Ladue, he pointed out. "They were the poorest family in the richest suburb."

After only a few weeks of decompression, barely enough time to shake the night sweats, *Monitor* producer Arnold Peyser, at the urging of Mike Zeamer, called with an intriguing question: Would Koch consider writing for Bob and Ray? With the Mutual series added to their weekend *Monitor* spots, Peyser explained, B&R were seeking some writing assistance. The cherry on top for Tom was that he could do it without ever having to leave home—his in-laws' home, that is.

Though he had never given a moment's thought to writing comedy, he had watched B&R's NBC television series and found them "hilariously funny," he recounted. Koch sent the team ten bits. "They bought eight," he said, "so I sent them ten more and they never did reject another one. . . . I just kind of fell into it." As for instantly capturing B&R's sensibility, he credited it to "kind of a knack to write in somebody else's style."

"It was a natural fit," said then-associate editor of *Mad* magazine, Nick Meglin, who would oversee around two hundred pieces Koch would later contribute to the publication. "He was such a polished writer, a very literate craftsman with a far-ranging wit that ran the gamut from hilarious absurdity to brilliant, wry commentary."

Koch went to work supplying the team fifteen spots a week for *Monitor* and Mutual, all by mail. He would write for the team on and off for the next thirty-three years, mostly from California, where he eventually settled. With the exception of a rare letter or phone call, or even rarer, an in-person visit, there was hardly any contact. "The check would come and that would be it," Koch said.

Tom Koch's sketches, turned out like widgets on a conveyor belt, were unfailingly funny and almost always performed exactly as written. His material arrived "ready to go," Bob said. "Tom's stuff couldn't have been more on-the-button."

To meet the schedule, Koch created dozens of concepts, essentially satiric templates which could be repeated episodically as regular features, each with its own premise and endearingly oddball characters. These were characters "that B&R could assimilate into their own personas," Meglin pointed out. "It became very clear after a while that even B&R didn't know where their voice began and Tom's ended. They were inseparable."

"Everything he did was funny," Bob agreed. "He was a gold mine of funny thoughts and exactly what we needed to punctuate what we had already been doing."

At three-and-a-half pages, the bits had to hit fast, with an immediately accessible premise. With parodies, Tom explained, there was only time to "pick the most easily attacked feature of the real show and then make a mockery of it." In Koch's *Squad Car 119*, the team's long-running *Dragnet* sendup, all plots were based solely on the original's signature clipped, monotone dialog about mundane subjects. Hence, detectives Sam Finch (Bob) and Ralph R. Kruger, Jr. (Ray) were too distracted by a chili-sauce stain on Kruger's necktie to pursue a bad-check artist. A hit-and-run victim could not be questioned because Kruger "gets the willies" in hospitals. Grabbing dinner at a drive-in, the two were unable to respond to a burglary in progress because they were unable to attract the attention of the carhop to remove the tray from their squad-car window.

> *Kruger:* Isn't that our waitress over there?
> *Finch:* No, our waitress is a tall brunette.

Koch's earlier involvement with *Welcome Travelers* was the genesis of the long-running B&R feature *Hard Luck Stories*, in which guests related personal tales of hardship and deprivation, after which they would be awarded, courtesy "of the generous Bob and Ray organization," a completely incongruous gift. Subjects were generally sobbing women (Ray's falsetto) in need of financial assistance for a desperate medical condition.

> *Ray (as a concerned mother):* My little Sandra has cuticles growing halfway up her fingernails, and the outstanding cuticle man has his clinic in Auburn, Indiana.
> *Bob:* There's nothing more touching than a mother's devotion to her child. We want you to have this beautiful set of burnished fireplace tools. There's a poker and a shovel and everything you'll need.

One of the team's most identifiable characters was their ace correspondent Wally Ballou, so named because Elliott's mother, Gail, worked for a period in Ballou Hall, Tufts University's administrative building at their Somerville campus. Wally (always voiced by Bob) brought his ego and adenoids to every story he covered; neither ever went into remission. Wally Ballou remotes were especially satisfying to write, Koch said, because "the whole world was open." B&R's afternoon Mutual listeners were treated to Wally's report from an atomic-energy plant that produced "bombs within the price range of the average consumer." Particularly memorable also was the Koch-scripted Ballou pickup from an Ohio paperclip factory that cut costs by eliminating machinery and having its workers—who earned fourteen cents a week and lived in caves at the edge of town and foraged for food—make the paperclips by hand from long strips of wire. Wages and prices were a frequent topic. Captain Wilmer Snavish (Ray), who operated an extremely small, ten-by-seven-foot ferryboat on the Wabash River, told Wally that his income was suffering because two bridges, one a quarter of a mile up the river and the other just down the river, neither of which charged tolls, had taken all his business. His only remaining customer, he said, was a farmer who had his barn on one bank and pasture for his two cows on the other. "I carry him and the cows back and forth every day," Captain Snavish explained. "I charge the farmer a nickel each way and three cents apiece for the cows. . . . I have a very low standard of living." On occasion, the very same theme would be turned inside-out, as when Wally Ballou interviewed the president of the Old Hoosier Doorstop Company, whose solid-gold doorstops retailed for $22,000. "We feel," the executive informed Wally, "the average person doesn't want to cut corners when buying a doorstop."

Self-important big shots were constant B&R targets. Typical of Koch-invented stuffed shirts was the executive secretary of the Parsley Institute of America, extolling the "fascinating story of parsley" while bemoaning that the "per capita consumption has been dropping steadily. . . . How often do you suppose that a factory worker's wife would think to put a sprig of parsley in her husband's lunchbox?"

Tom Koch's premises, always supported on a bedrock of deliciously abstruse logic, were nothing more than "reality carried a step further," he said. "If you accept the premise, it's all logical." Thus, Wally Ballou's report from a prefabricated-house factory in Greenland, where the temperature was kept at thirty-below to prevent their pre-fab igloos from melting before shipping, seemed perfectly plausible, as did his remote from the Bodenhaimer Rabbit Farm, where, through training and diet, "watch rabbits" are bred to protect property and chase off intruders.

"Failure or disaster of some kind," Koch said, was also a productive arena, as with Wally's interview with the chief engineer of the newly completed Franklin Pierce Memorial Bridge, which linked two points on the same bank of the Missouri River. "I had a general idea of what I wanted to do here," the befuddled engineer told Wally, "but I didn't have anything down on paper." Other Koch-scripted remotes were reported by Biff Burns (Bob's gravel-voiced sportscaster), including his coverage of the annual Soda Fountain Stool Spinning Derby in Crown Point, Indiana, and his interview with the owner of a parimutuel cat-racing track in Muncie. "He had stuff no one else was doing," Nick Meglin said of Koch. "His cleverness was understated, droll, wry, and sometimes minimal, creating big laughs from small moments."

Bob said that he and Ray had grown up listening to all of the top comedy shows of the day, which—with the exception of Don Quinn on *Fibber McGee and Molly*—never gave writers' credits. "We never thought to do it," he said. "And we did accept the accolades of people when they would flatter us with words about *The Gathering Dusk* or any of the other things that Tom created. Still now, I feel we didn't give him a real shake that he should have had. It was not our intention to hide him, or for us to hide behind his bits. . . . They certainly played a big a big part in the success we had."

As for Koch's opinion: "I never thought about it," he said. "I never even thought about it years later." (For the record, *Inside Bob & Ray* and all of their TV series contained writing credits.) In the Tom Koch hierarchy of recurring B&R features, which also included *Mr. Science, Anxiety, Fred Falvy—The Do-It-Yourselfer*, and *Widen Your Horizons*, the most enduring was *The Gathering Dusk*, the ongoing saga of Edna Bessinger (Ray, of course), a confused Midwest spinster who encountered misfortune "by hunting for it where others have failed to look." Residing alone in the small village of Red Boiling Springs, Edna, always under the spell of her own delusions, continually invoked the memory of her dear bootlegger father's life on the lam from the Feds, and her impetuous, "roscoe" packing brother, Waldo, and his shootouts with "the fuzz" until finally put away for keeps; she was convinced that her long-missing fiancé, David, was still living nearby in some barn.

In 225 episodes, initially sponsored by "Grime, the magic shortening that spreads like lard," Edna called to her home a parade of excruciatingly patient town administrators (always played by Bob) as she sought relief from her chronic, unwarranted assumptions, and, without which, she would have had no life at all. Treasury Agent Witherspoon assured her that the "counterfeit bill" she discovered was only a soap-flake coupon. Alcohol tax investigation chief Fundy explained that the mysterious man renting the upstairs bedroom was not a bootlegger; the "bottle of hooch" she discovered was just after-shave lotion. FBI Agent Shwip informed Edna that the "Communist underground cell meeting" across the street was merely sewer workers going about their job. Once her fears were put to rest, she would exclaim, "Oh my stars! It's as if I'm no longer standing in The Gathering Dusk."

"Those used to crack us up," said Bob, explaining that often when a bundle of Koch's scripts arrived, he and Ray would immediately rip open the envelope just for a "quick peek" to discover what calamity Edna would be facing next.

Unlike other Koch parodies which could be traced to actual programs, Edna Bessinger sprang from real life, in the person of his elderly, maternal aunt Esther, who lived in Olney, Illinois. "She was a little off-center all her life," Tom said. "She never married and stayed at home a lot. . . . I even had a mental picture of what the area looked like when she sat there staring out her windows, imagining all these things." Esther's father had run a department store in Olney and she often referred to him as a "merchant prince," as did the fictional Edna when recalling the days when "Daddy ran white lightning into the village." Aunt Esther, Koch said, was "still talking about 'the swain' that took her to the high-school prom, and things like that." Koch wasn't sure if his aunt ever knew she was the model for an eccentric radio character. He was positive, however, that *he* never told her.

By the autumn of 1955, NBC Television's five-year Sunday-night franchise, *The Colgate Comedy Hour*, was in a downward spiral. A name change to *The Colgate Variety Hour* apparently was not the answer, and with the company's decision to stop throwing its money against their competition on CBS, *The Ed Sullivan Show*, the program vanished after the last Sunday of the year. Its doddering stars—Eddie Cantor, Jimmy Durante, and Abbott & Costello—had already moved on, happily under their own power. Viewers of that final broadcast had to count on host Fred Waring and his Pennsylvanians for the laughs.

Its hastily assembled successor was the brand-new *NBC Comedy Hour*, inaugurated, the network explained, with the intent of discovering new, fresh, young talent. Why the indomitable baseball icon Leo Durocher and sixty-three-year-old William Frawley were selected to headline the first program was left unexplained. On January 8, 1956, Bob and Ray joined series regular Jonathan Winters in Hollywood as guests on the premiere. Like Liz Goulding, Winters grew up in Springfield, Ohio. The two had met through Liz's older sister, Barbara, a close friend of Jonathan's mother, Alice, who hosted a radio show in Dayton.

During a rehearsal break at NBC's El Capitan Theatre on Vine Street, Bob and Ray and their wives found themselves—along with two of the week's other "new talent" discoveries, Henny Youngman and female bandleader and songstress Ina Ray Hutton—comprising an impromptu audience for Jonathan Winters. "He was entertaining everybody," Bob said.

For Liz and Jonathan, flashbacks to their Springfield days were inevitable. Back then, she recalled, unable to suppress a laugh, "Johnny was a pain in the neck because he was always 'on.' But we were friends and acquaintances." On an earlier visit home, she said, Ray had even been a guest on Jonathan's mother's program.

The Elliotts and the Gouldings turned the boys' first major prime-time guest-shot into a fun week in Hollywood. "We shared dinners and went out together," Liz said. But, she added, she and Ray were not with Bob and Lee as constantly as they might have been as "they were kind of newlyweds, so to speak."

Also stepping off a New York flight was a short, reed-thin twenty-year-old prodigy, a recent graduate of the NBC Writers Development Program named Woody Allen. At the time, he had just been added to the staff (on trial) and was pulling down $169 a week. Another *Comedy Hour* writer, Danny Simon, older brother and former collaborator of playwright Neil Simon, had been so impressed with Woody's writing samples submitted by one of the Development Program's honchos, ex-agent Les Colodny, that he responded, "Les, I think the kid is my next brother."

Woody Allen first discovered Bob and Ray during his teenage years, which had only ended a month earlier, on his last birthday. He was "an enormous fan and listened to them or watched them on television at every opportunity," Woody stated in 2012, "and of course saw them when they appeared on Broadway. . . . They were clearly brilliantly funny—always hilarious, two original and authentically funny men." (Discerning members of the Bob and Ray cognoscenti have long delighted in pointing out that two of the team's charter cast members, Fielding Lovely and Mug Melisch, had their distinctive names lovingly combined in Woody's 1971 film *Bananas*, in the person of his own character, "Fielding Melisch." No, said Woody, "Fielding Melisch was not an homage to Bob and Ray at all.")

While Elliott and Goulding and their wives enjoyed the luxury of the Beverly Hills Hotel, Woody and the cabal of transplanted New York writers—which, for a period, also included Earle Doud—were assigned $290-a-month, one-bedroom digs up on Yucca at the Hollywood Hawaiian Motel. The group provided B&R's two spots for the show: a *Wide Wide World* takeoff with Elliott as Dave Garroway visiting Goulding as a resident of the Arctic, conducting a tour of his igloo; and a *Meet the Press* sendup featuring Ray, in his maniacal Joe McCarthy persona, being grilled by Bob and his panel of "newsmen." It was the first time the eerie impression was seen by a national television audience. In private, Liz said, her husband did the voice only with very close friends. "Of course," she noted, "I'm sure Ray added a few words that he'd like to have said to Joe sometimes, too."

In the following weeks, the program's concept endured endless tinkering. By then, B&R were back in New York and their WINS, Mutual, and *Monitor* commitments.

In early 1956, Bob and Lee and their three girls had moved to a newly purchased duplex on East Seventy-Ninth Street. At WINS, Elroy McCaw's belt tightening was increasingly tying Bob Leder's hands. That spring, when McCaw was in town visiting his GM's New York apartment, he felt strangely at home. It did not take him long to figure out why: the chair he was sitting on was his very own. Furniture from Leder's WINS office "wound up in his living room," Les Keiter said, and when McCaw discovered it, he "blew a fuse." Soon after, Leder fled to WOR, replaced by Jock Fernhead, who continued the fire sale, dropping the *The Bob and Ray Show* at the end of May.

Whatever McCaw and Fernhead determined about the station's morning needs, it apparently no longer included comedy. Replacing Bob and Ray was former NBC sportscasting legend Bill Stern, anchoring a music-and-newsmaker-interview program called *Contact*. WINS in-house reaction, according to Les Keiter, was "total shock."

B&R had drawn a devoted audience in the morning, but WNEW and Klavan and Finch still ruled the roost, with all pursuers—for the last year also including Ernie Kovacs on WABC—fighting it out a rung or two below. "It was the most successful radio station in the country due to the personalities on it," said Bill Persky, who, together with Sam Denoff, wrote promos, jingles, and interstitial material at WNEW from 1955 to '60 (and would later share three Emmys as writers and producers of dozens of TV series, including some of the funniest episodes of *The Dick Van Dyke Show*). The station even had a live show at noon. It was, Persky said, like "a localized version of the great days of radio as they were fading. . . . And the other stations hadn't really caught up to that."

WNEW's power was "enormous," said Jonathan Schwartz. "It was a one-station city. They were playing the music of the street—the music everyone listens to. And the people who presented the music were considered gods, especially William B. Williams and some of the others." (From 1971 on, those others would include Schwartz himself. His scholarly, five-hour Sunday show, in fact, still survives today, which is more than can be said for WNEW.)

The second-floor walk-up at 46th and Fifth was a "Mount Olympus of broadcasting," as Gene Klavan dubbed it in his memoir. The talent radiated star power. Dee Finch had "a voice made to make a million dollars in radio," his partner wrote, with "an open, absolutely contagious laugh. . . . When he laughed, you laughed."

While Dee never played anybody but himself, Bill Persky said, Gene was a master of voices whose characters mostly included people at the station. "If I walked into the studio, he would do me. If Sam walked in—whoever walked in, he would do that character." Klavan's characters mocked the station, the music, and particularly the sponsors. Frequently, a character was a sponsor, as live commercials were woven into the fabric of the show. The fun was in knowing it was really Gene. On the air, as themselves, the two were sharply differentiated from each other. B&R, by contrast, came across as tongue-in-cheek interlocutors who largely subverted their own identities, content to let their "supporting cast" upstage them. "The teams were really not competitive in terms of their approach," Persky pointed out. ". . . I think Bob and Ray were much more interchangeable in terms of nobody being a straight man. They were both funny and they both did characters. . . . Bob and Ray had more of a broader horizon to work on."

A wake-up show was not a good fit for Bob and Ray, in the opinion of Jonathan Schwartz. Morning programs, he pointed out, are "designed to create energy in the listener . . . choppy, quick pieces of fun. Bob and Ray were just the opposite in every possible way. They were quiet, they were thoughtful, and what they had to say was soft. . . . The morning shows on the New York dial were people, in effect, helping people to prepare themselves for whatever dark moments they might experience during the day. And Bob and Ray were satirizing those moments. . . . They were satirical without being venomous." It's a difference of "humorous intellect," Schwartz observed. "It's Letterman against Leno." David Letterman's view is "richly satiric. He's always sending-up someone, and it occasionally can be construed as a little on the vindictive side. But it's still wonderful." Jay Leno, Schwartz noted, has a larger audience, but "he's not going to hurt anyone, or hurt you. . . . Leno is Klavan and Finch; Letterman is Bob and Ray." For that reason, Schwartz happily tuned in B&R every morning. "I set the alarm and sat there and listened until their program went off. And I did this day after day."

Of the original group of 1954 WNBC émigrés to WINS, only Peter Roberts, signed by Leder to a longer contract, remained. "When the three of them vacated the premises," he recalled, "I was left with my tongue hanging out."

Later, Alan Freed would be gone, too. On the heels of the late-'50s quiz-show scandals, attention focused on rumors of payola in the record industry. As grand jury indictments swirled, it was a time for DJs, program directors, and song pluggers to get their stories straight. For Elroy McCaw, with investigators combing his files, an FCC license renewal on the line and antacids at his side, it was time to look for a buyer.

Alan Freed was ultimately charged with twenty-five counts of pocketing record-company bribes and would plead guilty. A subsequent WINS program director and a record librarian were also named. Bob and Ray, on the other hand, were never roiled in any scandal—though the scope of the U.S. House Oversight Committee's probe did not extend to accepting free steak-and-egg breakfasts.

It would be another seven years before Bob and Ray would take another early morning shift. Klavan and Finch would be waiting.

During the team's second year at Mutual, kidney disease struck once more. Ray's brother, Phil, the person who had influenced him the most, died on March 29, 1957; he was thirty-nine. Ray had planned a vacation in the Virgin Islands for himself, Liz, Phil, and his wife, Thelma. They wanted to get Phil away, Liz said, but at the last minute, WMGM refused to give him the time off. "Ray was devastated, and it was a real rough time. I think because of their both being in radio, the connection there was quite strong. Phil was his best friend and the only one he could talk to."

"I remember my dad being upset because they were treating Phil for his heart problem when it wasn't his heart at all," said Ray Goulding, Jr., today vice-president of marketing and special events for the Glendale, Arizona, Chamber of Commerce. "There are some pictures of Phil that you would swear are my father, younger. Uncle Phil was Dad's hero, by far. He was my favorite uncle, my godfather."

Nat Asch, a ten-year colleague who produced Phil's WMGM record show, remembered his friend as "outgoing, witty, an excellent announcer, and, of course, a Goulding—meaning that he thought funny."

After Phil's services at St. Margaret's in Lowell, one of his closest friends, former CBS colleague Sandy Becker—who had announced *Young Doctor Malone*, and later starred as Dr. Malone himself—told Ann, "You may have lost *a* brother, but I lost the only brother I ever had." Phil and Thelma had no children.

When, after thirty-nine weeks, McKesson and Robbins did not renew their sponsorship, Mutual's Los Angeles flagship, KHJ, dropped the program, causing such listener uproar that it had to be reversed a week later. *The Los Angeles Times'* headline announced: "Bob, Ray, Returned to KHJ After Fans Stir Up Protest." The concerted campaign resulted in *The Bob and Ray Show* being brought back in the evenings at ten-thirty. Referring to the reverberating "howls and screams," the *Times* called it a "victory for the oppressed. . . . Stations and sponsors do pay attention . . . if the complainants yell loud enough."

Ten-thirty at night was past the required bedtime of young Harry Shearer, who resorted to a green, Bakelite portable radio slipped under his pillow. "It was the size of a toaster," he said. "It must have been a big, big lump . . ." Though his parents would occasionally check on him, with the sound only an inch or two from his ear, he could easily hear Bob and Ray. "The door would open a little crack and I would see the light coming in," Shearer said. "I was, to all intents and purposes, asleep, but obviously I was listening."

Happily for Harry Shearer and Judy Garland, KHJ stayed with the program—eventually moving it up to seven o'clock in the evening—until the end of its two-year run, September 20, 1957. He loved them on *Monitor*, and loved them everywhere, said Shearer, adding that that Mutual radio show was probably his favorite. "Something about the apparent looseness of it always struck me as their best work."

Meanwhile, B&R were being stalked. Their replacement at Mutual—having followed them from WINS—was once again Bill Stern.

11

BABY BOOM

Bob was back at St. Vincent's Hospital, this time for the birth of his first son, Robert, Jr., on May 23, 1957. On May 31, 1960, following a few gracious remarks at a luncheon in the Roosevelt Hotel's Grand Ballroom honoring Bob and Ray as Radio Fathers of the Year, Bob again raced to St. Vincent's. He arrived just in time to discover that his second son, Chris, had been born during dessert.

Ray and Liz welcomed a new son, Bryant, on May 24, 1958. "We were really looking forward to a baby because we had lost quite a few," Liz said. "So he was quite a gift to us." Their fourth son, Mark, was born on February 1, 1960. "Now we have a good infield," Ray told Liz. On March 1st of the following year, the couple welcomed their second daughter, Melissa, whose first car ride was in a chauffeured Rolls-Royce that her father had arranged as a surprise for Liz for the ride home from the hospital. Combined, the two families now totaled eleven children, each one satisfying all requirements for membership in the (not yet coined) Baby Boomer Generation.

A few Maine summers around Popham Beach was all the convincing Bob and Lee needed to purchase a vacation house of their own. The home commanded one-and-a-half acres on a tentacle of land jutting into Casco Bay, with the Atlantic Ocean as its back yard. The view was spectacular, or so they were told. We bought it in "a complete fog," Bob said. "I had contacted a real-estate guy and the day he showed it to us, it was foggy and he said, 'You have to take my word for it, the ocean's out there.'"

A year later, working with a designer/contractor, Bob added an additional room, and did it all without power tools. Because Chris was only a year old at the time, and Bob, Jr., was four, Bob senior was afraid to have a power saw around. (Almost thirty-five years later, Chris and his family would be only a few doors away, having purchased the former vacation home of Senator Margaret Chase Smith.)

As a family of seven, the Elliotts now also sought more room in the city, which led to snapping up a five-story townhouse from the estate of New York City arts patron Walter Naumberg. "It was this giant sort of Edwardian, Tudor, Gothic, New York City mansion," as Chris described it. "It was sort of like living in the Hearst Castle in New York City. . . . English living room, and then sort of an Italian library and a French bedroom. . . . On the surface, it was kind of an absurd place for Bob Elliott of Bob and Ray to live. But it was like a fairy tale, and it seemed perfectly normal to me."

The home on East Sixty-Fourth Street featured large, thirty-six-by-nineteen-foot English oak-paneled living and dining rooms, and was the scene for many festive family occasions, including Bob's fortieth birthday party. "They threw a big one," Collie said. "I remember the boys dressed in their little red jackets and bow ties 'helping' the bartenders; that was great fun."

The townhouse also had an elevator, which was anything but a luxury for the Elliotts' youngest daughter, today Amy Elliott Anderson, a graphic artist and illustrator: "Having two brothers, it was often used as torture." By purposefully keeping the door open, she explained you couldn't ring the elevator to come down. "You'd have to walk up five flights."

"We were terrible," admitted, Bob, Jr., now semi-retired after thirty years in retail management. "My brother and I used to throw everything imaginable down that elevator shaft. I'm sure at the bottom there's tin soldiers, cars, any number of little toys . . ."

The elevator made a particular impression on Vic Cowen's oldest daughter, Terri, who, with her sisters, accompanied her parents to the Elliotts' home on various occasions. Terri also remembers "being told to 'Get lost'—particularly if it was so-called 'martini hour.'"

The place came with a "hefty" price tag, Bob said, which combined with the new summer home, took a big bite out of 1961, a "year I can easily pinpoint because it was one in which we didn't have our own show."

At home, "Dad's humor was just part of the fabric of our conversation," Collie said. "He can still have me roaring. It's effortless; it just kind of happens, which is the way it happened professionally as well, at least that's how it sounded."

His father was "always funny," Bob, Jr., said, but he was never someone who sat around, telling jokes. "He is very reserved; not someone who would hold court in a corner."

It was Chris's feeling that his mother's very sardonic humor "influenced" his dad, particularly "his ability to point at the absurd as if it's normal." Many of "his rejoinders and comments on things that just happened," Chris said, "were pretty sardonic and pretty full of hidden meanings."

With his family, Bob was not averse to some broader forms of humor. Recalling Saturday-night TV watching in Maine, Bob, Jr., said, "Late into the evening, and usually after a couple of drinks, my father used to stand up and start walking towards the kitchen to get a refill on his drink. He had loosened his belt and undone his trousers at the waist—which we couldn't see—so that as he walked away from us, his trousers would slowly drop to his knees, and then to his ankles, to reveal his skinny legs and white boxer shorts. . . . I can remember that never failed to get a huge laugh from us kids, though I don't think my mother thought it was too funny, or at least pretended like she didn't."

"The fact that he is this sort of mild-mannered person," Chris said, "whenever he did do something more broad than you would imagine, it was funny because it was him doing it. . . . And then at other times he could be sort of cocktail-party funny, and very charming and sort of eloquent in his humor that raised the level a little bit. He seemed to know his audience, whoever he was playing for."

Often, it was his kids he was "playing for," at least according to his daughter Shannon Elliott, now a speech language pathologist and yoga teacher. On one occasion, a large "surprise" box was delivered, Shannon recounted, noting her father's fondness for ordering items from magazines. "It contained lots of packing popcorn and a pair of plastic shoes with laces imprinted on them and an inflated balloon."

Collie was not aware of what her dad did for a living until "I started listening," she said. "And I thought, you know, they're really funny. . . . It wasn't a dumbing-down kind of humor; they assumed they had an intelligent audience."

As a boy, Chris, too, was not sure what his father did for a living. "He'd leave in the morning, wearing a suit and a tie, carrying a briefcase," he once told NPR's Terry Gross, ". . . then come back in the afternoon. But I never made the connection that he was a performer. . . . It was a very normal—*dull*, I guess is the word I'm looking for—childhood."

"I don't think Dad ever set out to be famous, to be a celebrity," Collie said. . . . "Mom liked the public life as long as it didn't invade her privacy. . . . They're both intensely private people." They weren't a show business family, she pointed out. "He just didn't bring it home that way. He didn't show the kids off."

But from time to time, others—non-family members—were hardly shy about presenting them, if sometimes inartfully. "There were occasions," Amy said, "where we were introduced as 'Bob and Ray's children.'"

Car trips to Maine figured prominently in the Elliotts' activities. During these excursions, the kids happily (if unwittingly) relived their father's childhood, minus the '32 Essex Super Six. Instead, they had "the longest Ford station wagon they made," Amy said. "Dad would always try to beat his best time. If it was six hours and fifty-three minutes, and if he could make it a couple of minutes faster, that counted." It was "important," she said, that there be only one bathroom stop. "We all had, like, five minutes to make our pit stop and, by that time, he would have filled up with gas and we'd be on our way. . . . It was always funny because it was such a big deal for him."

"And I swear," Chris said, "that we passed like ten gas stations before it was the one that we could go to."

"We spent a lot of time in that car—not just us, but we always had a dog, we had birds," said Bob, Jr., adding that what they lacked was air-conditioning, so by the time they got near Boston the windows would be down. "We'd be in the back seat fighting, of course," he continued. "At a certain point, my sister Amy always got carsick. Once we were in Maine, we'd go through a toll and take this sharp exit ramp and my sister, without fail, would lean over and vomit. . . . Yeah, those were fun trips—I'm not sure for my parents, but for us."

"I didn't even know that either of my parents had been married before," Chris said, alluding to a "somewhat traumatic" station-wagon ride when he was twelve. "I was with my dad in the car . . . and figuring out when he was married to my mom and how old Collie and Shannon were and what years they were born. And to this day I can remember my dad saying,

160

'Well, you know your mother was married before,' and just basically sort of going into shock. And then a mile down the road, he said, 'And you know, I was married before.' . . . Being the last one—being the fifth—the youngest one, I think everybody just assumed that somebody had told me. I was pretty upset, I remember."

In a happier Maine episode involving the same '58 Country Squire, the family could not figure out what Bob had up his sleeve. "We kept driving around and not going anywhere," Chris recounted. "Finally, we hit a stretch of road and he started counting down: 'Five . . . four . . . three . . . two . . . one . . . everybody look!' We all had to look at the odometer. The car had just turned 100,000 miles! That was, like, a huge thing. He pulled over to the side of the road and he had little gifts for all of us, each wrapped like a little present. We had a little celebration in the car. . . . It's something I recreated with our kids when our car hit 100,000 miles because it's a memory I'll never forget."

Family Thanksgivings at Bob's grandparents' house in Somerville evoked equally fond memories. Collie and Shannon would be in the kitchen with their grandma and great grandma, Collie said, making all kinds of cookies and floating islands. "I don't know how much we were actually cooking, but we were up to our elbows with flour."

Shannon's culinary recollections centered on "Dad's mother's molasses cookies, Mom's mother's coconut cake" and, on hot summer days, reaching into the Coca-Cola chest at Spinney's, in Popham Beach, for "icy Maine-made sodas." In the city, Horn and Hardart's macaroni and cheese and baked beans automat lunches "from the little self-service windows" rated high, Shannon said, not to mention New Year's Eve treats "off of Mom's beautiful blue-and-white platter" and "dancing on Dad's feet while watching Guy Lombardo."

"He's always been someone working on something," Amy said, "a project . . . a way to do this or that." This industriousness included restoring the turn-of-the-century soda fountain, complete with the original-labeled spigots and taps, inherited from his uncle Al Pilley's pharmacy in Brooks, Maine. As a child, Bob spent summers sitting at the fountain's tiny, two-stool marble counter, inhaling the atmosphere of the place. That atmosphere, which is no less alive today in the Elliotts' kitchen in Maine thanks to the fountain's well-preserved ice-cream-soda glasses, gold-labeled medicine jars, apothecary chests, and prescription scales, together with the ledger for the scripts themselves. Sharing Bob's upstairs office is a section of an 1890s New England post office—the metal clerk's cage, comprising thirty-two letter-size cubbyholes on each side. The townhouse's furnishings included a liquor cabinet Bob antiqued and modified from a cigar humidor, painting vivid cherubs and figures on its sides. "He could have his own antique shop, really," Amy said.

Citing another project, Amy recalled that, after moving into her first apartment, she discovered that something was missing: a place to sit down. Bob designed and constructed an entire wood-framed sofa for her and her roommate. An impossibly narrow stairwell was no problem. "He came over and built it right *in* the apartment," she said. He also leveled the out-of-plumb kitchen counter and fashioned and installed custom-made, hinged shutters, effectively converting the one-bedroom apartment into two bedrooms.

"Then she moved," Bob said.

He's always "challenging himself," Amy said, and yet still types on his Olympia 1960 standard manual, "the one where the 'G' is three-quarters the way up."

A fun project Shannon shared with Bob, she recalled, was "helping him come up with names for racehorses when he entered a yearly contest to name and win a racehorse." The two used to hit Aqueduct racetrack, she added, and her dad placed bets on horses "I picked out."

In addition to his cheery watercolors, Elliott's pastel or oil portraits of his children, and most of his grandchildren and great-grandchildren, are cherished family possessions, Collie said. All have a "softness and charm about them."

Bob was a close friend of the late, celebrated watercolorist Dong Kingman. Together, on painting jaunts around New York with their side-by-side easels, the two captured a collection of whimsical cityscapes. "Dad credits Kingman with teaching him how to paint a little more spontaneously," Amy said. "He learned a lot from Dong. . . . He's still constantly sketching, making notes to himself, but there will always be a little character he's drawn, some face or whatever."

By attending the Rudolph Steiner private school, all the kids were exposed to an art-based education. Even boys in the first grade learned how to knit, Amy said.

"I've always hoped," Bob, Jr., remarked, "that someday in a survival situation, it might come in handy."

All five are exceptionally talented artists. "Part of that was our schooling, part of it was the home we grew up in," Collie said. "It was just something you did."

"It was a very creative environment without being a sort of bohemian creativity," said Chris, "a very middle-class family who, on the outside, might look almost conservative and standard. . . . I always felt that my talents, whatever they were when I was a kid, were appreciated."

The Elliott children's Upper East Side upbringing was in marked contrast to that of the Gouldings' six in the suburbs. Both had enticements: The residential setting was ideal for Ray's kids' sports interests and for riding bicycles, while Bob's five, each with an artistic bent, adapted to life in the big city. "I actually learned to ride my two-wheeler by riding around the dining-room table in the house," Amy said. "It's funny, in growing up in New York City, I think we all grew up fairly protected. . . . My mom and dad made sure we had a normal life. But, in terms of life experiences, I think we were still pretty sheltered."

As a father, Bob was an involved, even-keeled, positive influence, who had a sympathetic ear and spoke in the lower case. What he was not was a "disciplinarian," Bob, Jr., said, ". . . My mother did all of the disciplining. And out of the five of us, I probably needed more than the other four."

"He would no more want a confrontation than anything else," Amy said, "which is often not the best route to take with things that you sometimes have to deal with. . . . I think he'd rather die than have to reprimand someone. . . . My mom was pretty good at keeping things under control, basically."

"He would get angry, and he would yell," Bob, Jr., acknowledged. "But," he added, "if I wanted something, I always went to my father first because I knew he was certainly the more likely of the two to say yes. But he learned quickly. After I had done that a few times, he would just send me to my mother."

The Gouldings had been seeking precisely what the sprawling estate of the late Ellis L. Phillips, co-founder and first president of the Long Island Lighting Company, had to offer: space, almost two and a half acres of it bordering Manhasset Bay. Their new home, a three-story brick English Tudor, at 107 Bayview Road, even included a boathouse and landing, plus an underground conduit linking the beach to the house, which Ray was convinced had been installed for the purpose of smuggling in Mr. Phillips's bootleg liquor when he settled there in 1926.

"It was beautiful," Liz said. "The kids had a ball. There were loads of rooms and they had clubs up on the third floor and did all kinds of things." These things included throwing the switch on the house's elevator, a favorite stunt of Ray, Jr., and Tom, to trap their sister, Barbara, between floors.

Playing catch with his father is a favorite memory for Ray, Jr., who was about twelve, he said, the first time he let loose with his fastball. I really tried to "wing it to him," and his dad "returned the favor. Yes, he showed me—he was still stronger than me."

Their dad's well-oiled first baseman's mitt remains a vivid image for Bryant. "It was gorgeous, like a masterpiece," he said. ". . . We treated it with nurturing respect." Playing catch and hitting grounders and pop-ups was his dad's "favorite baseball thing," according to Bryant. "When it went, like, *plop* right next to me, that's where I learned the term: 'Get off the dime!'" Playing catch was one of the "most intimate ways" Bryant hung out with his dad, he commented. "Just me, him, our two mitts, and a nice hardball—that was awesome." When Bryant was around ten he "mildly obsessed" about wanting to be a catcher, he recounted. When his birthday rolled around, he discovered a beautiful catcher's mitt and all the equipment hiding inside some wrapping paper. "I still have it in my garage. It's a bit snug, though."

The front yard was perfect for football, Ray, Jr., noted, either "two-hand touch or just throwing long passes." In the side yard, a driveway and a grape arbor provided natural boundaries for whiffleball games on a section of perfect grass, which their dad called his "beauty spot," he said. "Over the arbor was a home run in left field. And into the driveway was a home run to right field. It was a lot further to right field, and, of course, I'm the only lefty."

When perfecting his swing, their dad could be spotted at the Kiddie City batting cage in neighboring Douglaston. As Tom recalls, "He used to stop by and whack a few out."

If a home fix-it job could not be solved with a screwdriver, Ray immediately reached for the phone. The house came with a huge spotlight that supposedly was capable of shining clear to the water. The lens was perhaps fifteen inches across, Tom said, but his dad was unable to get it to work. Finally, electricians isolated the problem. It required a power load strong enough to cast a lighthouse-type beam. "Dad used to talk about screwing in a seventy-five-watt bulb or something."

The seven-year gap between the family's third and fourth child had once been the source of idle curiosity on the part of a certain "imperious" woman neighbor, Liz said. Because of her, "We started calling them 'Group A' and 'Group B.' Group 'A' attended Catholic schools; 'B,' public schools."

Each year the graduating class submitted names of peers whom they felt excelled in various categories. Bryant, Mark, and Melissa were all proclaimed "The Wit of the Year" in their high-school yearbook. When the youngest, Melissa, graduated, under a childhood picture of herself, submitted by her parents, the yearbook editor added the notation: "At wit's end."

"You weren't allowed to be funny at St. Mary's," Ray, Jr., said, "so Tommy, Barbara, and I didn't get that. . . . I'm convinced we had the Sisters of St. Lucifer as teachers."

"Definitely stricter," Tom agreed. "There's nothing funny when you've got a cross on the wall, come on!"

"My dad was bigger than life," commented Ray, Jr. "It was very hard to differentiate radio personality and father."

"At home, the guy was hilarious," said Mark, a semi-retired ad man. "But if you weren't in his inner circle, you wouldn't know." At a gathering, cousins and uncles, old friends of the family, would stand around and listen to him. "He'd keep them in stitches."

One of his favorite stories, Melissa recalled, occurred when he and Bob were new in the city, with hours to kill between their morning radio and evening TV shows. Ray, then barely thirty, started visiting midtown auction houses. During one such visit, he spotted a particular painting that appealed to him. After talking it over with their mother, Melissa recalled, "They decided, 'Let's splurge. Let's spend, like, four hundred dollars; maybe we'll go to five.'" At the auction, she continued, the "first bid was fifteen thousand dollars. It was a Renoir! He didn't know; he just thought it was pretty."

Another picture that attracted Ray's attention, a charming sketch of a lighthouse, cost him nothing. He simply cut it out of a magazine and showed it to Melissa, then in junior high. "It was pretty," she said. "I really liked it." Shortly thereafter, it started showing up on a shelf in her room, in a coat pocket, or in a book she was reading on the train. "It would go back and forth," Melissa said, recalling that she stashed it in one of his suits, his glasses case, and such. "It was actually really funny. We never planned it or talked about it. . . . It was the sweetest thing. . . . It went on for years."

"He saw humor in everything, and we kind of picked that up," said Tom, noting that his dad loved Robert Benchley, S. J. Perelman, and Laurel & Hardy. "He was a fun guy. Even if it was a bad thing, he was finding some humor there. All those damn TV shows he'd watch, he parroted everything. It was such great fodder for their takeoffs."

"We're all relatively ridiculous in our own kinds of way," said Bryant, recalling his dad "completely losing it at some of Benchley's stories—just hysterical. . . . It's really a nice thing that gets handed down."

"It's everywhere," Melissa agreed. "It's in everything we do, no matter what." In Melissa's case that even included her wedding-rehearsal dinner at the home of her future in-laws, an incident she prefaced by noting that her parents were "not thrilled" with her choice of a husband. "They were right, but at the time I didn't know it," she continued. "At one point I looked across the room and my dad was sitting in a chair by himself. . . . He had his glasses going diagonally across his face instead of across the bridge of his nose—cockamamie glasses. It was, like, this little subtle joke: 'These people are crazy!' Like an 'I don't want to be here' moment. I remember trying not to laugh out loud because it was so unexpected. It was a little shout-out to say, 'Hey, I've had it!'"

Ray was not one to let an opportunity pass to get a rise out of his kids. When they were in the depths of the end-of-summer blues, Melissa recalled, he "pulled out the 'Back to School' ads and read them aloud with a hokey salesman's pitch. Sometimes he would clip them on the fridge. We would all cringe."

Noting that much of Bob and Ray's comedy is based on "crazy tangents, and then another tangent, and another tangent," Bryant said that, at times, his father interacted with his kids in the same way. "Sometimes we got it, sometimes we didn't," he said. "If you're little, you don't know you're being 'had' necessarily." Bryant, who is in the title insurance business, recalled one brutally hot summer car ride, returning home from somewhere during the pre-AC era with his fellow Group 'B' siblings, then between ages seven and ten. "We were so thirsty," Bryant said, "and my dad just broke into this story about a lemonade stand. He was describing this generous, beautiful stand of barrels of lemonade and floating lemon chunks, blocks of ice, and this wonderful, kind man serving it with a big ladle and spilling it, and saying, 'Oh, drink up! Drink up! There's plenty more.' . . . And we were all dying in the back seat for want of this lemonade. But, of course, we couldn't get any. . . . It was only in our minds. He was having a hilariously fun time. . . . Probably when we were getting close enough to home, we knew we'd be getting lemonade."

A special pancake recipe of Ray's was the subject of a similar episode involving Tom's son—also named Bryant—when he was just a toddler. Ray combined a quarter-cup of milk with a quarter-cup of seltzer to create "an airier, lighter pancake," said the elder Bryant, "describing them as he was making them as being 'so airy, so light, you actually have to hold them to keep them on your plate.' So this little kid, captured by the story, is eating the pancakes, but he has one thumb on each side of the pancake so it doesn't lift off the plate."

"Food is linked to everything," Melissa said, "every celebration we had, every place we went; it was always [about] looking forward to certain foods." Dad watched *The Frugal Gourmet*," she explained, "but could not stand the guy's voice. So he would watch what he was cooking with the volume off, pay attention . . . and then go out and shop and make something that he'd been taken with that day. . . . He made fabulous fettuccini."

He used to bring home "amazing breads," said Bryant, recalling an early childhood memory. On those occasions, "He had us convinced that he'd flown to France and back that day just for the bread."

At the end of the day, home is where Ray Goulding wanted to be. "Fame was not something he was looking to drink in," Bryant said, recounting an exchange he witnessed between his father and a fan in Grand Central Station: "'You're Bob Elliott!' 'No I'm not.' 'Come on, you look just like him.' 'I'm sorry, no I'm not.' He never, never said, 'I'm Ray, the other guy.' He just denied that he was Bob Elliott. And that was the end of it. He just went on his merry way."

He understood what being a show-biz guy entailed and "wanted no part of it," Mark said. If approached in public, he was pleasant, but avoided such encounters whenever possible. It was not always easy, as Mark discovered when playing high-school football. With all the parents and booster clubbers seated on the home side of the field, Mark said, his dad sat on the opposing team's side, with perhaps one-fifth of the crowd, so he would not be recognized or "hear parents make jerky comments about other kids that would upset him," as Mark put it. "He just kind of buffered himself from that. It was almost like he was standing in the corner watching, but didn't want to be seen."

"Really, really private," is how Melissa, now an immigration specialist, describes her father. "I remember even in restaurants, when people would come up, he would almost tense up because that was, like, family time. . . . Mind you, he was gracious and kind, but you could see the body language; he wasn't comfortable with it."

With the two families' eleven kids, the scenes at both homes were often similar: total bedlam. "I'm not sure how I lived through it," Liz said, recalling many evenings Ray returned from work by train, only to have to wait at the Manhasset station because his children had the phone tied up. "He wanted to string up one of his sons," she said.

"And it was me," said Ray, Jr., "because I was probably on the phone with my girlfriend. Sometimes I think my father's fuse was micro-inches. It would just go off."

It was "nitroglycerin-ish," Bryant said, explaining that, when his dad had to walk home from the train station, "Somebody that night had to be sacrificed. There were probably a lot of siblings I've never heard of."

Although their dad kept the family laughing, Tom said, he was also "a father trying to bring order and discipline to his sons, who were trying to break and bend the rules through high school and college." As teenagers coming home late on weekends, a hanging layer of cigar smoke from one of their father's select Cuban stockpile portended trouble, said Tom, who usually got in earlier than Ray, Jr., thereby getting only a token dressing down. "He'd be waiting for Ray like the Cheshire cat." Tom continued, laughing at the sheer hyperbole. "You'd see this orange glow in the living room, lights out, the hanging smoke. It's so vivid I get chills in my back just thinking about it. You'd see that glow and go, 'Oh, damn it! Someone's going to die tonight!' . . . And sometimes it wouldn't happen. It would be, like, he wants you to know that he knows that you know he knows—one of those type things."

Upstairs, a main hall linked seven bedrooms, including a master suite at one end with two sets of doors. If his dad opened those doors, Tom explained, he could observe the entire hallway. If someone came in late, they could see the glow of his TV, but nothing beyond it; they could not tell if he was awake. "But you had to break the plane to get anywhere," Tom said. "He could be long gone, counting Z's, but we didn't know. So basically, you'd fall asleep standing against the wall so you wouldn't break the plane, or get really low to the floor. . . . You never knew for sure if he was there on patrol; but, with the cigar, you knew he was up and around."

One weekend morning when Ray, Liz, and Melissa were at the breakfast table, Bryant came in the front door carrying a fabulous melt-away ring from the bakery. "It was just like a crumb cake with this really delicious vanilla icing dribbled on it," Melissa recalled. "We were so excited." But Bryant looked like "a wreck," she said, ". . . ragged, in sneakers and sweats or whatever. . . . I remember distinctly looking at him and thinking, 'What in the heck is wrong with him?' . . . Later, come to find out, he was out the whole night. But smartened up and decided to make it look like he went running and picked up this melt-away ring. . . . My parents didn't pick up on it or anything. He didn't have to sneak in. He came in blatantly late and tied it into his jogging . . . and buying us this treat."

Bryant wasn't inclined to initiate what he termed, "Hey, dad, can we talk?" conversations." It may be that he opted not to, he said, because "I was afraid of Wolf Larson."

Solving an issue yourself was simply "easier," Tom explained. Otherwise, you could "trip another wire. . . . You could turn a phrase wrong and hit one of those mines."

Conversely, Melissa recalls having had "really cool talks" with her dad. "I think my father, in some respects, worried that I was too sensitive, too soft in a way. I remember him always telling me it was really important not to show my Achilles' heel . . . and then later going into my room and trying to look up what an 'Achilles' heel' means."

The subject of grades fell into a category of bad news to be avoided, as Ray, Jr., ruefully discovered. "Most of my anecdotes revolve around my report cards. . . . It was always a disappointment if I ever brought home a D. . . . One of the first books he gave me to read was *The Rise and Fall of the Third Reich*. I was a freshman in high school, maybe. I still have that thing; it weighs a ton."

"He was smart, brilliant beyond my understanding," Mark said. ". . . He knew facts out of nowhere. He'd fill the *Times* crossword puzzle with a pen and never make any mistakes."

When friends and family would gather, they sometimes engaged in a fun competition called *The Dictionary Game*. A dictionary would rest with each player for one round, Mark explained. That player would then try to find a ridiculously absurd and difficult word that nobody would know. Everyone would proceed to write down their own definition, trying to get the others to think theirs was the correct one. They could not play with their dad, Mark stated. Finding a word for which he did not know the definition was "fruitless," he said. "It was a sucker's bet to test his intellect."

It was due to his father's Red Sox paranoia, Mark recounted, that he learned to always expect "something bad to happen" when watching the team, a lesson in abject fatalism imparted—fittingly—during game seven of the 1967 World Series against St. Louis. He was seven, Mark remembered, and sitting down for the game on the sun porch. "Just before the first batter, a cardinal lands on our patio and just kind of prances, and jumps up and down outside the screen door, plainly visible just beyond the TV. And my dad, like, 'That's it! We're done!' There was the omen. And, sure enough, they did lose game seven."

Sometimes, Ray, Jr., said, his father "would talk to my mother about whatever I said, and my mother would come to me: 'Your father's worried about this or that.' . . . She controlled everything that way—kept everything flowing."

"For the most part, she took care of business," Bryant agreed. "She was very much a great, fun mom, and a *mom*. She had her rules."

Dad really did have "a soft side, but he didn't like to show it," Ray, Jr., said, recalling his uncle Phil's funeral. "Coming out of the funeral home, we all got in the cars and waited for the hearse to go by to go to the church. And Dad took off his hat, and it was the first time I ever saw my father cry. I mean, it was, like—*wow!*"

Tom remembers his dad as "that laughing, really crazy guy that used to run around the living room with Ray and me and just do silly things." But, when Phil died, he said, it "kind of took something out of Dad. He was never quite as light." Phil was "a warm, wonderful, friendly guy—like a tempering balance weight for Dad," Tom explained. "And when that was gone, there was no one that could call him out. He would listen to Phil, but no one else could tell him anything; I can't say that for sure, but that's my visceral feeling."

"The irony," Bryant pointed out, is that their father's nitroglycerin-ish episodes are always recalled in an amused, even comedic, context. "We developed a certain 'lens' through which we all saw our version," he said. "Because of his light side, we are able to laugh at his dark side—maybe not when it was happening, but later on. That's a true gift he passed along. I'm very blessed to have it."

"The things that ticked him off," Mark said, had a way of sounding "hilarious" in the mouths of his dad's characters.

Referring to Ray's irascible correspondent character, Artie Schermerhorn, Tom said, "We *knew* that guy." At the same time, he noted, the laughs and fun "certainly outweighed" everything else. "But for great stories among the kids, it was always when you got in trouble. Those are the ones that you remember . . . even though they were isolated events—mere moments."

"We knew he was a sweet, kind, and wonderful man," Mark said, "so, we are able to look back at these incidents and laugh."

Everyone had to be home for dinner and on time, Ray, Jr., said, recalling a night when Mark—his junior by fourteen years—ate in a hurry, then excused himself from the table, explaining that he was due at friend's house. "I asked my dad, 'How come you let him get away with this?' He turned to me and said, 'After awhile you mellow, Ray. Mark owes you an awful lot.'"

12

MAD MEN

Departing GEG on a spring day in 1957, Al Feldstein, then in his first year as editor of *Mad* magazine, clutched a box of Bob and Ray scripts as he headed back to the publication's dreary offices on Lafayette Street. After the war, Feldstein, like *Mad*'s creator and previous editor, Harvey Kurtzman, had gone to work for Bill Gaines, the eccentric owner of the magazine's publishing house, EC Comics.

Mad, the magazine, had evolved in 1955 from *Mad*, the comic book, a "bastard son," said Nick Meglin, former associate editor and liaison to all its artistic and writing talent. "It was never created out of some kind of vision. It was a default decision taken because of the demise of the comic-book industry." In the wake of the 1954 Senate Subcommittee's hysteria about the "delinquency-producing effects" of comic books, Kurtzman and Gaines more than doubled the price to twenty-five cents and converted *Mad* to a slick magazine format to avoid the sharpened blue pencils of the newly created Comics Code Authority.

"The new *Mad*" appeared with the July 1955 issue and sold out immediately, requiring an unprecedented second printing. For immediate recognition, Kurtzman's first four issues contained contributions by celebrity humorists, including Ernie Kovacs, Stan Freberg, and Steve Allen. Of course, none of them had time to drop everything and write for Bill Gaines's bargain-basement rates, but salvaging material from their respective trunks was another story. "They liked the inclusion," Meglin said. "I think they did it more for their own publicity and to keep their name and face and work in the public eye in other formats." Ernie Kovacs, for one, participated simply because he loved the way artist Jack Davis drew him.

When Kurtzman had departed, lured away by Hugh Hefner's budding *Playboy* enterprise, he took some of *Mad's* top artists with him, touching off an instant talent search. They did not have to look far for a gifted young artist—Mort Drucker found *them*. "They had an ad in the paper," Drucker said. "About three hundred people showed up. Myself and one other artist were hired. . . . In those days, everybody wanted to work for *Mad*. They were at the zenith—the first of its kind in satire."

Starting with issue number twenty-nine, Kurtzman's replacement was the intensely focused Al Feldstein. "Al came in in the morning and just worked all day," Tom Koch said. "He might have gone to the bathroom once."

He was a "wonderful editor," Mort Drucker agreed, "because he was *hands on*. He didn't let anything slip by."

Under Feldstein, *Mad* continued showcasing iconoclastic humorists, with the celebrity names now featured on the cover to add more adult appeal. Ensuing issues included Eddie "The Old Philosopher" Lawrence, Al "Jazzbo" Collins, Henry Morgan, Jean Shepherd, Sid Caesar, and Danny Kaye. When Feldstein approached Bob and Ray, there was still no budget for original material. "But," he recalled, "I did think that sketches they had already performed could be easily—and cheaply—adapted. I don't remember exactly, but I have the impression I offered to pay them a pittance. . . . Much to my surprise and delight, they happily agreed."

Feldstein then selected and adapted the pieces to an illustrated continuity format, with Bob and Ray depicted as themselves. Mort Drucker drew the two from a few eight-by-ten publicity stills. In every caricature of any celebrity he draws, Drucker said, "I look to see what makes them who they are as opposed to other people. You latch on to certain features in their faces. Or, if you're doing a full body, you look to how they stand and so forth."

"He was drawing us long before he met us," Bob said. "He got all the angles from those pictures."

"Mort became the best caricaturist in the U.S.," Feldstein said. Several of his original *Time* magazine cover drawings reside in the National Portrait Gallery in the Smithsonian.

"Other artists would just capture a photograph," Nick Meglin said, referring to Drucker's technique. "He gave it a feel. . . . It was a caricature of sorts, but it wasn't. Everyone didn't have the big nose and the big feet. It really looked like them doing different things."

Drucker's detailed, nearly photographic likenesses were energetic and playful. "When it comes to Ray," he said, ". . . the nose was a little longish, the double chin—that's about all I did with him. Bob has a more rectangular shape. . . . His eyes are larger and a little more distant from the nose. . . . The eyes are the most telling thing about Bob. . . . I try to work with just a slight exaggeration, that's all. I don't like to make people look bad."

Beginning with the August 1957 issue's adaptation of a Mr. Science script, a Bob and Ray satire appeared in every Mad, except one, for the next two years. (The long-running Mr. Science was a B&R spoof of TV's then-popular Mr. Wizard. Don Herbert, Mr. Wizard himself, was delighted by the satire, a fact which many years later would even find its way into Herbert's New York Times obituary.)

Each Mad piece "conjured up a particular mind's eye scenario," Meglin stated, such as the March 1958 issue which featured Wally Ballou reporting from the National Bannister Sliding Contests in Newton, Illinois. Drucker's Bob and Ray renditions "flipped everybody out," Meglin said, including Bob and Ray. "They went nuts. . . . This stuff that was only in script form, and only in voice form, suddenly visual. . . . The marriage was perfect."

On an NBC 1959 Hawaii junket, B&R, to their surprise, heard themselves introduced as "the stars of Mad magazine," instead of Monitor, for which, at considerable expense, they had been flown across an entire continent and half an ocean to publicize.

In culling through the initial B&R material, remembered Feldstein, "I noticed a guy named Tom Koch had written most, if not all, the sketches. His name was on almost every script. So, after asking Bob or Ray or both for permission, I called Tom and asked if he'd like to work for Mad." Since the job required that Tom write at home, his decision was a no-brainer.

On Koch's rare visits to the magazine's New York headquarters, he was easy to spot. "He wore a shirt and a tie and a business suit," Meglin said.

"He looked like an executive. He was conservative—very smart mustache and trimmed hair, and we're walking around with jeans and sneakers and sweatshirts and stuff." Tom Koch's pieces appeared for the next thirty-eight years, during most of which he also continued his radio output for B&R. "He was selling us everything and anything," Meglin said. "The stuff just kept coming out."

Perhaps the most fondly remembered is a sports spoof, "43-Man Squamish," a new amateur game played on a five-sided field known as a Flutney, with shepherds' crooks, diving flippers, and fiendishly complex ground rules. In fact, it had roots in a couple of Koch's previous Biff Burns segments on B&R's Mutual series. "Klishball" was a game in which the team captain, after being elected by a two-thirds majority, then calls the best four-out-of-seven coin flips to start the game. Another, "Stiffleball," featured 108 players on a side, including twenty-seven left wedgies, thirty-one right wedgies, sixteen snugglies, twelve double backs, nineteen middle drifters, and three roving utility men. The game's inventor, Arnold Stiffle (Ray, naturally), was concerned, he told Biff, because they were expecting a crowd of seventy thousand for that night's opener and there had not been enough time to work out any rules. "I think the fans are going to be pretty upset," he said, "when the players just trot out on the field and stand there for a couple of hours."

Koch's name appeared on nearly two hundred *Mad* satires, however Feldstein did not include it on the earlier radio adaptations, more "as an effort to avoid confusion than anything else," he noted. He then added, "I am sorry that Tom did not get the credit he deserved for writing those B&R pieces." The boys split Feldstein's "pittance" three-ways, sending one-third to Tom. Considering that the income was from Bob and Ray's recycle bin, for all three it was found pittance.

There was a cozy symmetry to Elliott and Goulding's association with *Mad*; both poked fun with blunted spears. Reflecting on the magazine, Meglin said, "We were mild. We didn't hit with hammers. As a matter of fact, we were faulted for not saying enough." It was mostly about taking mild shots at the movies, advertising, celebrities, and some politics, he pointed out. "But I don't think there was much commentary in there." Bob and Ray appealed to all demographics; however, like *Mad*, they uniquely resonated with one cultural subset in particular: smart, clever, perhaps disaffected—mostly male—adolescents of the era. For this bunch, Bob and Ray's off-center cosmos was especially seductive. Upon first tuning in, they would become instantly addicted. As in the case of fleebus, there was no antidote.

—

Ed Sullivan's reputation as a television host was legendary. He was notorious for commanding novelty acts and comedians to trim their material just before going on-air. After once ordering an animal trainer to cut three minutes from the act, the angry guest replied, "How am I going to explain that to the lion?"

Of all stand-ups, Bob's former drama school classmate, Jack Carter, had the most Sullivan appearances to his credit: "Maybe about forty-five," he claimed, and consequently was a frequent victim of Ed's obsession with timing. "He never knew when an elephant would shit on the stage and he'd have to have five extra minutes," Carter explained. "You'd have six minutes, and when you got down on the stage, the stage manager would say, 'Four minutes.' Then, when you're out there, from the wings you'd see [someone waving] 'Get off!' You'd have to jump to your big joke. . . . Ed would stand onstage while you performed, which was murder, because the audience would look to him for his reaction to the jokes. So that made it twice as tough. . . . He did everything wrong and it worked out right."

Ed's standards were as rigid as they were unpredictable. Comedians were constantly lectured on what they could, and could not, say. "I once said 'bellybutton,'" Carter recalled, referring to a Sunday run-through when he told a joke concerning someone's navel. "And Ed said, 'That's an aperture in the human body!' I said, 'So is an asshole, but I'm not going to say it.'"

George Carlin recalled that, whenever appearing on the Sullivan show, he always stayed at the Americana Hotel (now the Sheraton) on Seventh Avenue. His Sunday-morning walk across the short block to the theater on Broadway—always racked with "fear and vomiting nervousness"—he called "The Last Mile." Carlin's anxiety centered on the show being live. "There were no second takes," he wrote in his memoir. "If you fucked up, all America saw it. . . . There were no do-overs, no cutaways, no edits. No apologies were accepted."

Like most performers, B&R had heard all the horror stores. "Neither Ray nor I ever vomited before a Sullivan show," Bob said. "After, maybe, but not before."

Introducing Bob and Ray's Sullivan show debut on May 12, 1957, the showman announced that the highlight of the recent Peabody Awards ceremony (at which B&R took home their second Peabody, this time for both the *Monitor* and the Mutual series) had been a baseball routine the two performed. Repeating it for Ed's audience, Bob as Biff Burns—"your eyes and ears of the sports world"—interviewed Ray as the ambidextrous pitching sensation Snag Sawtelle, who does not decide which hand he's going to throw with until he is into his wind-up.

"It must," Biff said, "make the batter feel pretty shaky up there."

"Well," Snag responded, "if *I* don't know what hand I'm going to throw with, you can imagine how the batter feels."

B&R's second Sullivan appearance, on October 6th, marked Ed's tenth-season opener and fell smack in the middle of the tight, New York Yankees-Milwaukee Braves seven-game World Series. Exploiting the city's baseball frenzy, the boys pulled out a tested bit they had recently aired on Mutual. Bob, again as Biff Burns, introduced Ray as Dusty Wilberforce, the Yankees rookie groundskeeper recently called up from their triple-A farm club. Asked by Biff what advice he would offer young viewers who might be dreaming of a career as a groundskeeper, Dusty, demonstrating with an imaginary rake, advised: "I use a big seventy-eight-ounce rake. I don't choke up on it. I grip it way down on the end. . . ." Taking a realistic attitude towards his future, Dusty told Biff: "I think I have two or three good seasons left, if my legs hold out."

The audience's lively response to the routine was especially gratifying considering where Sullivan had placed the pair in the show's batting order, following killer stand-ups by Alan King and Danny Thomas.

Guesting on *The Perry Como Show*, on May 3, 1958, in a sketch written by Goodman Ace and his Como staff, Bob and Ray played employees of a small-town, two-man, single-studio television station. The multi-tasking team had to man the single-boom microphone, turntable, and camera, while simultaneously delivering the sports, weather, and news. With their weatherman, Clifford Fleming (Bob), supposedly on the line from Mount Washington, New Hampshire, Dave Garroway (Ray), inquired, "Cliff, how does it look for the weekend?"

"Afraid not, Dave" replied Fleming. "She's coming home Friday."

Reporting on a tiger that had escaped from its cage at the zoo and was presently wandering around the city, Ray warned viewers to keep their eyes open. "The tiger," he reported, "is described as being orange in color with black stripes."

***

"Hi, Bob and Ray," said Victor Borge, passing Ray in the hallway at 30 Rock. "He never passed one or the other that it wasn't 'Hi, Bob and Ray,'" Liz said. "I suppose he thought it was funny. . . . It became an irritant after awhile."

Being perceived collectively was a "constant annoyance," said Mike Smollin. "Occasionally, mail would arrive addressed to 'Mr. Bob Andre.' It would really frost them."

On *Tonight*, Bob told Jack Paar, "We come into a room and people say, 'Hang up your coat, Bob and Ray.' 'Take off your hat, Bob and Ray.' 'I hear you just had your appendix out, Bob and Ray . . .'"

Many gifts the team received had to be divided, said Bob, recalling a book that Ernie Kovacs gave them, inscribed, "'For Bob on Monday, Wednesday and Friday, and Ray on Tuesday, Thursday and Saturday.' It ended up in my library."

Knowing their sensitivity, Ed Graham had a special gift bowling ball especially designed with two different sets of finger holes drilled on opposite sides, and sent it to the GEG office a few days after the team's Perry Como show guest appearance. One set of holes was marked "Bob" and the other "Ray." It was enclosed in a stylish bowling-ball bag, together with a card reading: "Bob and Ray, Thanks for being on my show. You two score a perfect 300 every time. All the best, Perry."

"It was brilliant," Smollin said. "They came out and opened up the gift and started cursing, saying, 'That guy is richer than God and he can't afford more than one ball for us,' and so on and so on. Oh, it was hysterically funny."

Ray was particularly steamed because he and Liz were friendly enough with Perry to stop and chat with him on Sundays, at St. Peter's in Port Washington.

"I had thought they would take it as a joke," Graham remembered. "But when Ray turned purple and threw a fit I decided not to own up to it."

The oppressive GEG overhead eventually necessitated some hard business decisions. A casualty was John Moses. By this time, he had left GAC and was on his own with a one-man office at Fifty-Seventh and Fifth. "He was good at selling and had a good imagination," said Grant Tinker, who after his earlier NBC stint had gone to work for Moses at $250 a week. ". . . He had to work hard to make a buck. Nobody was going to carry him." In addition to B&R on his client list, he had added Allen Ludden, a young game-show emcee from Hartford. He would go on to host *College Bowl* and *Password*.

John was getting a commission on everything Bob and Ray did, Ed Graham said. "And we didn't want to do that with GEG, and he did. And for some reason, we settled on twelve thousand bucks. I remember writing out the check and he was glad to get it. . . . He was getting a commission on the Piels contract, which he had worked out. And I guess maybe that's where the twelve thousand came [from]. . . . We arrived at that figure. And the deal was, then, we could go ahead and do all our stuff at GEG. . . . I was selling it anyway." The parting was bitter, Graham acknowledged.

Moses had a lot of "interests," Bob said, "one at least, and maybe more, with Bob Leder that involved racehorses and stables. As I remember, he appeared to be pursuing a direction that was very removed from what we were hoping to have. . . . And maybe we shouldn't have severed with him, but we did."

In terms of Bob and Ray's early New York successes, Tinker said, "John was the prime mover. . . . He was the guy who said to them, 'Gee, you guys are funny. You could be on the network,' and brought them to New York. . . . He planted some ambition."

On that score, there was never any argument from Elliott and Goulding. According to Bob, "The second-most important figure [after Bill McGrath] in launching the B&R career and bringing us to national attention was John Moses. . . . John was an enthusiastic champion of anyone and anything once he embarked on a project."

As the end of the 1950s approached, CBS was the only network at which the boys had yet to set up shop. But, with the sudden departure of the man perhaps most identified with CBS's burnished image, that was about to change.

TOP: Ann and Bill King's wedding in Lowell, April 19, 1954. (Top row, from left) Ray, Liz, Peg and Joe Goulding, and Bubby "Paul" Regan, Jr. (Middle row) Paul Regan, Sr., his younger son, Mark, and wife, Mary Goulding Regan. (Right of Ann and Bill) Thelma and Phil Goulding. (Bottom row, left) Marie Regan. (Right of Ann) Joe's son Philip, and Ray's kids Ray, Jr., Tom, and Barbara. (Courtesy of Ann King)

RIGHT: Phil Goulding said his most memorable radio experience was covering Boston's Cocoanut Grove fire, which claimed 492 lives. His most embarrassing, a station ID at the Metro-Goldwyn-Mayer-owned WMGM: "This is WMGM New York— the Metro-Goulding-Mayer station." (Courtesy of Ann King)

"Sleeping" during one of their unremitting weekend shifts in their Radio Central booth at *Monitor* in 1955.

Ray, Ed Graham, Jack Sidebotham, and Bob (left to right), checking original Bert and Harry storyboards in 1955.

"If that sells beer, I'll quit!"

Jack Sidebotham's illustration of Bert (right) and Harry.

"Jack had a natural warmth about him that he communicated in his work. Even an angry Bert became loveable when Jack drew him."

Goulding-Elliott-Greybar Productions, Inc.

SOLE MAKERS OF BOB AND RAY STUFF

April 24, 1981

Desr Tom:

Sorry not to have gotten back to you with a
progress report/critique, etc.   st
spent four
(bac   n-
ing   mbo--
"Ins   be
the
doing
bits.

"Buck
sion   "
spots.
mainin   ey
like a   )
and th   t
Also,
among
etc.
was it
going
even be
or "Nor   as,
and hop
commitm

The fir
what we
using it
removed.

Thanks f   en
anything

Best from us both,

Bob

Tom Koch wrote for Bob and Ray for thirty-three years, mostly from California. Their
only communication was an occasional letter or a rare phone call. (Courtesy of Carol and Dan
Gillespie)

Receiving their second Peabody Award, April 16, 1957, for Outstanding Radio
Achievement from John Drewry, dean of the Grady College of Journalism at the
University of Georgia, and Bennett Cerf, Peabody board chairman (right).

*" . . . By reason of their unrelenting excellence, Bob and Ray has stood as the lone magnificent
palm tree in a vast and dreary desert."*

Adapted Bob and
Ray scripts, such
as *Mr. Science*,
appeared in *Mad*
magazine from
1957–59, all
illustrated by Mort
Drucker. (From
MAD #34 © 1957 E.C.
Publications, Inc. Used
with Permission.)

Artist Mike Smollin's storyboards for Andersen's Pea Soup combined with Bob and Ray's soundtrack for Second Prize at the Cannes Film Festival.

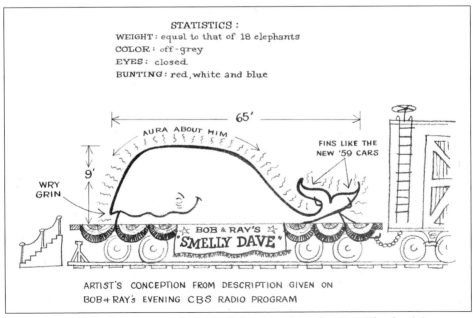

STATISTICS :
WEIGHT : equal to that of 18 elephants
COLOR : off-grey
EYES : closed
BUNTING : red, white and blue

65'

AURA ABOUT HIM

FINS LIKE THE NEW '59 CARS

9'

WRY GRIN

★ BOB & RAY'S ★
"SMELLY DAVE"

ARTIST'S CONCEPTION FROM DESCRIPTION GIVEN ON
BOB & RAY'S EVENING CBS RADIO PROGRAM

Mike Smollin's "artist's conception" of the whale-napped Smelly Dave. If sighted, listeners were advised to contact Bob and Ray immediately "at your own expense."

"Life is so crowded with serious problems; we need an outlet of some kind. What's a better outlet than looking for a dead whale?"

With Ray vacationing in Europe, Bob (back row) flanked by Sir Cedric Hardwicke (left) and Robert Kennedy, accepted the Radio Fathers of the Year Award for the team on May 31, 1960. Other winners in their respective fields included Art Linkletter and Johnny Unitas (front).

"For reasons that remain a mystery, the Committee also chose to salute Anne Bancroft, then starring on Broadway in The Miracle Worker.*"*

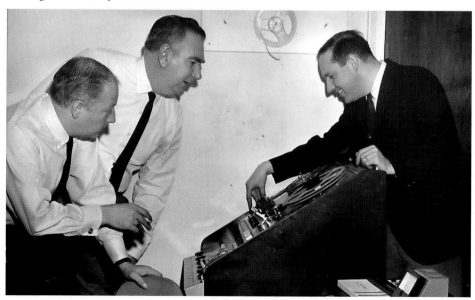

In GEG's studio with Vic and their workhorse Ampex 350 tape machine.

"Vic Cowen was of inestimable help in our careers for ideas, scripts, and overall organization… He was Bob and Ray."

LEFT: "Finlay Llewlyn Goulding 1653–1736." The painting is signed, "Bob Andre."

BOTTOM: Following orders from WHN's promotion director in 1962.

13

THE SMELLY DAVE CAPER

Edward R. Murrow's nightly quarter-hour newscast had been a seven-forty-five CBS Radio mainstay since 1947. Signing off his final program on Friday, June 26, 1959, Murrow announced that he planned to spend the next year "receiving instead of transmitting. . . . I will return with at least the illusion that I know what I'm talking about."

In Murrow's spot the following Monday was Wally Ballou, a self-described "highly regarded" reporter who never let not knowing what he was talking about get in his way. This marked the beginning of a new fifteen-minute Bob and Ray show, "CBS's decidedly offbeat replacement," *Newsweek* called it. At the time, the radio network had been hemorrhaging money for three years. A recent housecleaning had included the long-entrenched daytime dramas *Our Gal Sunday*, *Road of Life*, *Wendy Warren and the News*, *This is Nora Drake*, and *Backstage Wife*.

Bob and Ray Present the CBS Radio Network was part of a new evening hour block called *Comedy Time*, which also featured Andy Griffith, recycled George Burns & Gracie Allen routines, and *The Amos 'n' Andy Music Hall*.

B&R knew that just two years earlier their friend Stan Freberg's satiric efforts had been strangled by the radio division's New York vice-president of programming, Howard Barnes, a "very serious, buttoned-down guy," in Freberg's opinion. "He had no sense of humor whatsoever." After hearing an advance tape of *The Stan Freberg Show* premiere, the network brass had gone into shock. "They demanded that I redo it," he said. "They couldn't believe how outrageous it was." Barnes finally booted the series after only fifteen weeks. Through a CBS friend, West Coast VP Bill Froug—unforeseeably in the right place at the right time—the comedian later learned that, from the start, Barnes "didn't like the idea of Freberg," Stan said.

Froug was "at the next urinal in the men's room; Howard Barnes was standing next to him."

Without an agent at the time, Elliott and Goulding were forced make their deal themselves with the very same Howard Barnes. They would later be represented for many years by Lester Lewis and his wife, Juliet, and for a period by Val Irving, whose comedy stable also included Audrey Meadows, Jack E. Leonard, and Phil Foster. Ray could be a hard bargainer, Bob said. "He had a technique in negotiations of appearing negative about the whole project under discussion when, together, we had already agreed to go along with it. His attitude frequently resulted in our getting more benefits than we originally sought." It was, Bob felt, a consequence of what some found to be his partner's intimidating quality, particularly "in negotiations and anything that involved points of agreement. . . . 'Good cop/bad cop' is a good description. We did it automatically, because of our temperaments," he explained. "Ray was of that temperament. I was quieter, a less strong personality when it came to an argument. Not between us, but over anything we were doing, or with an agent. . . . If he got into a negotiation, he was adamant about the position. . . . And usually he won." We ended up with a "pretty good deal for the time," Bob said.

One round that Goulding did *not* win involved the frequently touchy issue of exclusivity. Barnes insisted that the team drop their weekend *Monitor* gig for the length of the CBS deal. Reluctantly, they complied.

The summer of 1959 saw the imaginary whistle-stop tour of Smelly Dave, "Bob and Ray's great dead whale on a flatcar." The tongue-in-cheek promotion, perhaps the team's most popular, heralded Dave, perched on a red-white-and-blue bunting-bedecked flatcar and shunted onto railroad sidings and displayed in every city with a CBS affiliate. Other than the crowds' vocal repulsion at Dave's overpowering "aura," as it was referred to, initial appearances at Quincy, Peoria, and Akron went well. Empty-suit station managers (all played by Bob) blathered on with tired promotional platitudes. However, in Albany, Arthur Shrank (Ray), the screechy-voiced announcer accompanying the exhibition, proclaimed to a stunned crowd that Dave had been "whale-napped."

A detective, Sylvester L. "Gumshoe" Flaherty (Ray, in his gangster voice), along with his limousine-driving assistant, Kato (Bob's Asian accent), was immediately assigned to the "case." By the middle of August, Flaherty had picked up a lead that a whale-oil syndicate was involved and that Dave had been spotted floating off Martha's Vineyard. An artist's conception (drawn by Mike Smollin) was offered, describing Dave as "off-gray" in color with a "wry grin" and "fins like the '59 cars." If found, printed instructions advised that he be packed in an adequate amount of ice—"approximately three tons"—his flat car kept in the shade, and fins "shellacked every three months, or one thousand miles, whichever comes first." Thousands wrote in for the Smelly Dave drawing, including the Chicago History Museum's curator of whales, who generously volunteered his expertise. Finally, on September 10th, Dave was discovered hidden behind a glue factory in Albany. The job, Bob and Ray discovered, had been pulled off "in a fit of petulance" by a former employee who, "much to his chagrin," had dared to correct them on something they said on the air. Listeners were left to guess exactly which employee—all fingers pointed to Webley Webster—but were assured that the individual would be turned over to the "proper authorities" and dealt with "summarily."

At the height of the caper, a large crate addressed to Elliott and Goulding was delivered to CBS Radio's studio building at Forty-Nine East Fifty-Second Street. When pried open in the lobby, the reeking container revealed a giant section of an actual decomposing whale carcass, a contribution from a zealous fan in Florida, who was apparently convinced that Smelly Dave's two creators would find it hilarious. The smell was beyond description. While an alert staff publicity man grabbed the boys for a quick photo standing next to it—holding their noses, of course, for as long as they could stand it—CBS found itself in the middle of a jurisdictional muddle over which city department was going to remove a dead whale from their lobby. Howard Barnes could not have been amused, though B&R never heard a word from him about it.

"It could be that people enjoy us because we let them join in our fantasy," Goulding told a reporter at the time. Life is so crowded with serious problems, he noted, that "we need an outlet of some kind. What's a better outlet than looking for a dead whale?"

By now, Elliott and Goulding had so thoroughly assimilated the quirks of their characters that improvised CBS segments with The McBeebee

Twins, The Amazing Follenger, Tex and the Smoky Valley Boys, Kent Lyle Birdley, Flaming Bombadeen, Charles the Poet, Señor Honduras, Natalie Attired & Eddie, and Professor Groggins could be set on automatic pilot. It was as if the characters themselves knew the drill. All Elliott and Goulding had to do was stay out of their way.

The key to Bob and Ray's voice characterizations was "commitment," said Harry Shearer, himself having voiced dozens of characters on *The Simpsons* and his own weekly radio program, *Le Show*. "It's almost an act of self-hypnosis," he said, that you *are* that other person that you are portraying. Bob and Ray weren't "voice guys," he stipulated. "They were *actors*." In some part of their brain, he continued, they were Mary, or they were Wally, or they were Artie, or these other people for a moment. It's a way of committing to *being* that person, and not just doing that voice, Shearer said, pointing out that "each of those people that Bob and Ray did had their own speech patterns, their own ticks, their own peculiarities. . . . That's what made it so vivid for me."

Many of Bob's characters, such as Mr. Science and Fred Falvy, the Do-It-Yourselfer, embodied tightly defined theatrical types. "Voices," Chris Elliott said, "that everybody that had been listening to the radio and going to the movies had grown up with themselves." In the *Anxiety* parodies, his Commander Neville Putney characterization was funny because it was so organic, so ingrained. "You know," said Chris, "he has muttonchops, and he's got a uniform on and maybe smokes a big horn pipe."

The byplay, of course, was reconfigured each time, but—as with Jack Benny's recurring trips to his vault to visit his money—the satiric schematics were basically the same. Indicative of this were thirty-three serialized *Lawrence Fechtenberger, Interstellar Officer Candidate* episodes, spread over the CBS run, each accompanied by elaborate and inventive production values, several involving the mysterious, always-marching "little people of Polaris." During one stretch, Lawrence and Mug Mellish orbited Earth for days without food until the commandant ordered a rocket bearing BLT sandwiches to be fired through the open window of their spaceship as it passed over Walpole, Massachusetts.

The entire July 31st broadcast was devoted to coverage of the much-promoted "annual Bob and Ray Employees Outing and Clambake" at

Smollin, New York. It was another example of Elliott and Goulding making themselves the targets of the satire. Ice cream for the picnic was delivered four days early, and the event went downhill from there. Wally Ballou and Artie Schermerhorn, working "under field conditions," reported on the stifling 102-degree heat and 98 percent humidity, accompanied by the sounds of dive-bombing mosquitoes. B&R's "high powered, chauffeur-driven limousine" arrived late to alternately reverential and resentful shouts of, "Bob and Ray waved at me!" and "How about a raise, Bob and Ray?!" As the scheduled "entertainment,"—a flamenco dancer with what sounded like a wooden leg, a softball game with an angry polecat sleeping next to the second-base bag, and an off-key flautist—continued, the event's star attractions, Bob and Ray, never once left the comfort of their air-conditioned limousine.

"Wealthy Chairman of the Board" Jacobus Pike (Ray) was called upon to read their prepared remarks. ("We hope you're having a crackerjack good time. Bob and Ray want me to extend to you their kindest regards and good wishes. In the coming years, this family of ours. . .") The booing and grumbling of the by-then thoroughly disenchanted employees were suddenly interrupted by a clap of thunder, followed immediately by the sound of the limo's motor starting. With the rain pouring, it was left to Ballou—who had just spotted a water moccasin—and Schermerhorn to sign off the program. Elliott and Goulding never appeared as themselves.

The network arranged for Bob and Ray guest-shots on its other programs, including Galen Drake's show and *Arthur Godfrey Time*, the latter with Robert Q. Lewis guest-hosting as Godfrey was recuperating from lung surgery. The Godfrey appearance garnered especially big laughs and none more so than from Robert Q. himself, who, while at WMGM in the 1940s, had been a colleague of Phil Goulding. Arthur Godfrey wielded tremendous power at CBS. Despite his magnetic and personable manner, he could also be unpredictably arrogant and cruel. After famously firing singer Julius La Rosa on the air six years earlier, the reverberations still lingered.

Upon Godfrey's September return to his mid-morning program, Elliott and Goulding did not know what to expect when they were again booked to appear on his show. Capitol Records had recently killed a Stan Freberg takeoff of the CBS star when Godfrey refused permission. By then, Bob had been doing his Godfrey impression for well over a decade, but never in front of him. A few years earlier, at an Overseas Press Club affair at the Astor Hotel, Ray had performed his Senator Joseph McCarthy impression, and Bob, his Harry Truman, with the former president seated at the center of the head table. The latter bit featured Elliott as Truman chiding *Washington Post* music critic Paul Hume for his scathing review of the president's daughter Margaret's singing performance at Constitution Hall. Both bits received an ovation from the Press Club crowd, and a pat on the back from Truman. "But, then," Bob pointed out, "President Truman didn't have as much clout as Arthur Godfrey."

As for the performance that morning on the Godfrey show, "He didn't object," Bob said, but noted that he only imitated him "a little bit—not much, though." Was it scary? "Absolutely, in front of him—oh, Jesus, yeah! . . . He could have given us the Julius LaRosa treatment."

On one of his subsequent programs, Arthur Godfrey played a tape of an entire B&R segment from one of their shows with Bob impersonating Arthur. "I swear to goodness he does it better than I do," said Godfrey, still laughing. "It's the most perfect; he even fools me every time I hear it—I think it *is* me."

With Tom Koch having joined George Gobel's NBC TV stable, by 1959 B&R had turned to Phil Green for writing help on *Monitor*, and later brought him with them to CBS. He had earlier churned out routines for Orson Bean, Kaye Ballard, and others, including then twenty-one-year-old-Maggie Smith's signature sketch in Leonard Sillman's revue, *New Faces of 1956*. More recently—and weirdly—Green, too, had been on the Gobel staff, for a brief period overlapping with Koch.

Like Woody Allen, Phil Green was an alumnus of NBC's short-lived comedy development program, which also included his future (and ex-) wife, Lois Balk. For many years, Green's name appeared on the Writers Guild Newsletter's "Unlocatable Writers" list of members for whom unclaimed residual checks were being held. Presumably for the same reason, he also did not want on-air writing credit on *The Bob and Ray Show*. He was avoiding "something or someone," said Lois, adding that she was never sure exactly "what or who." When things did not go well, she said, "He was comatose."

"He liked to be around comics," said Kaye Ballard, recalling Green's frequent presence at Hanson's drug store, a comedians' refuge at Fifty-First and Seventh, located close by a cluster of drab, mostly single-room agents' offices. "Let's face it," she said, "Jack E. Leonard, Red Buttons, Phil Foster—they were fun to be around." Not that Kaye could tell by observing Green. He was "always depressed," she said. "He was a hypochondriac and a nervous wreck, and he was very funny."

Phil was "a big talent," recalled writer George Atkins, who later worked with him on the variety series *The Entertainers*, featuring Carol Burnett and Bob Newhart. Green wrote "terribly funny pieces," Atkins said, "exclusively for, and with, Bob Newhart."

When *The Entertainers* started production, Newhart was shown a "list of writers," he said, "one of which, I think, was Buck Henry, and another, I think, was Woody Allen who were staff writers at the time, and Phil Green. And then I saw Phil's résumé and he had Bob and Ray; that was the thing that did it for me. I said, 'I want Phil Green.'"

The Bronx-raised Green, whose bald head always seemed to be tucked under a Bogart-style fedora, even when indoors, was slender, likeable, and enigmatic. He was "eccentric," Newhart said, recalling a day when the two were collaborating on a sketch and Phil showed up with a black eye. "He said he got in a fight. I don't know over what, but he was in a bar and got into a fight."

A few comedy writers felt their reputations were enhanced if they appeared a little crazy, explained George Atkins, referring to a few contemporaries who were fond of wearing leather suits. "Phil didn't have to feign being crazy; he was the real article." On *The Entertainers*, Atkins said, he "would bring little toy cars and gadgets into my office and start playing with them on the floor."

"We never could figure him out," said Elliott, who was never quite sure what Phil's mood would be when he came up to 2545 with his scripts. "Sometimes he was serious, sometimes flip. He fought for his favorite pieces when we might have preferred others."

A defining Phil Green sketch for both was a soap spoof, *The Secret Heart of Sayville*, involving a plot so convoluted that the announcer's opening summation of the previous episode took up all the allotted time.

The recollection of his "audacity" in presenting the piece, Bob said, was, in itself, laugh-provoking, a "thought that plagued both of us as we tried to read it in soap-opera fashion."

Bob: You'll remember Chester Olson and Jack Craven expected to find a message left in the arm of the Statue of Liberty. A message left by Earl Piro.

Ray: But, you'll recall, the message never turned up, because Lela Spotts got to the arm first . . . and found the messages left by Earl Piro.

Bob: So, naturally, Chester Olson and Jack Craven left Bedloe's Island, a bit wiser for their experience in the arm.

Ray: And now, Lela Spotts had the message—a message really intended for Edmund Gronek . . .

Bob: . . . But Gronek had a clue. And he had more than that, as you remember. He had some friends at the International Hotel.

Ray: That's right. Staunch friends—ones you're all familiar with: Bennett Blanco, Nadine Corey, Constance Cordova, Linda Bisby, Jean Piper . . .

Bob: . . . Clara Dietrich, Glen Finney, Nick Catlow, Emma Milhouse, Paul Hope, Samuel Bean, and Cletus Wofford.

Ray: So we understood that Gronek was not alone in New York City . . .

It went on for pages, Bob said. "We never could get through it without breaking up. . . . We figured later they must have been people Phil had known or knew."

New recurring B&R routines with the Phil Green sticker included *Mr. I-Know-Where-They Are*, *The Adventures of Charley Chew*, *This Place for Heroes*, and *Johnny Braddock's Sports-o-Phone*, the latter being a rigged quiz show in which increasingly irate callers vied for "a valuable twelve-page sports encyclopedia." There were others: Critic Ward Stuffer (Ray) was a master at sidetracking Bob's interviews, as attested by his review of a World War II memoir which evolved into a meandering digression about a mistake-prone Allied commander who dropped three divisions of paratroopers on London, and his belief that if a certain staff sergeant had been relieved of his command, the "war might possibly have been shortened by fifteen or twenty minutes." *Grand Motel* spotlighted its proprietors, "uncompromising" Leonard Humphrey (Bob), and his daughter, Naomi

(Ray), and their relentless cost-cutting efforts—on one episode, cutting the size of the coffee-stirring sticks to three inches—to turn a profit on the continental breakfasts.

A B&R *Overstocked Warehouse* offer promised sets of *The Encyclopedia Book of Wonder*, covered in genuine pigskin "from pigs selected at birth and nurtured on the finest slops available." The color of the covers, the offer continued, was a "deep, rich maroon—which is about the color we turned when we checked the publication date of these books: December 3, 1899." As always, focusing on the positive—"Our loss is your gain"—the pitch pointed out the thrill of rediscovering that "there are twelve gas stations in the United States" and learning "the correct procedure for dumping sandbags from a balloon."

Green even took a swing at an obscure 1950s anthology series, *The Silent Service*, which was evidently tailor-made for his *Underwater Service*, featuring the dramatized naval exploits of the U.S.S. *Spectacled Bass*, the "submarine too proud to stay on the bottom."

Tom Lowell (Bob) answered listeners' questions about vacation planning ("Deportation is the cheapest way to travel"); The *Book of the Month Club* provoked *The Bob and Ray Thought of the Month Club* ("We'll ship you five thoughts a month, plus a free bonus thought every three months . . . with a guarantee that unused thoughts may be returned after ten days.")

The pre-recorded shows routinely included additional effects and voice tracks from the GEG library, all lovingly hand carried by the boys and Vic Cowen, hiking the ten short blocks from 2545 up Park Avenue to CBS for each taping session. These included a sequence known as the "Locking the Studio Doors Ceremony"—a recording of a military cere-mony with marching boots and barked commands of "Last call for the keys!" meticulously put together by Vic Cowen—and another featuring Wallace, the "Bob and Ray midget" (in reality, the British tenor David Whitfield, singing "Good-bye" in an operatic style).

In the control room were three men: director Cowen, network associate director Kirby Ayers (whose main function was timing), and Joe Alonzo, a thirty-four-year CBS veteran staff engineer who ran the board. In the twenty-by-forty-foot studio with Bob and Ray was sound effects man Joe Cabibbo, a quiet, slender Long Islander with thirty-two years at the network, and, at a console on wheels, thirty-seven-year CBS lifer Ciro Torchia, manning three turntables for themes, incidental music, and commercials.

During ad-libbed bits, it was every man for himself. Occasionally, Joe Cabibbo "wouldn't know what to do," Alonzo recalled with amusement. "He'd be running all over the place—slamming a car door or something, and then Ray or Bob would say, 'Oh, I forgot my keys. I've got to go back in.' And he's, like, six or eight feet from there and he'd have to run back and slam the car door again."

B&R would alert the soundman with obvious references within the spontaneous dialog. "Let's say they were indoors," Cabibbo explained. "Bob would say, 'It's kind of stuffy in here. I think we'd like to go outside.' And Ray would say, 'Okay, let's go.' So then I'm ready to open a door and maybe [add] some traffic sounds as we go outside."

Typically, cues were also exchanged through eye contact. In a sketch, when they needed a musical bridge, said Ciro Torchia, "They'd glance at me—just a glance and it was ready to go. . . . It was so close. I was fifteen feet away from them." As for technical glitches, Torchia added, "Some little thing—they'd just leave it in."

"Nothing was ever done over," Alonzo said. "If they made a mistake, or I made a mistake, everything just went. That was it."

"I don't ever remember going over a show," Cabibbo agreed. "They always liked the unexpected because they could ad-lib around it. They were so great at that."

"They could make a skit out of nothing," Torchia said.

"Ray was a lot of fun," Cabibbo said. "Bob was quiet. You never heard a peep out of him until he got on the air."

The opening sketch of a February 1960 broadcast—a raucous edition of their game show *Ladies Grab Your Seats*—was actually off a disc cued up on one of Ciro Torchia's turntables, a cut from the new RCA Victor album, *Bob and Ray on a Platter*. The same label had previously released *Bob and Ray Throw a Stereo Spectacular*, demonstrating the company's new Living Stereo line. In early 1954, Unicorn Records in Boston issued the ten-inch LP, *Write if You Get Work*, a selection of eight pieces from the original NBC radio series. In November of the same year, Elliott and Goulding also recorded several sides for Coral Records, including their *This is Your*

Life sendup, *This is Your Bed, You Made it, Now Lie in it.* Coral's A&R chief, Bob Thiele, had signed B&R along with fourteen other comedians, including Steve Allen, Phil Foster, and Buddy Hackett, for two compilation albums, *The Laugh of the Party* and *Fun Time*, released in 1955. Some routines were also issued as singles.

The late 1950s and sixties saw a huge surge in comedy albums by the likes of Shelly Berman, Lenny Bruce, Nichols and May, and other new performers not necessarily embraced by guardians of the status quo. One front of the establishment's first line of defense, *Time* magazine, labeled them "sickniks," and referred to the trend as a spreading "virus." Increasingly, younger audiences, who couldn't afford nightclubs, had little in common with the old mainstream stand-ups—or with *Time* magazine, for that matter.

"'Take my wife, please!' and mother-in-law jokes had no relevancy to their lives," said Bob Newhart, a major beneficiary of this sea change upon his first album exploding onto the scene in 1960. "So they'd get a six-pack of beer, sit around the record player and have a pizza and listen to comedy records. That was their nightclub." Besides the material being more relatable, Newhart added, "Nobody could steal it. . . . Anybody could come along and steal a joke. But they couldn't steal a style. What we were doing was very stylized."

With clouds having already gathered over network radio, local jocks grabbed more of the spotlight and jumped on the comedy-album boom. Nobody beat the drum louder for Bob Newhart than Dan Sorkin on WCFL Chicago. Within days of the release of *Bob and Ray on a Platter*, San Francisco's top morning man, Don Sherwood, was spinning the "Charles the Poet" cut on KSFO. Bob Crane's entire four-hour morning show on KNX Los Angeles consisted of cuing in wacky tracks from hundreds of comedy albums, including all of Bob and Ray's.

It has been said that there was not much going on during the Eisenhower '50s, Newhart noted. "Well, there was a lot of stuff bubbling that was a part of comedy. . . . Bob and Ray were a part of that, and the anti-authority movement."

All the airplay, naturally, generated more sales for comedy records. Immediately following the release of *The Button-Down Mind of Bob Newhart*,

it shot to number one on the *Billboard* charts, with Newhart winning Best
New Artist and Best Performance Grammy awards, in addition to squeezing
past Frank Sinatra to grab Album of the Year honors. "It got back to me
later," Newhart said, "that Frank apparently was not thrilled with the fact
that a comedy album beat him out. But then it didn't take a lot to upset
Frank—a bird, or wind, or something, that's all it took."

In 1960, ad sales of all radio divisions had plummeted 75 percent from
their 1948 high. To stop the bleeding at CBS, its chairman, William S.
Paley, devised what he termed "a dramatically new program pattern." Its
concept was amazingly simple: All weeknight entertainment shows were
canceled. Robert Q. had already been shown the door with little more
ceremony than that afforded the dead whale which had been hauled away.
Then, on Friday, June 24, 1960, the axe fell on the back-to-back Burns &
Allen, Andy Griffith, and Bob and Ray programs, plus the daytimer, *The
Romance of Helen Trent*. Five months later, on November 25th—"black
Friday"—all four still-surviving daytime soaps, including "Oxydol's own"
Ma Perkins, were sent packing, together with the one remaining evening
show, *The Amos 'n' Andy Music Hall*. The latter marked the end of a
thirty-four-year continuous run—much of it on NBC—for its creators and
stars, Freeman Gosden and Charles Correll. To Bob and Ray fell the honor
of having the second-to-last evening comedy program in the celebrated
history of CBS Radio. But it was left to Gosden and Correll to turn off
the lights for good before leaving. The creative result of Paley's bold new
"program pattern" had been achieved: a void, which, without fanfare, was
then turned over to the affiliates—all 191 of them—to fill.

Happily for B&R, NBC still had a radio network—at least on the
weekends—so in the fall the boys resumed their *Monitor* appearances.
They also accepted a couple of invitations from Jack Paar, pocketing the
Tonight show's then-standard late-night AFTRA rate of $320 each.

B&R's successful appearances with Sullivan and Como—both perenni-
ally top-ten rated shows—opened the door to bookings on other big-ticket
programs. In the early sixties, Bob and Ray popped up on *Omnibus* and an
ABC holiday special, *An Old-Fashioned Thanksgiving*, with Gene Barry,
Eddie Foy, Jr., and Richard Kiley. On a prime-time version of CBS's
Calendar, with Harry Reasoner and Mary Fickett, the boys appeared in

sketches written especially for them by the program's staff of one, Andy Rooney. Prior to his *60 Minutes* career, Rooney had been on the writing staffs for Arthur Godfrey, Garry Moore, Victor Borge, and others. ("I had my scripts bound," he noted. "Looking for immortality, I suppose.") Two decades later, Andy Rooney would contribute the foreword to a published compilation of the team's routines, *From Approximately Coast to Coast . . . It's The Bob and Ray Show.*

Until the quiz-show scandals grabbed the headlines, the biggest TV flameout of the 1959–60 season had been CBS's *The Big Party*, a lavish get-together set in the "living room" of a different major star, joined by celebrity "guests" for a scintillating ninety minutes of scripted spontaneity. Alternating with the prestigious *Playhouse 90*, it suffered an immediate thrashing by the critics and was dumped at midseason. From its ashes emerged a little opus called *The Revlon Revue*, a series of live variety specials airing at ten o'clock on Thursday evenings. The salvage operation was directed by Abe Burrows, co-writer for the book of *Guys and Dolls*, and the reigning Broadway show-doctor of the day.

As guests on the April 7, 1960 show, Bob and Ray pulled out an old stand-by from their "Willful Denial of the Obvious" file: In the *Revlon* version, Bob, upon bumping into "Charles de Gaulle" (Ray in horn-rimmed glasses), proceeds to make small talk as if chatting with the president of France, never catching on (as the audience does immediately by the disjointed nature of the conversation) that it is obviously *another* Charles de Gaulle—as it turns out, one who runs a linoleum tile company in Port Washington, Long Island.

One of the draws of the *Revlon Revue* for Bob and Ray—in addition to being reunited with Peggy Lee, another of the guests—was working with a giant like Abe Burrows. During rehearsals, they were invited by the director for a lunch of radio "war stories," said Bob, who recalled that Abe did most of the talking.

Burrows had considerably less to say at a series of tension-filled luncheon meetings with Revlon executives in the office of Charles Revson, the company's powerful founder. Though he had the feeling that "everybody's job was on the line all the time," he recalled in his memoir, the Revlon Company lunches proved fortuitous. By capturing their corporate lunacy,

Abe Burrows was able to create many hysterical moments, not, unfortunately, in time for *The Revlon Revue*, but rather for his next Broadway hit, *How to Succeed in Business Without Really Trying*, which opened the following year.

The team's third appearance on *The Ed Sullivan Show* fell on a brutally cold Sunday, with Arctic-like conditions somehow managing to penetrate the theater. In the late morning of January 8, 1961, huddled in the otherwise-empty audience seats, Bob and Ray, Bob Newhart, and other headliners on the bill watched one another rehearse. It was pretty much standard procedure, as the only other choices were hanging out in their tiny dressing rooms or ducking next door to the Cordial bar (which for a few, was also standard procedure).

Sullivan observed the acts close-up from the apron of the stage, standing just to one side. Nothing got by him. Despite his amiable—if stiff—on-air demeanor, he could also be a brusque, intimidating presence.

That Sunday, the run-through of the boys' segment—mock-audience interviews with Bob (in different mustaches and wigs) as the presidents of both the Fast and Slow Talkers of America, and Ray as a children's book author who speaks as he writes ("I gave my friend a dog for Christmas. A brown and white dog. He calls him Spot. He loves to run and play with Spot . . .") had been well received by their fellow performers. But their laughs were soon overshadowed by two acrobats, introduced by Sullivan simply as "Two Janbaz from Iran." The muscular father-and-son duo had evidently just arrived in this country. Despite the freezing temperatures, the two men, Bob recalled, were "dressed for summer in Iran."

As Sullivan watched from just a few feet away, they started their act. On a bare stage, except for a small magician's prop table behind them, and accompanied by the Ray Bloch orchestra's lively up-tempo beat, the Two Janbaz performed several daring balancing stunts, including one in which the son—upside-down and playing a violin—balanced directly on the head of his father, who stood beating a side-slung conga drum. But before they could finish, an assistant appeared and whispered something to Ed, who then went to the side of the stage to take a phone call. Troupers that they were, the Two Janbaz—to the amusement of the other performers and crew—held their precarious positions.

"Nobody told them to quit," said Elliott, to whom it seemed that Sullivan was on the phone for twenty minutes. ". . . And these guys, shivering to begin with from the cold, are standing there getting redder and redder, the son balancing on his father's head. Nobody told them to cut."

In another Sullivan appearance, this one on October 13, 1963, Bob Elliott asked his interviewee, the would-be inspector in charge of the United Kingdom's then-ongoing Great Train Robbery investigation, if Scotland Yard had turned up any leads.

"We're working on the theory that this is the work of thieves," replied the inspector. Then, referring to their artist's composite, he added, "We have built up an extremely good likeness to the Archbishop of Canterbury."

"He is your number-one suspect?" Bob asked, incredulous.

"Let me say, he is the man we are currently beating the living daylights out of down at the Yard."

Yes, edgier than their previous *Sullivan* appearances, but then the inspector was played by Peter Cook of the British revue, *Beyond the Fringe*, which recently crossed the Atlantic and was the talk of New York. The troupe also included director Jonathan Miller, *The Establishment*'s John Bird, plus Jeremy Geidt and Eugene Troobnick. All were part of a new, thirteen-minute Sullivan segment, "What's Going on Here?" written by Cook, Bird, and Miller, and co-anchored by Bob and Ray.

Opening the bit in a newsroom setting, Ray, referring to a globe on their anchor desk, explained that "we've divided the world into two portions. The land part will be my beat." And, added Bob, "I'll be covering everything that happens on, in, under, over, around, and through water." Turning to sports, Ray reported, "Alabama moved ahead of Mississippi last night in the race race, arresting seventy-four more civil rights demonstrators to move their total since the beginning of the year to 1,432, seven notches ahead of the spunky Mississippians."

The following Sunday, John Bird, as commander of Berlin's British sector, was grilled by Bob about his country's ineffective military equipment. The commander fixed the blame on the East Germans' new Berlin Wall, which, he explained, is "eight or ten feet high. This, of course, completely knocks out our missiles. They simply haven't got the height."

On the political front, former vice-president Richard Nixon, reported Goulding, again denied that he was a candidate for the 1964 Republican presidential nomination. "Nixon now leads Goldwater by two denials, Rockefeller by four denials, while Romney and Scranton trail with six denials apiece."

Elliott and Goulding generally avoided political or controversial subjects. Yes, there was the episodic Army-McCarthy lampoons, but, in reality (that is, the "reality" of the fiction), that particular flap merely centered on a matinee idol's construction of a sixteen-story summer home, and a badgering, demonic zoning commissioner who just happened to sound like a certain Wisconsin senator.

The "What's Going on Here?" experiment was shaky from the start. Sullivan and Jonathan Miller continually battled over the material. Miller repeatedly walked out, refusing to make cuts that Ed demanded. It was a "big mêlée," Bob said; at one point he and Ray were not even sure they would be going on.

Ed always feared alienating viewers. To take the sting out of a "What's Going on Here?" mock Vietnam news conference with footage of President Kennedy, Sullivan announced afterward that Kennedy had granted permission for use of the clip, pointing out what "a good sport" the president was. The era of innocence still had a few months left. *That Was the Week That Was*, *Monty Python*, and *The Smothers Brothers Show* were not yet on the horizon, not to mention *Saturday Night Live* and *The Daily Show*.

Sullivan's producer, Bob Precht, eager to cash in on the British satire craze, had scheduled several segments of "What's Going on Here?" It got the hook after two, deemed too radical for 1963 viewing appetites—as it turned out, Ed Sullivan's included.

Ed also had been offended by what he perceived as the Brits' truculence. "You young men," he snapped, "are the most discourteous people with whom I've ever worked, and it is a pleasure to part company with you."

"You," replied Jonathan Miller, "are the stupidest man with whom I have ever worked, and it is a pleasure to part company with you."

The following week, it was back to the status quo; Topo Gigio, the little Italian mouse, never gave Ed any guff.

—✦—

"Nothing work related ever affected our personal lives," Liz recalled. "Ray never brought concerns home."

"I didn't either," Elliott said. "I think I thought more about it than Ray did, but there again, I don't know. Ray was very close to the vest in most everything in his life that I could see."

And there definitely were concerns at the office. At GEG, a disagreement led to Ed Graham terminating his six-year relationship in September 1961. However, Graham never had any differences with Bob. "My difference with Ray," he explained, "was over selling Ed Sullivan . . . material from a pilot I'd produced and directed and put up one third of the money [for]—only to be dropped when Sullivan wanted to use the material. It would have been nice if Bob had pointed that out to Ray. But he may have felt it was fruitless. At any rate, I argued with Ray. Bob remained silent, and I walked out."

"I vaguely remember that being an element," said Bob, adding that it had more to do with Ed wanting to have "an empire. We just didn't see eye-to-eye. It happened and probably, maybe, we were wrong, in part or wholly, I don't know."

"They didn't need me and I didn't need them," Graham noted. "But there was something special that happened when we worked together."

All parties were intractable; there were no winners, unless you count Vic Cowen, for whom Graham's departure was an opportunity to begin scripting some of GEG's commercial copy.

Now in his early thirties, and with a wife and three young daughters, Cowen had been eager to shed his roles as simply a production facilitator and Bob and Ray's all-purpose aide-de-camp. In Vic's mind, *one* Wilbur Connally was enough. Given the environment in which he found himself, comedy writing was the natural—if not the only—path open to him. In fact, he had already taken a crack at submitting B&R *Monitor* bits—a few of which were just concepts, and, in some cases only notions, while others were fully developed scripts. Early contributions included takeoffs of Lloyd Bridges's popular underwater-adventurer series, *Sea Hunt*. In a couple of Cowen's versions, called *Sea Search*, the "freelance skin diver" Flipper

Martin (Ray) was unable to retrieve a wealthy countess's missing pearls from the ocean floor until he had first waited an hour after eating. In another episode, Flipper was prevented from diving deeper than twelve feet due to perforated eardrums.

Vic Cowen was just getting started. His output would continue, but he still did not give up his day job. One of his additional roles involved coordinating the team's increasing number of guest bookings, which, through the spring and summer of 1962, included multiple *Tonight Show* appearances with various guest-hosts filling in until Johnny Carson's October arrival. Peter Lind Hayes and Mary Healy were at the helm for one; Hugh Downs, another. On July 3rd, B&R were the guests of a most affable Jerry Lewis, who off-camera told them how much Billy Wilder—a longtime neighbor of Jerry's on the Paramount lot—admired their work. Lewis was understandably upset that night because his hotel suite had been robbed of $185,000 worth of jewelry, though on the air he managed to laugh it off. The visit united three comedy team members—two current, one former— whose first-ever appearances with their eventual partners occurred through sheer chance, and both only weeks apart in the spring of 1946. Ray happened to be introduced to Bob while he was on the air, and Dean Martin and Jerry Lewis popped up at the same time on the same bill at a New York nightclub, the Havana-Madrid. Dean was the singer; Jerry, the comic. One night, in the middle of one of Dean's dreamy renditions of "Where or When," Jerry, then barely twenty, appeared from the wings as a waiter with a napkin over his arm and a huge hunk of raw meat stuck on a fork, yelling, "Who ordered steak?!" Obviously, Dean was forced to interrupt the number.

Describing Bob and Ray's first-ever on-air performance, Ray said, "We just fell into it." Jerry called his and Dean's "an asinine prank."

With Ed Graham's exit, Elliott and Goulding were suddenly left running a company without a name. The second "G" in GEG had just walked out the door. Quickly dismissing the easiest fix—calling themselves "GE" and hoping General Electric never finds out—they felt it was imperative to retain the GEG banner under which they had been so successful for six straight years.

Upon returning to their office one afternoon, the name of the building suddenly jumped out at them. They had their solution: From that point forward, they would do business as Goulding-Elliott-Graybar. The issue had been resolved in a flash—only slightly longer than it took the Greybar Building's attorneys to threaten legal action for name infringement. They backed off only when the boys agreed to spell Graybar with an "e."

Free of the network commitment, one of Vic Cowen's challenges as curator of the Bob and Ray tape archive was the creation of a GEG radio syndication library, a massive cataloging, dubbing, and editing operation. Sales and distribution fell to Hollywood-based radio syndicator Harry O'Connor and, outside the U.S., to packager G. N. Mackenzie, Ltd., of Toronto. In fact, the vignettes ended up in more major Canadian markets than in the United States. Trinidad, Australia, and South Africa were also Bob and Ray countries.

Of course, O'Connor and Mackenzie each took a healthy bite, but it was still found money for B&R. They discovered, however, that once the tapes were out there, other stations and local jocks could easily pirate them. "And they did," Bob said. Asked how one protects himself, he replied, "You don't."

For decades, Bob and Ray's bits, in whole or in part, had found their way to the programs of many striving, young DJs. Derivatives of their characters and voices had been both knowingly and unknowingly appropriated by local, early-morning zanies and wannabe two-man teams who taped and studied the pair's techniques, hoping to extract some sort of alchemy. For years, it was as if Wally Ballou was the public-domain name for any personality's "roving correspondent."

But what could they do?

"If a guy wants to put our stuff in his morning show in Bo Peep, Ohio," Elliott said, "how are we going to know?"

One particularly egregious venture did come to the attention of their attorney, Stan Schewel. When a Portland, Oregon, outfit began marketing a Bob and Ray orange drink, Schewel, like an axe-wielding Prohibition agent, promptly closed the operation down with one of his patented "thank you note" cease-and-desist letters.

~~

Among the furnishings in the library of the Elliotts' townhouse was an easel on which rested a large, three-by-four-foot canvas. As an artist, Bob was fond of classic paintings. One that had always "stood out," he said, was Sir Anthony Van Dyck's *Charles I at the Hunt.* The elegant 1635 masterpiece, set against a lovely English countryside landscape, depicts the king in velvety red pants, silvery doublet, tan riding boots, and a dark, wide-brimmed hat.

Bob got the oils out and painted a copy of the same figure and background and colors, and then finally, he said, instead of King Charles, "I painted Ray's face in it."

From a Third Avenue antique shop, he and Lee purchased a large, gilt frame and added a specially made brass nameplate: "Finlay Llewlyn Goulding 1653–1736." He was supposedly a long-lost, distant relative possessed of the typical Goulding features, which, Bob said, "I could do blindfolded. On the air, I used to scribble cartoons of Ray's face. During a three- or four-hour show, wherever we sat, I was always looking at one side or the other."

Using Vic Cowen's station wagon, Vic, his wife, Joan, Bob, and Lee drove the painting out to Long Island for Ray's fortieth birthday party. He was "completely surprised," said Bob, who had signed it "Bob Andre." The portrait enjoyed a prominent spot in the Goulding's foyer for over three decades. One recent Christmas, a framed photograph of it arrived in Bob's mail, a treasured surprise gift from Liz. To this day, Bob's painting hangs in her dining room. Van Dyck's original hangs at the Louvre, in Paris.

14

A FRAGILE DYNAMIC

Entering the sleek, glass skyscraper at 400 Park Avenue, on July 30, 1962, for the premiere of WHN's new *Bob and Ray Show*, Ray Goulding was instantly embraced by the specter of his late brother. The fifty-thousand-watt station had been Phil Goulding's on-air domain for thirteen years. Now, with Storer Broadcasting's $10,950,000 purchase from Loew's Theatrical, WMGM was being dropped in favor of its pre-1948 signature, WHN. For Elliott and Goulding, it was a return to the same spot on the New York dial where their 1949 appearance with Phil, pinch-hitting for Morey Amsterdam, had been pivotal in bringing them to New York.

Foremost among a series of changes by the new ownership was the mounting of a large oil portrait of George B. Storer above the reception desk. The swank offices, noted Rick Sklar, another WINS refugee at WMGM/WHN during the changeover, were completely redecorated to reflect the company's prim image. Secretaries were instructed on office comportment, telephone etiquette, and how to eat lunch discreetly at one's desk.

General Manager John Moler, however, was less concerned with appealing to the eye than the ear. WMGM's Top-40 sound, in place since 1958, was scrapped in favor of a standards-and-easy-listening format, billed as "The Sound of Music." WMCA, WINS, and WABC were left to chase the pop charts. A follow-up Moler staff memo advised against programming music "even suspect" of being teen oriented. WHN would pursue an adult demographic and go head-to-head with WNEW and WOR. Bob and Ray in the four o'clock to eight o'clock evening block, Moler concluded, would go a long way toward turning the station around. To promote the changeover and help expunge their musical past, WHN threw a splashy, kickoff concert in the Grand Ballroom of the Waldorf, featuring Hugo Winterhalter and his orchestra, and The Kirby Stone Four. It was about as far as they could distance themselves from the Chiffons and Jimmy Gilmore and the Fireballs.

B&R welcomed the opportunity to work with Ted Brown, their former morning competition and practical-joke victim from the WINS days. Brown had remained as the WHN morning man, however briefly. One day, he announced he's "got plans," Elliott recalled. "I'm going to the best radio station in New York," he told the two. It was WNEW, and an afternoon slot, once again, opposite Bob and Ray.

From a small, third-floor, mustard-colored WHN studio, the pair introduced some new features, including *Wayside Doctor, Hawaiian Eye, Ear, Nose and Throat Man*, and Wally Ballou's daily *Pigeon Saturation Report* ("Normal to heavy in the metropolitan area") with suggested alternate routes for harried Manhattan foot traffic. During the winter, a similar service was provided for pedestrians seeking momentary relief from subfreezing temperatures by standing on a hot grate.

In addition, of course, there were the usuals—the Bob and Ray "A" package— standard equipment that comes with the team, everything from *Matt Neffer, Boy Spot Welder* to *Jack Headstrong, All-American American*. The latter, of course, mimicked *Jack Armstrong, All-American Boy*, and the role's originator, Jim Ameche (brother of Don). More recently, Jim had been an L.A. disc jockey on KLAC and the announcer on *The Amos 'n' Andy Music Hall*. Serendipitously, in 1962, he was added to the new WHN lineup, immediately preceding B&R.

On Ameche's midday program, his live commercials were prerecorded— in radio, not an oxymoron. As a throwback to the medium's Golden Age, Ameche felt that stumbling on the air was out of character with his formal style, Bob said. So he routinely pretaped his spots and simply started over if he made a mistake, or, more typically, laughed, which was his habit at the slightest provocation. "It started from a snort," Bob explained, "and grew into a full-fledged laugh which he tried to repress. . . . A great laugh—the Peter Roberts of WHN." Engineers at his recording sessions, under instructions from Vic Cowen, always kept the tape rolling. Vic then had the breakups dubbed and spliced into a continuous loop, ready for injecting into B&R's on-air proceedings whenever the moment demanded something they could just as easily do without. Like Peter Roberts and George Putnam, Jim Ameche never complained.

Tom Koch had just finished a stint on *The Tennessee Ernie Ford Show* when Elliott tracked him down in L.A. to write for the new WHN series. Tom was thrilled; he could once again work from home. With Ford, he had been commuting weekly by train. Ernie had determined that he was fed up with L.A. and yearned for a spot more in keeping with his "pea-picking" roots. So he moved to San Francisco.

Resuming many of his old standbys, including *Bridget Hillary and the News*, a takeoff on the CBS soap *Wendy Warren and the News*, Koch also created several new, recurring parodies of hit TV series of the period: *The Defenseless*, mocking *The Defenders*, featured father-and-son attorneys, Millard (Ray) and Ferdy (Bob) Shifton, representing such clients as an embezzling accountant found in his office "holding ledger books disclosing a shortage of $582,618 in one hand and cash amounting to $582,618 in the other," and a bank-robbery suspect arrested for speeding during the getaway. *The Orderlies*, a hybrid of a couple of medical dramas, featured compassionless Chief Orderly Schnellwell (Ray) as he castigated his whimpering subordinate, Winecoup (Bob), for putting patients' needs ahead of profits. His infractions included discharging a patient with surgical benefits still remaining on his insurance; dropping a tray when the patient was not even asleep; and failing to put up partitions between beds so "we can charge for a private room."

You and Your Symptoms was a Koch sendup of call-in shows addressing listeners' medical issues, such as one raised by a "caller" claiming that he regularly sent his dentures to a San Francisco dentist who routinely added California sales tax to his fee. "Is this ethical," he wondered, "when he works on my teeth in a state where my mouth has never been?" *You and Your Income Tax* featured Bob as tax authority Claude Flabbert answering imaginary listeners' IRS questions. ("I held up the First National Bank of Prairie View, South Dakota, and escaped with eighty-two hundred dollars. I know I have to pay tax on this money, but can I deduct the cost of the getaway car as a business expense?")

Noting the volume of B&R mail WHN had received, *Newsweek* reported that their return was "as popular as MacArthur's was in Manila."

It was good hearing Bob and Ray and their "brainchildren," Mary and Webley, Matt Messina of the *Daily News* wrote upon their return, saving his criticism for the format. "It hardly gave them time to get out of low gear," he stated. "Comedy was incidental to records, weather reports, news and an avalanche of commercials." In 1962, the prescient Messina was, in fact, describing the ultimate fate of AM radio.

By 1963, WHN concluded that Bob and Ray's success in the second-most lucrative time period warranted a shot at the first. They were offered the morning slot, from five-thirty to nine o'clock. Neither was keen on the idea of getting up at three-thirty in the morning, nor going to bed right after dinner six days a week, nor was Ray thrilled with the long commute. For Bob, walking ten short blocks down Park Avenue from East Sixty-Fourth Street was not particularly burdensome. But, for Ray, the trek from the North Shore of Long Island was another matter. But program manager Roy Schwartz had answers for everything. He announced that they could pretape their show the day before, all three-and-a-half hours of it. Instead of slipping into the city when the roads were empty at four-thirty in the morning, Ray could rise at a sane hour and drive in like a normal person in bumper-to-bumper traffic.

Each day, the next morning's program was taped in real time, including all music, commercials (both live and recorded), and even time checks. Holes were left only for weather and traffic updates and, of course, newscasts, all integrated as live cut-ins in the morning by John Connally, Ed Stokes, or Dick DeFrietas. Though not unprecedented, it was a system somewhat fraught with potential problems. However, for Bob and Ray, it clicked along each day without incident—except once.

On Friday, November 22, 1963, they were in the middle of prerecording their Saturday-morning show when President Kennedy was assassinated. The taping session immediately stopped, Bob recounted, as everyone gathered around a control-room TV monitor to watch Walter Cronkite. Before long, Roy Schwartz entered and wanted to know what was happening.

"The president's been shot," Vic Cowen told him.

"We won't be on tomorrow," Bob and Ray added.

"Who said you won't? *I'm* the program director," Schwartz responded.

"And we said, 'Well, we're not going to finish the show.'"

There would be nothing else on air but continual coverage of the tragedy for at least four days.

Bob and Ray's greatest quality, Vic Cowen told a reporter at the time, is not only their ability to assume the characters they create, but "to think like them." That, combined with the audience's greatest quality, their willing imagination, had the effect of turning listeners into a third collaborator, each supplying their own images of Clifford Fleming at the Bob and Ray weather station high atop Mount Washington, Charles the Poet's tattered manuscripts, or The Amazing Follinger's mind-reading act.

"Imagination sets all the backdrops," Ray told the *National Observer* in 1963. "We can have such wonderful, fanciful fun."

However competitive WHN was in the mornings, it was never able to overtake WNEW. B&R's WHN run, which concluded the last week of June 1964, would be the last time they would go up against Klavan and Finch. Though each team had its loyal following, it was easy to be a fan of both, as was the case with actor/comedian Jack Riley. Long before his role as, in his words, the "socially maladaptive" Eliot Carlin on *The Bob Newhart Show*, Riley and partner Jeff Baxter were a wake-up duo at WERE, Cleveland. In fact, it was Riley being a keen student of both teams that had precipitated the advent of Baxter and Riley.

"I was always a big Bob and Ray fan," Riley said, "but I'd never heard Klavan and Finch until I moved to New York. . . . Bob and Ray were more organized and saner, more disciplined," Riley said. "They seemed to have control of their bits and nobody ever went nuts and went crazy . . . which Gene Klavan did. . . . You'd toss him any kind of a question or some line from a commercial and he would run with it and he'd always be funny as hell." Once in New York, Riley landed a job as a promo writer at WNEW, where he observed Klavan and Finch close up. "It kind of rubbed off on me," he said. "I felt, 'This is for me. I love this.'"

Another fledgling team had a more ignominious beginning. In 1963, WNEW's ownership, MetroMedia, having just purchased KLAC in Los Angeles, wanted to duplicate their New York success and began a search for a new morning twosome. Two KLAC jocks, Al Lohman and Roger Barkley, fearing they would soon be victims of the changeover, quickly put together an audition tape, and the new owners bought it. MetroMedia found the two fresh, inventive, and clever. There was only one problem: they weren't Klavan and Finch. So KLAC flew Lohman and Barkley to New York for a week with detailed instructions to monitor Klavan and Finch every morning, carefully noting every aspect of their technique and style. Once in Manhattan, Lohman and Barkley dined and hung out at some of the city's nicest restaurants and late-night haunts, oversleeping every single morning without hearing one second of Klavan and Finch.

"You really can't create anything for somebody until you know what their working style is," Lohman later told the *Los Angeles Times*. Once on the air together, Lohman and Barkley relied on their own instincts. "As young men," Barkley said, "we both idolized the same two-man team, Bob and Ray. So we had a sort of frame of reference on how to start the show." Lohman and Barkley were at or near the top of the L.A. morning ratings for almost a quarter-century.

The wake-up slot continued to be a drain on WHN. Finally, by February 1973, Storer chucked "The Sound of Music" and went country and western.

◄~

The boys typically relied on their own material for guest appearances. But occasionally on prime time variety shows, the program's writing staff prepared spots for the two, as was the case on their earlier *NBC Comedy Hour* and *Perry Como Show* visits. It was what they anticipated when reporting for a guest-shot on a 1965 Jonathan Winters NBC special. "We expected a script," Bob said.

To Bob's annoyance, Winters told biographer Gerald Nachman in 1999, "I idolized Bob and Ray. . . . I thought everything they ever did was improvised. . . . So I said to them on the set, 'Okay, here's what's going to happen. I'll ride up as George Washington and you'll be two Minutemen and I'll interview you. They just looked at me. Then, I finally realized, nothing was happening. They were stumped."

"We weren't hired to go and write his material, and play against him," Bob said. "Jonathan was playing a Revolutionary general or something. And we didn't know what the premise was for any of this stuff."

Though the hour came off well enough (*Variety* called the Minutemen sequence "very funny"), particularly galling to Bob was Jonathan's gratuitous swipe at two fellow performers—ones that had always been friends and admirers. "There never was a time I didn't laugh at Jonathan Winters," Bob said, adding that Liz—who had known Jonathan and his mother growing up in Springfield—"was livid" when she read the quotation. "I know what he was saying: 'Here are these guys who are supposed to be ad-lib champions and all that crap,'" Bob continued. "That wasn't why we were there."

Winters was possibly influenced by articles about the team during their earlier years in which the two said their routines were spontaneous, Bob conceded. "We might have been trading on the fact that we *had* ad-libbed so much of the stuff. . . . Anybody listening to *The Gathering Dusk* would know we were not ad-libbing it as we went. But a lot of people would think we were reading *Mary Backstayge*, too."

Whatever Winters's opinions about material, when it came to his own two network series—on NBC from 1956 to 1957, and CBS from 1967 to 1969—they certainly did not prevent him from hiring a platoon of talented writers, two of whom on the CBS series, Tony Webster and Tom Koch, had previously written for Bob and Ray.

Hugh Downs was anchoring *Today* when Elliott and Goulding resumed weekly appearances in 1966 and '67. With the format tailored for an audience busy dressing and preparing breakfast, the pair's radio-specific interview segments were ready-made. Little visual attention was required to enjoy Bob interviewing Ray as the managing director of the new International Home Movie Film Festival, one of many *Today* premises from Vic Cowen. Over ten thousand home movies, Ray explained, were divided into categories: "Best performance by a child on a swing . . . feeding an animal at the zoo. Best performance by a male parent at a Little League game, and best performance by a mother holding up an infant's hand and waving."

Johnny Carson's *Tonight Show* staff arranged a super-glittery guest lineup for the week of April 17, 1967, to throw against ABC's newest late-night entry, Joey Bishop. Wednesday's show included two Bob and Ray routines, one featuring Wally Ballou's interview with the president of The Ambiguous Sign Company ("Don't stop for school children except in crosswalks, but only not between 8:00 a.m. and 4:00 p.m., excluding Saturdays, except when patrolman is not on duty").

They were back six months later, with Bob interviewing Ray as Nelson Malamon, an enterprising Vermont farmer, who, on Friday the thirteenth, when his delivery truck went over a cliff, lost his entire crop of four-leaf clovers, which he sold as good-luck novelty items. Then, his second crop came out rather badly, Malamon explained, when he could not tend to it properly because he was laid up. "I got hit in the head with a horseshoe that was hanging over the door of my greenhouse."

Johnny Carson, like B&R at NBC, had ascended from radio and spent much of the 1950s bouncing all over the CBS TV dial, leaving a kinescope trail of local and network, prime-time and daytime series. He was a pushover for even the most subtle of Bob and Ray's broadcasting-based spoofs. "He'd just fawn over them," said Tom Goulding, who worked summers as a page at NBC while in college. "He just loved their stuff." On a couple of their visits, Tom recalled personally escorting his dad and Bob to the green room. "I'd say, 'What are you doing tonight?' And they'd go, 'Oh, we don't know.' And I'd get all panicked. But somehow they'd pull it all together. . . . And when you're a page," Tom added, "Carson was like visiting the pope. You don't want to make eye contact. Maybe kiss the ring, or something."

Both he and Ray felt Johnny was a "master," Bob said, when setting up their bits. His introductions provided a "feeling of authority, and the sense of his approval." Two to three annual B&R *Tonight Show* guest appearances would continue for the next eighteen years—each usually comprised of two vignettes, either at center stage or on the couch.

As a student of comedians, a favorite Carson topic was the social aspect of Bob and Ray's relationship. Ray pointed out during one appearance that "it's natural for people to think if you're a comedy team that you're Siamese twins." He added, "It's not true."

"We don't socialize particularly," Ray explained to Johnny on another occasion. "He lives in New York City and I live on beautiful Long Island."

"There's something I learned tonight," Bob said. "I never knew where he lived before."

Ed Graham recalled an occasion when Piels executives were arranging a limousine to escort the two to a distributors meeting at the brewery in Brooklyn. The limo was to first pick up Ray at his house in Plandome, and then he was to direct the chauffeur to his partner's home in Manhattan, from which they would be driven to the brewery. "Well, I know Bob lives on the Upper East Side somewhere," Ray told the Piels execs.

They did socialize to some extent, Bob said, particularly when it involved business. The two families were together on various work-related junkets and major birthday parties.

"Ray and Bob both valued their privacy and family lives," Liz commented. ". . . While there was a fondness and closeness due to the relationship between Ray and Bob, we also were raising families of our own and were kept busy outside of the business relationship. . . . There were times when Lee and I would spend time together while our husbands were working. We were good friends. Our family get-togethers were infrequent but always lots of fun when they did take place."

On a 1958 winter junket to Miami Beach, the group was put up at the Belmar Hotel while taping *Monitor* pickups around town, including the horse races at Tropical Park. On the air in the winner's circle with *Monitor's* Don Russell following the running of the featured Belmar Stakes, the boys draped the traditional blanket of flowers over the winner, Thin Ice, before heading back upstairs to rejoin their wives in the turf club, leaving Russell to interview the horse. What listeners did not know was that both had money riding on Thin Ice.

The following year, the two families were off to Hawaii on another NBC junket, this one including executive producer Al Capstaff and former *Duffy's Tavern* creator-turned-*Monitor* contributor, Ed Gardner. The three-week expedition was bookended by stays in Los Angeles (including a Disneyland visit), San Francisco, and, on the way home, Phoenix. The latter was an added, last-minute destination as it was then the Red Sox spring-training site. It was only when arriving in Phoenix, Ray, Jr., said, that they discovered "the Red Sox were spending that weekend in San Diego."

From the beginning, the Honolulu stay was cursed by sloppy planning, a super-tight NBC budget, and a fast-talking PR man who had made the arrangements, all of which ignited when the Elliotts were checking in at the Royal Hawaiian Hotel. Bob and Lee had a problem with the location of their room. It was in another hotel—one with a commanding view, Bob said, of "the backside of the city."

As for Ray and Liz's Royal Hawaiian accommodations, there was no problem. Their room, with a breathtaking view of the Pacific, was ready and waiting—even though they were still in San Francisco, and would continue to be for a couple of days. Their son Tom, then nine, had come down with viral encephalitis following a bout with mumps, Liz said. "It just happened there was a medical convention in the hotel and I went down and asked for a doctor. And they had him in the hospital and on an I.V. right away."

Recalling the experience, Tom said, "I was lying in the hospital and this Andersen's soup commercial—which we never saw in New York—comes on and I go, 'Hey, wait a minute! That's my dad!' And the nurse goes, 'Oh, yeah, sure, kid.'"

By the time the Gouldings and their three older children arrived in Honolulu, the PR man had the Elliotts and their two older girls back in the Royal Hawaiian. All the children had dinner together every night in the dining room, Liz said. "And we felt free to do our own thing with the adults."

"We had a ball," Collie said. "I can remember playing spin-the-bottle in a hotel room in Phoenix with Ray, Jr., and Tommy. Ray was two years older than me, and Tommy was one year older than Shannon. We thought it was all very romantic. . . . We didn't socialize with the Gouldings, but when we did see Ray's kids, we always had a good time."

"I think the unusual thing is we never had any great upheaval between us," Bob said of his forty-four-year partnership with Ray. "We differed on a lot of small, everyday things—not even important things—as far as the business was concerned."

All comedy teams are held together by a fragile dynamic. Their interrelations are complex, with each member's individual integrity constantly on the line. Both can feel inextricably superimposed into one being, as if fixed in a never-ending cinematic dissolve.

In 2012, Jerry Seinfeld told Richard Sandomir of the *New York Times* that, as a stand-up comic, he could not fathom being part of a two-man team, let alone one that worked together for decades. "I think it's pretty well acknowledged that it's way tougher than marriage," he said. Setting aside the iconic vaudeville twosome of Smith and Dale—Joe Sultzer and Charlie Marks—who performed together for over sixty years, actuarial figures for double acts are not pretty. Celebrated fellow vaudevillians Weber and Fields split up while still in their early thirties, and Gallagher and Shean's constant backstage battles were as legendary as their onstage routines.

Gene Klavan, B&R's perennial morning neighbor just up the AM dial, once said of his relationship with partner Dee Finch, "We have never had a single serious difference of opinion, depending on your definition of serious."

"They stayed out of each other's way," said Klavan and Finch's WNEW colleague Bill Persky, later the assistant program director. "They didn't spend time socially either. They didn't avoid each other, but in the studio was the primary thing, and whatever else was courteous and respectful. . . . But there was no great bond between them."

The greater a team's success, the higher the stakes, and inevitably, the more suffocating is the team interdependency. For many—Abbott & Costello and Martin & Lewis, to name two—it proved fatal. The latter duo, while hugely successful, was together only ten years. As Jerry Lewis gloomily expressed it in his memoir, "Just try doing comedy with someone when you're not on speaking terms."

Laurel & Hardy were more fortunate. "We seemed to sense each other," Stan Laurel told their biographer, John McCabe. "Funny, we never really got to know each other personally. . . . When we made the pictures, it was all business even though it was fun. Between pictures we hardly saw each other. His life outside the studio was sports—and my life was practically all work, even after work was over. . . . But whatever I did was tops with him."

Similarly, Elliott and Goulding managed to successfully separate themselves from the *Bob and Ray* franchise. Their relationship was rooted in an "on-air business," Elliott said. "That we weren't closer privately, I think, was because of our diverse natures."

Ray's interests were mostly sports related, particularly when it came to baseball. When not working, he was ever-present at his kids' Little League games. He often said that his hobby was "rooting against the Yankees." The Boston Red Sox were "a mania" with him, according to his partner. For better radio reception, he would sit in his car in the driveway at night to pull in their broadcasts from the Hartford affiliate. During some anguish-filled games, he could not bear to listen or watch. Recalling the '86 World Series, Ray, Jr., said, "Dad never saw the Mets bat. He walked out of the room when the Mets came up."

If not at an easel, or scouring an antique shop in one of New England's far-flung precincts, Bob Elliott was attending a rare coin auction on Fifty-Seventh Street. He remains the family's self-appointed curator of unique conversation pieces, including an impressive collection of their past New Year's Eve champagne corks.

"It may be that the separateness helped," Ed Graham suggested. "Perhaps meeting at the studio, doing their work and going home to different lives alleviated some of the usual team strains." Both were proud of their longevity as a team. One of the reasons for this, Ray claimed, was that the two spent only business time together.

"When they were working," observed Graham, "I think each of them thought the other guy was a terrific performer. . . . Each of them could make the other laugh so hard that continuing a studio session was pointless. So it seemed strange to me that each of them could just get up and leave every day without even a goodbye to each other. Now that the years have passed, I realize that may have been one of their many strokes of genius."

At one of the infrequent family get-togethers, this one in the summer of 1968, the Gouldings were the guests of the Elliotts for a benefit at Bowdoin College on behalf of Park View Hospital in Brunswick, Maine. Ray and Liz came up with Bryant and Mark, then ages ten and eight, respectively, recounted Bob, Jr. "We horsed around terribly, all of us, Mark, Bryant, Chris, and I. . . . We were all dressed up to go to this thing at Bowdoin, and it was raining. And Mark somehow got outside and got his suit and everything wet and muddy. When Ray saw him, he was furious. I just remember Bryant and me laughing over that whole thing."

Unfortunately, the laughs during both the afternoon and evening B&R appearances were not as robust. If there was a lesson to be learned, it was that a college gymnasium is perhaps not the ideal venue for nuanced satire. Years later, Bowdoin featured an exhibit of many of Bob's paintings. "All was forgiven," he said.

Dick Cavett announced on his original ABC daytime series that he was dispatching Bob and Ray to send back exclusive, daily, on-the-scene reports from both the Republican and Democratic conventions. With campus unrest and draft-card burning over the raging Vietnam War, then in its fourth year—depending on when one started counting—the 1968 political conventions were expected to be two burning fuses. "Coverage" began with the August 5th opening of the GOP gathering in Miami Beach.

Each day, B&R conducted probing interviews with those on the political fringes, including a cagy assistant hotel manager (Ray) who refused to divulge the "fast-breaking story" taking place "behind closed doors," which, when ultimately opened, revealed a linen closet. Another was with the Republicans' official shrimp deveiner. The latter bit was a favorite of Cavett's in spite of his not remembering one single thing about it. "Nothing," he said, "other than I laughed myself sick."

Making him even sicker is the fact that he can never, ever see it again, nor many other favorite moments from his earlier shows. "In those days," Cavett said, "ABC was stupidly—and illegally, I think—reusing the tapes to record *Let's Make a Deal* or something. . . . So many, many, many treasures don't exist."

A cousin of Cavett's had first introduced him to B&R on *Monitor*. "Natalie Attired," he said, "just put me on the kitchen floor. . . . I'm sure a lot of people didn't get it." In Cavett's opinion, Bob and Ray "never hit a false note." Despite their broadcast format, he said, there was "sort of a wonderful sense of overhearing what they're doing. It's not thrust at you. It just seems to come alive without any noticeable effort or push or ambition to be funny. It just happens; it's just a magical thing." Cavett felt that someone not speaking the language and hearing one of their bits, would probably assume it was "just two people talking, and maybe not even aware that they are being overheard."

Each was a genius in his own way, he said. "In talking with Ray, you never would have guessed what a great talent he was. . . . Ray was just a stunningly brilliant actor. The boobs he played were just dead-on. . . . My late wife and I had dinner with Bob at his home. I don't remember what we talked about, but I just remember being so thoroughly entertained and delighted by him." Cavett also recalled "envying" Lee, he added, because "she got to be around him all the time."

Bob Elliott's lasting impression of the evening was that it was still going strong at one-thirty in the morning.

"Oh, God, yes," said Cavett. "I never wanted to go home."

Following the head-cracking riots and ensuing turmoil at the Democratic convention, B&R's final Cavett appearance had to be canceled. "Chicago became a very unfunny place," Dick said. "It would have been like coming on two hours after the Kennedy assassination and doing humor."

"Mr. Cavett," wrote Cleveland Amory in *TV Guide* about the convention segments, deserves high marks for putting them—and us with them—on."

The pair was back on the show in September, beginning a week's worth of appearances in a hospital-based soap takeoff, *Today is Yesterday—Tomorrow*. Madeline Kahn played the female lead, and Dick Cavett was an intern. "I'd love to know what I did," he said ruefully, flashing back to those lost tapes.

Working around GEG studio sessions for Pillsbury biscuits, Vise-Grip, and GE Plastics, there were more Cavett guest-shots, with Bob and Ray's "coverage" of the Summer Olympics in Mexico City, and in November, the last days of the tumultuous Humphrey-Nixon campaign. However, it was America's eighth president who was receiving B&R's attention. Ray, as an uninvolved interviewer successively asking the very questions that Bob has just answered, introduced his partner as an authority on President Martin Van Buren. Bob then proceeded—as the bit had been structured by the two—to inform viewers that the president was called "Old Kinderhook," that he had been born in the small town of Kinderhook, New York, from which it is believed we get the word "okay." Then, totally out of the blue, Bob said, "And he favored muttonchops."

Completely thrown, Ray could only think to respond, "And what did he like for breakfast—muttonchops, I guess?"

"It was one of rare times Ray and I ever broke up," Bob said. "Ray looked at me and I looked at him in complete deadpan, and we both started to laugh. . . . And Cavett broke up, and the band could see we were breaking up. We really had to cut it short."

Dick Cavett recalled a conversation he once had with Woody Allen about Bob and Ray. Allen remarked that it seemed odd that, when people have to list "the great comedians, they'll say, 'Oh, Benny, Hope, Berle'— some idiots will even say George Jessel—and they never mention Bob and Ray. And then you say, 'What about Bob and Ray?' And they go, 'Oh, great, yes, oh my God, yes, yes!' It says something good about them that they don't fall into the category of everybody else."

15

B&R INK FOR PIC IN STIX

In early 1969, the boys received an offer from Hollywood producer Norman Lear to appear in his forthcoming film, *Cold Turkey*. The timing could not have been more propitious. Local AM radio was giving way to all-talk- and twenty-four-hour-news formats. Like two polar bears on an ever-shrinking ice floe, Bob and Ray's longtime base was melting out from under them. Norman Lear's invitation was a welcome—if interim—lifeline.

Cold Turkey is a satire of small-town America and the tobacco industry. Dick Van Dyke heads the cast as a minister rallying citizens of Eagle Rock, Iowa, to quit smoking for thirty days in order to win a $25-million prize. When the publicity stunt—hatched by Bob Newhart, a cigarette company's ad exec—makes national headlines, the town is overrun by a pack of famous newscasters. Each of these newscasters is portrayed by either Bob or Ray.

It was "a dream come true," said Bob Newhart, recalling his days on location in and around Greenfield and Ames, Iowa, with B&R. "They were very heavy influences on me." When first contemplating a career in comedy, Newhart listened "religiously" to Bob and Ray on *Monitor*. "I saw their success, and the success of George Gobel. Their much subtler form of comedy was what I chose. It wasn't bombastic, or over the top. You didn't have to put on women's clothes and walk on your ankles on television."

At one point, Newhart and a close friend, Ed Gallagher, put together a syndicated radio program, basically "a poor man's *Bob and Ray Show*," he called it. "We were only on in three markets. It actually cost us money to do the show, what with tape and postage." When the bottom line finally caught up with them, the enterprise was scrapped and he faced a decision. "I had wasted so much time," Newhart recounted, "knocking around

Chicago trying to make a buck, I said, 'Okay, I'll become a comedy writer.' If I'd become a writer for Bob and Ray that would have been just fine with me."

One can see Bob and Ray's influence in Newhart's work, he stated, defining their comedy as "these two very calm people blithely going on about horrendous events" in an "insane society that obviously doesn't exist." Illustrating the correlation, Newhart cited his routine as the submarine commander whose crew just broke the speed record for firing at a target and re-submerging—pointing up the parallel of a "disastrous trip, described in very calm tones." ("I want to congratulate you men on the precision and teamwork. At the same time, I don't mean to slight in any way the contribution made by the men we had to leave on deck. . . . I doubt if any of us will ever forget their somewhat stunned expressions as we watched them through the periscope.")

There are also "traces of Bob and Ray" in his original telephone routines, Newhart pointed out, explaining that, after his radio enterprise folded, "I took what were two-man routines and turned them into one-man stand-ups." Recalling his role as Abraham Lincoln's press agent on his first album, he said, "I was still part of a comedy team. It's just unheard what Abe is saying, but the audience can infer the unheard portion. In McLuhan terms, it would be *hot* because the audience isn't passive; they're very active and involved. . . . You presume certain intelligence on the part of the audience."

Chatting informally between setups on *Cold Turkey*, Newhart recalled that Bob "could start going in a certain direction, and Ray knew exactly where he was headed. They would play off of each other, almost like Ping-Pong. It was second nature. It was just one brain that they both shared— one comedic brain."

Upon its release in 1971, the film was generally well-received, but, almost without exception, Elliott and Goulding's contributions were mentioned as being a standout. "Bob and Ray," noted Roger Ebert in the *Chicago Sun-Times*, "do a ruthless job" on Walter Cronkite, David Brinkley, Hugh Downs, Sander Vanocur, Paul Harvey, and Arthur Godfrey. *Daily Variety's* man wrote that the team "is as talented as it used to be at 1:35 p.m. weekdays on WHDH, Boston, some 25-years ago." The *Los Angeles Times* film critic Charles Champlin called the pair "multi-threat commentators," adding that Goulding's Walter Cronkite is "a gem of impersonation," and that Elliott is "likewise deft" as David Brinkley.

Having been panned enough times during their combined career, B&R had adopted a philosophy similar to that of the French film director Claude Chabrol, who, on the subject of uneven critical reception, is said to have remarked, "You have to accept the fact that sometimes you are the pigeon, and sometimes you are the statue."

"I admired them enormously," Norman Lear said, reflecting on his casting of Bob and Ray. "I probably never had another thought but using these guys as multiple anchors and newscasters and so forth. It's like, how could I have done it any other way? . . . That's what I had in mind when all of American media descended on this little town in Iowa." Though it was the first time Lear ever worked with the boys, he said, they had long ago "influenced" him. "On radio, Fred Allen and Bob and Ray were my idols. They shared a wit that was above the other players, and a dry and sardonic one at that."

The team had lunch with Norman one day, Bob said. His deal for *All in the Family* had just been made with CBS, but he had conflicted feelings.

The word swiftly making the rounds was that "they would never keep it on," said Lear who had just rejected a three-picture deal from United Artists to write, produce, and direct, so thrilled was the studio with *Cold Turkey*'s dailies. "Everybody in my life—my wife, my friends—everybody said I was out of my mind."

Returning one night from the location site, Elliott and Goulding, along with some of Bob's kids, stopped for dinner at a place where diners select and grill their own steaks. Ray, who was starving and liked his steaks on the rare side, pulled his sirloin off first, Bob recalled. "My kids were aghast. They said, 'Ray ate that and it was blue!'"

When it came to ordering steaks, Tom remembered his dad always saying, "Just warm it up in the palm of your hand."

"Ray missed the Cape like crazy," said Liz, who remained with the children at their brand-new summer house in Hyannis Port. Often visiting Cape Cod as a boy, Ray had become attached to the place. His older brother, Joe, and his wife, Peg, also had a place there. During previous summers, Liz and Ray had rented on Craigville Beach. This year, however, they had finally bought a place of their own, which only added to Ray's yearning.

It was at Joe's house a few summers later that yet another Goulding steak-related incident occurred. Preparing to leave for a family barbecue at his brother's home, roughly four miles away, Liz momentarily placed a frozen one-and-a-quarter-inch-thick first cut of a top round, Ray's absolute favorite, on the bumper of their car. Halfway to Joe's, she realized that she had forgotten it, but she could not bring herself to tell her husband. Had he learned that his steak was lying somewhere along the road, Liz said, Ray would have "blown his stack." It was a reaction Liz was ultimately spared; upon arriving, she discovered the meat somehow had managed to stay on the bumper.

Upon *Cold Turkey*'s release, Johnny Carson gave it a nice plug during Bob and Ray's next *Tonight Show* guest-shot. The appearance, when spoofed some years later on a *Mary Backstayge* episode, supposedly hyping Norman Lear's fictional remake of *Treasure Island*, featured the nervous Backstayges—after several days of build-up—arriving at the *Tonight Show* only to discover that Carson was away, and that the guest host was Lassie.

It was an easy mistake. After all, the names on the two dressing room doors *did* read "Bob" and "Ray." However, they had been reserved for Bob Eberly and Ray Eberle (the former had changed the spelling of his name), revered vocalists with the Jimmy Dorsey and Glenn Miller bands, respectively. As Bob Elliott and Ray Goulding would discover, their dressing rooms were just down the hall.

The two sets of Bob and Rays were at CBS's Studio 43 in Hollywood in April 1970 to tape segments for *Happy Days*, an hour-long Thursday-night summer placeholder for *The Jim Nabors Hour*. The ten-episode series, hosted by Louis Nye, premiered June 24 and was premised on a nostalgic escape to yesterday—the 1930s and 1940s swing era of the Big Bands and heyday of radio. For series regulars Bob and Ray, no time-travel was required. Their bits were already there. For that reason, co-producers Jack Burns and George Yanok felt the team would be perfect. Initially exploring the

Acclaimed caricaturist Mort Drucker illustrated GEG's 1964 holiday greeting to agencies and clients. (Courtesy of Terri Collin)

Bob, with Chris (left) and Bob, Jr., in Central Park in 1967.

From *Bob and Ray—The Two and Only*, Biff Burns interviewing resentful, old-time ballplayer Stuffy Hodgson, a routine with roots reaching back to their Somerset Hotel appearances.

Bob as *The Slow Talker*—the Broadway show's Act Two curtain raiser.

Ray, as a diner ordering from a rabbit-shaped kiddie menu—a routine always performed as a *Two and Only* encore.

"…I'll have Turkey Lurkey with Gravy and Cat and Fiddle Mashed Squash…then for dessert, Curds and Whey Pudding with a lollipop on it. …Oh, and for openers, I'll have a Shirley Temple—straight up!"

One of dozens of appearances spanning eighteen years with Johnny Carson on *The Tonight Show*.

Bob and Ray: A Night of Two Stars, Live at Carnegie Hall, May and June, 1984.

"We went both nights, and I remember when Dad and Ray walked out on stage, the entire audience rose to its feet, clapping. And that was really quite extraordinary."

GEG's Arizona Bank campaign ran for four years with Bob and Ray portraying spokesmen for the competing "Bank of Bob and Ray."

Bob, Jr., Shannon, Bob, Collie and Amy, November 2012.

At the Grand Canyon for Arizona Bank's *Say Howdy to Bob and Ray* celebration, with Liz (left) and Lee in 1985.

In Suite 2545's studio, stacks of their sound-effects cartridges behind them.

TOP: Tom (back left), Melissa, Barbara, and Ray, Jr.; Mark (front left) and Bryant, in 1987.

LEFT: Bob, portraying Bob Newhart's father on the comedian's CBS sitcom in November 1988.

project in New York at the GEG office, it was, Burns said, an instant flashback to his days at Brockton High.

"The last time I saw you guys," he told B&R, "I was standing outside the Somerset Hotel in Boston trying to get your autograph and I didn't have a pen and paper." The two were "so unassuming," Burns said. "They were never *on* offstage."

On *Happy Days*, Bob and Ray recreated their originally improvised parodies of Golden Age radio programs. Standing behind vintage microphones, they read directly from the transcribed scripts. Sound effects, when required, were provided by CBS soundman Ray Erlenborn, also visible in the "studio." Aside from the set and period wardrobe, there was no concession to television; nobody played to the camera.

"They had so much material," noted Burns, "I said, 'Well, you guys just pick what you want to do.'" In all, thirty-six B&R bits were taped, including five episodes of *One Feller's Family* ("written and produced by T. Wilson Messy. This is a Messy Production."), four editions of *Jack Headstrong, All-American American* ("The secret plans for Jack's atomic fertilizer spreader are missing!"), and four installments of *Mr. Trace, Keener Than Most Persons* (including "The Case of the Hiccoughing Tragedians"). "They did everything in one day," Burns said. "It was amazing."

The series was performed without an audience in the same "block-and-shoot" system employed by executive producers Frank Peppiatt and John Aylesworth on their other show, *Hee Haw*. A laugh track was then added. Thus, in the case of B&R's bits, the canned reaction was added to the very routines which, when originally improvised live years earlier, had been perfect without laughs. The program made a "sad debut," reported *Variety*, with "only the musical content and Bob and Ray's spoofery coming over favorably."

During a break, Bob and Ray had a brief chat with another of the shows' guests, Edgar Bergen, just as he was preparing to leave the studio. Bergen deposited his wooden partner, Charlie McCarthy, in his battered trunk, Bob recounted. "As he closed the lid, he said, 'There you are, Charlie. Don't play with yourself!'"

While in town, the boys joined other CBS stars performing at an affiliates gathering at the Century Plaza Hotel. After doing a stand-up and returning to their table, the two discovered everyone had been served but them. After waiting patiently, Ray finally asked the waiter where their dinners were.

"What did you order?" the waiter asked.

"I ordered a steak," Ray said.

"Well, this man over here took it," replied the waiter, pointing to the next table.

"It was Junior Samples, the fat guy on *Hee Haw*," Bob said. "He ate Ray's steak."

In describing the unique relationship between a comedian and his writer, veteran scribe of *The Bob Hope Show* and *The Carol Burnett Show* Gene Perret said, "It's a lot like a boy and his dog. They both have each other, but only one gets to eat at the table."

After sixteen years with Bob and Ray, Vic Cowen wanted a seat at the table. But, by 1970, it had become clear that this was not going to happen. Cowen's frustration was understandable. Not unlike a second-story man, writing comedy is lonely work, performed in the shadows. All in the trade crave recognition; however, most come to accept their membership in a largely invisible brotherhood, once labeled by one of its most distinguished members, Larry Gelbart, as "Writers Anonymous." In fact, as Gelbart once explained to journalist Eric Lax, producers, too, can have a generic view of writers: "Years ago, Norman Panama and Mel Frank were a writing team at MGM. One day Mel Frank was walking alone and [producer] Arthur Freed passed him. 'Hello boys,' he said."

Ed Simmons, producer and head writer of *The Carol Burnett Show*, once summed up the situation for his staff: "We're not in show business. We *work* for people in show business."

"Vic felt unappreciated," Ed Graham said. "He was a worker bee."

Though Cowen tended to "overwrite" and "needed editing," Elliott said, he "contributed a great deal. . . . Vic had a lot of funny ideas."

On one of B&R's *Tonight Show* visits, two Cowen-inspired bits provoked huge laughs. One featured Ray as a recent bankruptcy victim who had lost his shirt opening a chain of twelve dance studios specializing in teaching the minuet. The other, an Elliott favorite, occurred at the height of the space program. It featured Bob as Winston Grebnick, the head of T.R.A.S.H., an acronym for the Tactical Rubbish and Space Haulage Program. Over twelve thousand pieces of discarded trash and odds and ends from previous missions, revealed Grebnick, were currently encircling the Earth, a thousand of which were officially designated as "garbage." Explaining the program's operation to Ray, he then referred to a large artist's conception of an orbiting space capsule with a rear-loading garbage truck-type compactor. Outside the vehicle, two tethered astronauts were holding sticks with large nails at the ends for stabbing drifting refuse.

Much of Vic Cowen's discontentment within GEG had to do with perception. Nick Meglin recalled, "Vic always confessed to me personally that B&R considered him the man in the booth that put it all together . . . and never a writer in the Tom [Koch] sense." As Meglin put it, "There appeared to be a 'Tom and everyone else' situation."

"True," confirmed Elliott. ". . . Vic didn't come to us on our doorstep as a writer. He was a music expert, and eased into that situation."

Koch's prolific output included the creation of dozens of long-running Bob and Ray features and characters, spanning four decades. Tom Koch, in Meglin's words, was "a writer for a living," whereas Cowen wore several hats. In addition to writing, he supervised the production of all the radio series. Following Graham's departure, he ran the GEG agency accounts, assembled the syndication library, wrote a B&R newsletter, and was the team's front man when arranging guest appearances.

"He handled an awful lot of stuff for us that saved us a lot of time and worry," Elliott said. ". . . Vic Cowen was of inestimable help in our careers for ideas, scripts, and overall organization. . . . He *was* Bob and Ray. He kept us where he felt we should be."

Cowen's oldest daughter, Terri Collin, today a successful playwright, recalled that her father talked about his Bob and Ray association "with equal parts pride, joy, sadness, and regret." Reflecting on his ultimate decision to sever the longtime relationship, she believes that a precipitating factor had been an awkward exchange with Goulding.

"It's Bob and Ray," Goulding told Cowen. "Not Bob and Ray and Vic."

"I think that probably did happen," Bob said. "But I think Ray was trying to be paternal in doing that."

It was Collin's feeling that her father had "discovered his own gifts over time," in what she described as "a long process of discovery." Collin simply adored her father, she said. "He was funny, but also the sweetest man you could ever know. . . . He found it hard to find the confidence to ask for his due—not secure enough in his own value; not a businessman."

Post-Bob and Ray, Vic contributed some pieces to *Mad*, and freelanced material for another radio team, Stan Freeman and Richard Hayes on WCBS. "His stuff read funny," Hayes said. "It was crazy, offbeat."

As the 1970s arrived, the boys were not exactly inundated with offers. "They had that little office, but things were very quiet," recalled theatrical producer Johnna Levine. That reality alone accomplished what she and her co-producer husband, Joe, had not been able to pull off in years of annual meetings. Reluctantly, Bob Elliott and Ray Goulding—the two introverts—agreed to star in a Broadway production.

16

THE TWO AND ONLY

The decision to launch any project in the theater invariably starts with a script. Such was not the case for *Bob and Ray—The Two and Only*. There was no script. Also atypically, a major pre-production phase was already completed: casting.

Johnna Levine immediately began an exploratory dig through decades of Bob and Ray material to be later integrated into an overall structure, yet to be determined. The plan made good sense—if you believe in building the foundation *after* the house. While some of the team's routines were on paper, most existed only as recorded air-checks which—as with the previous *Happy Days* series—had to be converted to script form. "I would visit their office," said Johnna, "and sit there, listening to tapes and talking to them about which ones they thought were usable and advisable." It was a rigorous process.

Unlike traditional Broadway comedies, Bob and Ray's humor was sometimes fragile and not laced with jokes. With the exception of some prime-time and late-night TV guest appearances, the vignettes had never been performed before live audiences. The laughs, it was felt, would surely be there, but exactly where, and how many, nobody could be sure. The bits were frozen-in-time renditions, premise driven, and largely populated by a make-believe cast that, once seen by an audience, would be instantly stripped of their imaginary status.

Of course, their "old-line characters," as Johnna called them, would be greeted as "old friends." But, she pointed out, "This would not work in the theater." This was not news to Elliott and Goulding. It was the same *Linda Lovely* issue the two had wrestled with twenty years earlier on their TV series. Listeners had already formed their own images of the team's regulars. But there were economic aspects to consider, too. To fill a Broadway theater for eight performances a week, it was necessary to reach beyond hardcore B&R fans. The sketches also had to appeal to the uninitiated. Everyone continued sifting through the material for a show which still didn't even have a title.

At home one evening, Lee offered Bob a suggestion: "Why don't you just call it what it is? You and Ray are one of a kind. Why not call it, 'Bob and Ray—The Two and Only'?"

"I knew instinctively she was right," Bob said. "Another case of her getting right to the crux of a matter and coming up with the answer I wished I'd thought of. . . . We watched TV and, on a lined yellow pad, I doodled 'Two and Only' logos over and over."

The next morning, the boys, the Levines, and Tony Award-winning director Joseph Hardy assembled in Suite 2545. Aware of the "negative reaction I could probably expect from Ray to the idea my wife had suggested a title," Elliott said, "I waited for an appropriate opening. Then, casually I repeated Lee's words. 'How about calling it 'Bob and Ray—the Two and Only'? . . . 'That's not bad, you know it?' Joe said. 'I like it,' Johnna agreed. Ray said nothing, but nodded. I knew this to be an indication of agreement."

From then on, *Bob and Ray—The Two and Only* became the official title of the Broadway venture, though, Bob pointed out, little "was ever said publicly by either of us about the origin of it, or how precisely it suited the production."

Home base for *The Two and Only* would be the Moorish-inspired John Golden Theater on West Forty-Fifth Street, conveniently located, as it turned out, directly across the street from another iconic Manhattan steak house, Frankie & Johnnie's. It was in the basement lounge—an anteroom, actually, at the base of twin staircases, rarely the backdrop for anything more creative than winding intermission restroom lines—where the show began to percolate. There, two or three afternoons a week, seated on somewhat uncomfortable chairs that had been pulled into a circle, Bob and Ray gathered with Joseph Hardy, stage manager Don Koehler, and script girl Iris Merlis.

"We talked quite a bit before we ever started working on it just to get the pieces in order," Hardy said. "That was fun, interesting, never difficult.

Ray would occasionally say, 'This isn't going to work! I know it isn't going to work!' But other than that, it was fine."

Many sketches were selected then later discarded for any number of reasons. The twenty or so that ultimately made the final cut included Wally Ballou at Times Square with Ward Smith (Ray), a cranberry bog owner who is surprised to learn that his crop—which he sells in a basket, like strawberries, for cranberry shortcake—can also be squeezed into juice, or served as a side dish with turkey or meats. Another routine featured Ray as celebrated raconteur Martin LeSoeur, whose anecdotes—including one involving "a man hanging from a ledge on the fifteenth floor of the Vaseline Building"—eventually fizzle when he cannot remember the punch lines. Yet another bit had Bob as an unvaryingly dull expert on the Komodo dragon, with Ray, as his disengaged interviewer, asking the very questions Bob had just answered.

The origin of the latter premise was from a tape a friend sent Elliott from San Francisco. This involved a similarly tedious, but completely serious, authority on the whooping crane, being questioned by a host who has scarcely heard one word. "I played it and laughed myself silly," said Bob, who then developed it into a bit for himself and Ray. "I took the four salient facts out of this guy's ten-minute interview, and we did it over and over again." Additional variations on the same format, employing equally obscure subjects—including the aforementioned President Martin Van Buren—followed. To make the bit seem more authentic, Elliott recalled, "I looked up some facts on the Komodo dragon."

Also selected for the Broadway show was a visit from Ray's Barry Campbell, the hard-luck star of *The Tender T-bone*, a "love story set in the Chicago stockyards." The play, Barry explained to Bob's Larry Lovebreath, opened and closed in one night because he could not remember his lines, causing all the other actors to just stand around, speechless, blankly staring at each other. ("There were twenty or thirty minutes in the second act when nobody said anything. . . . The audience ended up walking up and down the aisles, visiting with one another.")

Two other Larry Lovebreath spots were adapted, one with Goulding as a dog trainer who has taught his large poodle to hold a hoop for him to jump through, and the other, from the CBS series, with Goulding as

Clinton Snidely, a New Yorker who keeps a pack of wild boars chained in his small apartment for hunting truffles in Central Park.

"We kept shifting stuff around," Hardy said, "deciding to do this then, and not that then, and to get rid of that and put something else in. They were very good about all that because they were used to that sort of editorial stuff, anyway, in their radio work."

Mary Backstayge and other dramatic parodies were also tried, but it was concluded that they did not come across as well, said Hardy. "The other stuff worked better on a one-to-one basis with the audience."

Given the immediacy of the theater, shorter, more intimate sketches were a better fit for the team's instantly recognizable character types. "They did these wonderful people," Hardy said. "They had this ability to get to the core of how people related to each other in a very simple, down home, terribly funny way." It was these same characters that inspired Hardy's cluttered attic setting. They needed "a background," he said. "You didn't want them in some cozy, Midwestern living room or any nonsense like that." Bob and Ray's characters and situations—"all so ordinary"— reminded the director of "pieces of things we all know about, sort of common and usual to all of us," he explained, referring to the items in the attic. "I just thought it would be great to have as kind of a background, all these pieces that everybody could relate to."

Other selected routines included Ray's resentful old-time ballplayer Stuffy Hodgson, Bob's dead-on David Brinkley, and Ray's quintessential empty-suit bureaucrat Clyde L. "Hap" Whartney. Whartney, the "regional Eastern Inter-bureau Coordinator of Administration for the New England States, and Southern Indiana,"—nationally known since the team's very first weeks on NBC—provided his interviewer, Elliott, with a set of his scripted answers, together with the corresponding questions designed to elicit his self-serving responses.

It is never advisable—especially with comedy—to give an audience too much time to think. "The material kept it moving more than anything," Hardy said. "We just jumped from one thing to another and were always ready with the next thing as soon as we'd done one thing—the next idea, the next 'joke,' if you will, the next whatever."

Frequently, either Bob or Ray would appear from offstage, on a large monitor. It was one of Broadway's first hookups with closed-circuit TV, and quite "hard to do," Johnna noted. "When it went out of order, there was hell to pay and a very expensive repair man who had to be brought in immediately." Though it was a two-man show with no elaborate sets or music, it was "expensive," Johnna said, because of the technology involved. "It was going to be thirty thousand a week, or something, which was money at the time."

Once into rehearsals, Hardy said, it was just a matter of making Bob and Ray "comfortable, and making it all simple enough." It would not be easy. "Ray hated the whole idea," he said. "So he grumbled and bitched all the time. . . . I'm not trying to say that he put up roadblocks and stuff; he was just pessimistic about it all. Said it wasn't going to work. . . . Bob was all for it, liked the idea."

That is not to say Bob was in-sync with everything that was put before him. During one preview which Lee attended, he said, "We tried an awful vignette involving me as an astronaut from Belize, interviewed on the rear screen while supposedly orbiting the earth at some ridiculously low level. She agreed with me that the bit should die before opening night, which it did."

It was Ray's basic nature to be "the grumbler," Hardy said, adding that what finally turned him around was when he saw how the first audience reacted. Hardy felt Ray had the "darker, more sanguinary personality." Bob was "sunnier," he said, "a good center to it all. . . . Bob was really a great assessor of the climate all the time and he had an ability to come in under the storm or ride on the top of the wave and calm it all down, or cleverly manipulate a way to use the material that might have been in question." To Hardy, it was "good cop-bad cop." "I think they operated that way, even with each other. . . . I had a feeling it was the way they always worked. . . . It never became unpleasant."

Hammering out production problems and the inevitable technical glitches with the closed-circuit setup did not allow for much social time. "I never got to know them personally, very well," Hardy said. "We didn't sit around jawing about our lives, et cetera, et cetera. There was none of that." To Hardy, they were more like "corporate lawyers or admen" he said, "and yet, much more real than that. . . . There was nothing show-biz about them whatsoever."

In the midst of the run-throughs, it suddenly occurred to B&R that they had not included a sketch that had rung the bell when they performed it on *The Tonight Show* just a year and a half earlier. The routine centered on interviewer Goulding's ever-increasing exasperation with the tortuously deliberate, unhurried answers of Elliott, as Harlow P. Whitcomb, president of the Slow Talkers of America. At one point, Goulding even attempts finishing Whitcomb's sentences for him—inevitably, in vain. The bit was actually a flip-flopped hybrid of a 1957 segment from the Mutual series, with Elliott interviewing Goulding as Humbert Gwill, president of the Loud Talkers of America.

"Bob or Ray said to me, 'Take a look at 'The Slow Talker,'" Johnna recounted. "But remember, 'The Slow Talker' is not effective in the reading, so I hadn't picked it out. But they said, 'Go back to it.' . . . That was something they knew the effectiveness of."

"We went through it for Hardy, and he said, 'Oh, jeez, you've got to put that in,'" Elliott said. "But we didn't know *how* it was going to go in. And then he came up with the idea of ending the first act with it." The intermission curtain fell on Harlow P. Whitcomb in the middle of a ponderous sentence, and, to the audience's utter surprise and delight, it rose fifteen minutes later with Whitcomb still talking, to a now sound-asleep Goulding.

"Oh, perfect laugh," Bob said. "Joe Hardy came up with that—that was him."

"As soon as we started doing that one, it took shape," Johnna said, "and, of course, became the runaway hit of the piece."

As with the leads in any Broadway enterprise, much was riding on Elliott and Goulding's health. Unlike other shows, if either became ill, there could be no understudies. The entire production would be forced to shut down, at a tremendous loss to the investors. The standard solution was insurance.

"Ray flatly refused to undergo a physical examination," said Johnna, who had been unaware of Goulding's family history of kidney disease.

". . . He had six children. He wasn't going to endanger any of the insurance he had by subjecting himself to another examination. . . . I think he was probably iffy about the state of his own health."

The producers had a "terrible problem," Bob recalled, "to the point where Levine said, 'You've got to take a physical!' Ray knew what a physical would indicate."

"That was a big deal," Liz said, "and made him very nervous."

At one point, it appeared "that was the end of the show," according to Johnna. The matter was only resolved when the investors reluctantly decided to be "self-insurers," she said. "They would take their chances."

They finally let us go on without insurance, Bob said. "Ray never missed a show."

If there were any doubts, the September 24th opening proved to all concerned that the laughs—huge rolling laughs—were there; they were everywhere.

"It was an electric, really cool thing," Bryant Goulding said. "But, it's preceded by a lifetime of, 'It's not a big deal; this is what I do.' So, there was some of that. But the moment is still the moment—really cool."

"I was a little kid," Bryant's brother Mark said. "I don't remember any of the show. . . . I remember seeing Woody Allen in the audience."

"When you're part of it," Liz said, "you can't believe this is my husband and his partner—and the audience is responding this way. I was more awestruck than they were. They just seemed to take it in their stride."

The key word, Liz might have added, is "seemed." Appearing to take it in their stride may have been Bob and Ray's best performances of the evening. Afterward, with everything riding on the notices, the two felt totally exposed. Unlike two leads in a play that gets blasted, Bob and Ray would have no playwright to absorb some, if not most, of the flack. It is hard to disavow a show when you're the stars *and* the authors. Their DNA was on everything. Sure, there had been laughs, but they, like everyone, had heard all the stories: Critics are not necessarily influenced by laughs. The *Times'* Clive Barnes, for example, had once panned a Neil Simon comedy that had wall-to-wall screams.

One of the first reactions the boys gleaned was relayed through producer Joseph Levine, who had been informed by friends and fellow producers Alexander Cohen and Hildy Parks that their special guest, Gina Lollobrigida, had not understood *any* of it.

Waiting for the reviews, everyone was very much "up in the air," Johnna said. There was no formal opening-night party. "We were running this thing very tightly," she explained. "We had to keep on budget, and stayed with it very closely. . . . We had a hard time raising the money. But our major backer, Hy Saporta, sent around a case of champagne, and everyone wandered around backstage, sipping champagne."

Bob, sipping Saporta's champagne, found himself reflecting on Harry and Mary Backstayge's favorite backer, the "wealthy Jacobus Pike." Not once, he mused, did he and his partner think to have Pike spring for opening-night champagne.

The Levines' guest, Gore Vidal—with "that terrible calm," Johnna added—continued assuring the couple that the notices would be wonderful. "And I said at one point, 'Are you always so goddamned sure?'"

Bob and Lee stopped off for an anxiety-filled Chinese dinner at Sun Luck East. Much later, at home, they received a call from their friend, the actor Hugh McPhillips. Through NBC, where he had been directing *The Doctors*, McPhillips had wangled an advance copy of the crucial *Times* review. Hugh McPhillips was well motivated: Besides being a B&R fan, he had invested in the show.

Elliott listened as McPhillips read Clive Barnes's opening line: "It is outrageous." It only got better: "The inescapable fact is that a two-man show called *Bob and Ray—The Two and Only* is one of the zaniest shows to hit town in many a season. It is also first-rate theater. These people are simply unfair to playwrights." Meanwhile, Edwin Newman on WNBC-TV was already proclaiming Bob and Ray "are expert funny men," and on WCBS-TV Leonard Harris was calling the show "a great evening of fun." Richard Watts in the *New York Post* was noting that Bob and Ray's "gift for humor is as engaging as they are."

Over the next couple of days, the love letters continued: "Bob and Ray touch real nerves," said *Newsweek*, dubbing them the "last gentlemen of comedy." *Time* found them "excruciatingly funny." Brendan Gill in the

New Yorker called it "irresistibly funny," adding that "the audience refused to go home until Bob and Ray provided them with several encores." "Never disappoints," stated the *Saturday Review*. Writing in the *Los Angeles Times*, Sandra Schmidt claimed that, if *The Two and Only* works at all, it is "Bob and Ray's fault." *Life* magazine's Tom Prideaux pointed out, "Bob and Ray seldom raise their voices. They disarm their audiences with bland smiles. But at the bottom, they are assassins, stalking a large mass of their fellow Americans with intent to kill. Bland? Sure, like vanilla custard spiked with cyanide." In a *New York Times* Sunday piece, Walter Kerr said Bob and Ray were funny men "interchangeably and surreptitiously," citing their "front-porch friendliness and easily swapped insanity."

Elaborating on Bob and Ray's methodology, Barnes picked up on perhaps the team's defining characteristic: "affectionate observation, coupled with the very minimum. . . . They work masterfully close to the very things they are gently mocking, and this gives their sensible nonsense its special flavor." Similarly, T. E. Kalem of *Time* observed, "They record things almost exactly as they are heard and seen every day—and then they take that one subtle, savage farcical step over the brink into the inane."

The heat from the ecstatic notices, combined with a New York reservoir of affection for B&R, became obvious to the Levines as they regularly bird-dogged the lengthening line at the box office. Such was the glamorous life of Broadway producers.

Johnny Carson, who attended the show during its opening week, visited backstage after the performance. A few nights later, when Bob and Ray were guests on *The Tonight Show*, Johnny gave it a rave. Seeing the show the same week, Henry Morgan told them afterward, "You could run forever with this!"

It was all exhilarating, but the boys knew they would eventually come back down to earth. And for that, they will forever be in debt to *New York* magazine theater critic John Simon. His blistering review, appearing two weeks later, described *The Two and Only* as "not only a stupid show but a cowardly one," appealing to "brainless nostalgia and ostrich-like escapism." Bob and Ray, he wrote, are "by standards of even minimal intelligence, unfunny."

"I had it framed," Bob said. ". . . Ray claimed he never read it. I'm sure he did."

Simon was later rewarded with a role in a subsequent incarnation of the team's *Mary Backstayge* soap. Never speaking, and making only ominous slurping and crunching sounds, the character was referred to as The Worst Person in the World.

Years later at a New Year's party, Bob met Clive Barnes and told him, "I've always wanted to thank you for that review." Only when relating the story afterward did Elliott learn that he had violated a long-established theater custom. "I guess actors don't speak to critics," he said. "Well, that deserved a thank you."

***

Though Toronto's Royal Alexandra Theatre had faded from its opening "Edwardian jewel box" glory days, it was ideal for the *Two and Only* road-tour kickoff, March 8, 1971. With the audience practically on top of Bob and Ray, the intimate Royal Alex seemed custom-made for the show. The two had always enjoyed a large Canadian following, thanks to the strong AM signals of the U.S.'s northern network affiliates wafting across the Great Lakes, plus the presence of their syndication package. But, as successful as the two-week engagement was, it could not prepare the team for their second stop, two weeks at the Parker Playhouse in Fort Lauderdale, the "home of the blue-haired," said Elliott, referring to the venue's large number of elderly women subscription holders. "They thought we were a dance team."

Because the ladies shunned late hours, the theater regularly scheduled extra matinees, performances distinguished by the distracting feedback of their whistling hearing aids cranked to maximum volume. Some walked out in the middle of the show, pushing open side-aisle doors which cast long shafts of daylight through the house before clanging shut.

To get through the matinees, it was finally decided to cut large hunks of material. A couple of times they went through the play "in, like, forty-seven minutes," Tom Goulding said. "They didn't have to wait for laughs; they just marched right through the damn thing."

One afternoon, Chris Elliott, then about ten and a half, was backstage with Lee during a performance, as they frequently had been during the

New York run. Both, of course, knew every line of the show. Listening over the speaker, Chris was suddenly alarmed. "They're skipping!" he told his mother.

"That was bad," Johnna Levine said, recalling the matinee disasters, and also pointing out that "it was Hell Week, or whatever they call it when the students are out in Fort Lauderdale during Easter time." The March 22–April 3 run fell dead center in the middle of Spring Break.

As the tour's next stop was Miami's nearby Coconut Grove Playhouse, Elliott and Goulding were able to catch the matinee of Mickey Rooney's show, *Three Goats and a Blanket*, which followed *The Two and Only* at the Parker. The two happily stayed to the end. The subscription ladies, however, again got up and left. Recalling their backstage visit with Mickey, Tom said, "He told Dad, 'You know what they call it down here? God's waiting room.' It's an old line but it was new to me then."

Though B&R never missed a performance, the same cannot be said for a key article of Wally Ballou's costume. An hour before curtain time on a rainy Saturday night in May, during a two-week run at the Locust Theatre in Philadelphia, stage manager Don Koehler was checking all the props and found that Wally's hat was not where it should be, on a coat hanger in the middle of the set. A frantic search ensued, but at the last minute, a standby hat had to be pressed into duty. Later, in a little vestibule just inside an entrance to the theater, it was discovered. "An inebriated fellow," Bob explained, "had taken cover from the rain and, I guess, needed a hat, too, and must have wandered onto the stage and took it—with the 'press' tag in the hatband and all."

A mid-July engagement at Stanford University in Palo Alto was "absolutely wonderful," Johnna said, "We sold out every single seat for an entire week of every performance—eight performances. Every last ticket went, and they were the hot shots of the town."

Four shows at Princeton University followed, and *The Two and Only* wound up the year with a two-week run at Ford's Theatre in Washington, D.C. In the middle of one performance, an audience member started bleeding profusely, Bob said. "They brought him back, looking for a doctor. He'd had an operation on his upper lip, and he'd laughed so much he had broken the stitches."

During the Washington stay, Ray became hooked on a seafood place Bob and Lee had recommended, returning several times for one of his favorite dishes, oyster stew. With each dinner, he would count the oysters in his bowl. On one particular night he became miffed, convinced that the restaurant had short-changed him.

Reflecting on a January 1973 booking at the Taft Theatre in Cincinnati, Johnna Levine's words came quickly: "The worst night of my life." First opened in 1928, the art-deco house seated twenty-five hundred, had two balconies, and a sound system that was "wholly inadequate," she said. "It stopped operating immediately." In the middle of the show, members of the audience started calling out, "Can't hear you! . . . Can't hear you! . . . Sound! . . . Pick it up!"

"It became a nightmare," Johnna continued. "People sitting in the rear, or sitting in the balcony, said they couldn't hear a thing and they wanted their money back. There was a line of ticket holders getting refunds at the box office by the middle of the first act. . . . Bob and Ray were shell-shocked. It was not something where they could start shouting to the audience. . . . They got quieter and more inhibited as the thing fell apart."

Given the structure of the show, there was nothing the two could do but keep going like two crash dummies trapped inside their own vehicle. The Barry Campbell spot, recounting the hellish *Tender T-bone* opening night disaster, took on a surreal quality. It was life imitating art imitating life.

"It was horrific," said Johnna, who feared that she and her husband would never get their two leads back on the stage. "But they calmed down by the next day." Other Ohio engagements in Dayton and Toledo came off without incident.

In addition to the sound problems, a lot of the Cincinnati audience, according to Bob, really "didn't get it." Then, to cap the run, when the theater manager asked the team for a signed picture for the backstage bulletin board, "He handed us a pen with red ink in it," Bob noted. "I've always assumed it was code for an unsuccessful engagement!"

If the Taft ended up with a little red ink, *Bob and Ray—The Two and Only* did not. With a five-month run on Broadway and a successful tour, the show "went into profit," Johnna said. "We returned the entire investment and it fell into the hit category."

17

WALLY BALLOU FOR MAYOR

The team had just completed taping their segments for a 1972 PBS ninety-minute *NET Playhouse* episode, *Between Time and Timbuktu* by Kurt Vonnegut, Jr., when Ray lost another sibling. His oldest sister, Mary—the surrogate mom who took in Phil, Ray, and Ann when they lost both parents in 1941—became the family's third kidney disease victim. Mary died, aged sixty, on Mother's Day. (Twelve years later, Ray's elder brother, Joe, would die of a heart attack at sixty-nine.)

After Johnny Carson uprooted *The Tonight Show* from New York to L.A. in 1972, Elliott and Goulding increasingly found themselves on the West Coast. They made the trip again that same year to be guests on Flip Wilson's show and *Comedy News*. The latter program was an ABC ninety-minute late-night sendup of "happy-talk" news teams. The boys covered "human-interest" features on a "news team" of Richard Pryor, Mort Sahl, Stan Freberg, Anthony Holland, Kenneth Mars, and Marian Mercer. The only time B&R ever had a drink before going on, Bob said, was when they were invited into Richard Pryor's well-stocked dressing room/bar (although not necessarily in that order). Over drinks, Pryor rhapsodized about his favorite Bob and Ray bits, which in itself was intoxicating to the boys.

Plundering their *Two and Only* trunk on Flip Wilson's show, B&R dusted off "The Slow Talker" and the punch line-forgetting Raconteur, which, like several other routines, had already proven TV-adaptable and audience-friendly. After nearly two hundred Broadway performances, both men knew exactly where every laugh was. Still, there were always concerns—particularly as guests on someone else's show—and usually involving details beyond their control. Given the intimate nature of the material, staging was critical. Studio audiences' attention could easily be hijacked by placing the pair too far upstage behind a scrum of technicians, cameras, and booms. Fortunately, the theater-in-the-round design of Flip's setup, with the boys practically in the audience's laps, played to their strengths.

Despite their successes in other media, by 1973 the boys had been without a steady radio series for nine years. That is, if you don't count a brief, weekly gig on WNEW-FM—and Bob and Ray didn't. With Ray, Jr., Tom, and Barbara now grown, the big house on Bayview Road exceeded the Gouldings' needs and was becoming more difficult for Liz to run. She was eager to move full-time to their home on the Cape, but Ray was reluctant to let go of the place. While he loved the Cape, he was fond of pointing out that "when you leave New York, you're camping out." They arrived at a compromise: They would sell the house, but only through word-of-mouth. No real-estate listings, no agents, no open house.

It sold immediately to a doctor and his family. Just as the property cleared escrow and Ray and Liz packed, B&R landed a new daily radio show in New York.

•••~

Exiting the elevator into the art-deco lobby of the Graybar Building, Elliott and Goulding cut through Grand Central Station before exiting onto Forty-Second Street and heading west. As usual, to keep up with his partner's long stride, Bob had to walk faster.

Crossing Vanderbilt Avenue, their route would take them just south of Times Square to the twenty-fourth-floor studios of WOR. The pair had recently joined Soupy Sales and other personalities taking one-week turns guest hosting the prominent three-fifteen to seven o'clock afternoon drive-time block, *Radio New York*, on the 50,000-watt station.

A small, unimposing deli on Forty-First Street, just off Sixth Avenue— selected only because it was more or less on a straight line between GEG and WOR—would be their only stop, just long enough to grab a couple of Taylor Ham sandwich take-out orders. "We got onto one of those things," Bob said, "where you eat the same thing day after day because you hit on something that you hadn't had before. And then we got to a point where we couldn't look at it again."

From the deli it was only a short block to the station in the 1440 Broadway building, where the two frequently stopped at the lobby's candy store for a bag of red-and-green pistachio nuts. By the end of their on-air shift, their fingers would be bright red, to say nothing of their smeared commercial copy.

That winter, *Radio New York* had been a nagging topic at general manager Herb Saltzman's program meetings. However, that came to an end when WOR executive producer Nat Asch received an impulsive call from Ray Goulding—as it happened, an attentive listener to some of the fill-in hosts—during which he casually dangled the notion of B&R's availability, say, between three-fifteen and seven in the afternoon.

Raised in Brooklyn and the Bronx, the trim, athletic-looking Asch had originally dreamed of a career in baseball. As he explained it: "The Yankees were interested—a Jew who could hit!" Asch had first met the boys through Phil Goulding, with whom he had worked at WMGM in the '50s. After then tuning them in, Asch said he was "enamored; loved them immediately. . . . And so the opportunity arose for me to mention the fact that Bob and Ray might be available. . . . Saltzman said, 'Okay, see if you can get them.' And I said, 'I *know* I can get them.'"

After first subjecting Saltzman to the obligatory corporate dance, RKO General's fourteenth-floor overlords—headed by chairman Tom O'Neil—approved Bob and Ray for a one-week tryout. They would be there for over three years. Having sold their house, the Gouldings moved—maybe four or five hundred yards or so—around the corner to another house on Bayview Road.

The March 12, 1973, debut of their new program—now renamed *Bob and Ray-dio New York*, another fourteenth-floor executive decision—occurred in the midst of a New York City mayoral race. By the second week, Wally Ballou was coyly dropping hints about entering the race, possibly with Mary McGoon on "the fusion ticket." A couple of weeks later, he stated that he would officially declare his candidacy on the second of April. "You don't want to announce on April Fools' Day," he said.

"It made perfect sense," Asch commented, recalling that he suggested to Elliott and Goulding that Wally throw his hat in the ring. "They loved it. . . . They jumped on it."

241

Henry Gladstone, one of the venerable members of the station's news-and-sports team (which also included Lyle Van, Roger Skibenes, and Stan Lomax) had been assigned to B&R's program. During several on-air moments, Gladstone took mock delight in exposing Wally Ballou's glaring lack of qualifications, a fact Wally himself seemed to verify every time he opened his mouth. In response to Gladstone's charge that he was "a carpet-bagger," and to prove that he, indeed, knew which subway to take to the Bronx, Wally got on a D train and ended up in Far Rockaway. One of his many gaffe-plagued statements offered the claim that "victory gardens" would put an end to the high cost of living. Another time, he blew an entire day stumping in New Jersey, only to discover that Garden State residents cannot vote for the mayor of New York. The farcical campaign—complete with "Wally Ballou for Mayor" posters, buttons, and bumper stickers—stretched clear through the summer of 1973. Finally, by Labor Day, a mere "125 votes short" of the amount needed to get on the ballot, Wally sadly threw in the towel, musing, "I can only blame myself. . . . I ran a clean campaign."

"You ran *no* campaign!" Ray snapped.

One of those "Wally Ballou for Mayor" posters hangs today in the office of Keith Olbermann. As a high-school freshman, Olbermann re-ran the team's best WOR bits on WHTR, his Hackley School, Tarrytown, New York, one-watt AM station, featuring himself, as he pointed out, as "the hilariously high-voiced announcer." He not only sought the boys' okay by letter, he said, but had the "temerity to ask them for a letter from management permitting it. And, by god, I got it, from none other than Nat Asch. . . . I can still see the WOR letterhead and can only wonder how *that* conversation went." Olbermann also used B&R as intermission features during broadcasts of the school's hockey games. "It does remain one of the odder programming decisions ever made," he noted, "even with the excuse that it was made by a fourteen-year-old."

Keith Olbermann even made it his business to attend a Bob and Ray broadcast in person one day after school. Witnessing that day's extemporaneous *Backstayge* episode from about twenty feet away, he "sat dumb-founded," Olbermann later recounted. "They trotted out, as if from some unseen storage area just outside the regular universe, eight different human beings to whom they gave voice and personality." It was "verbal prestidigitation," as Olbermann put it, adding that what he observed "at once made permanent my desire to go into broadcasting, in the same way Ray expressed it to me that very afternoon ('it was radio, it was all I ever wanted to do')." Soon after the studio visit Olbermann began recording the team's WOR programs. "Not merely to enjoy them again," he pointed out, "but to create an archive—for whom, I didn't know. I managed to put away around one hundred hours' worth of cassettes."

He wasn't alone. Movie critic Jeffrey Lyons, too, made sure the reels of his recorder were turning every afternoon when Bob and Ray came on. "Understand," he stated emphatically, "*every* day I taped their show." Once having stumbled onto Marshall Efron's mother lode of discarded B&R tapes, Lyons had been bitten by the collecting bug. With additional acquisitions—some from as far away as the U. K.—plus a demo reel of the team's commercials, all of their LPs and videos of their TV appearances, Lyons today is the self-appointed curator of, in his words, the "largest collection of Bob and Ray tapes in private hands; I'll wager it." His Manhattan apartment serves as a reliquary of Bob and Ray memorabilia: an inscribed photo of the team and "Wally Ballou for Mayor" buttons complement a proliferation of Piels beer antiquities, including a Bert & Harry clock, bow tie, and wallet. Two "prized items," Lyons noted, are a rubber Bert & Harry statue and a dual cup holder. Jeffrey Lyons attests to being "Bob and Ray's biggest New York fan—even more than Keith Olbermann! . . . I treasure my friendship with Bob, and remember my friendship with Ray fondly. Or," he asked dryly, "is it Bob? I always get those guys mixed up."

Six flights below *Bob and Ray-dio New York*'s twenty-fourth-floor headquarters was a large, windowless audience studio that had not been used for years. Asch convinced Saltzman to open it up and invite listeners to attend the broadcasts. "We had lines of people virtually around the block—down Broadway and around Fortieth Street," Asch said. ". . . Either Bob or Ray brought in a picture window and hung it on the wall, so it looked like a studio with a window. And then, of course, they did their magic—just remarkable, just overwhelmingly good." When the number of guests started to dwindle, the studio audiences were dropped and the show retuned to its old twenty-fourth-floor studio, the same one that a decade and a half earlier had been B&R's home during the two-year Mutual run.

"We left them completely alone," Asch said, "because they did everything we asked. Every commercial we sent down to them, they did. There would be occasions when Ray would say, 'Is it okay if we do this in our style?' And he would suggest something, and we would say, 'Sure.' But there never was any tension." Being team players, however, did not necessarily extend to meeting up with clients—which hardly set them apart from most on-air talent—or hanging out after hours.

Ray was "reluctant in company," Asch recalled. "I guess he expected that everybody wanted to ask him to do bits. Whatever it was, he was just a very, very quiet man in social terms—the total opposite of his brother Phil, by the way, who was gregarious and social. . . . Bob, of course, was shy. But Bob at the very least had a smile on his face." They were "workmanlike every single day," Asch added. "They showed up and they did their job and they left. I don't remember any other aspects of it, although, more than likely, had they gone down to the bar with me I would have."

A brand new *Mary Backstayge* episode was performed live every day at four-twenty, and then repeated on tape at five-twenty and six-twenty. The serialized storylines and subplots could turn on a dime. From Skunk Haven to the Casbah to the Dry Tortugas, the hilariously innocent Harry and Mary Backstayge, "America's Favorite Family of the Footlights"—abetted by Calvin L. Hoogevin, their neighbor; Pop Beloved, stage doorman; and Greg Marlowe ("young playwright secretly in love with Mary") starred in matinee and evening performances of *Westchester Furioso* while at the same time hosting a daily four-hour morning TV talk show. In addition, they sang and danced in a musical, *The Zachary Taylor Story*; they blithely delivered mysterious brown-paper bags with contents unknown; they set sail for Africa with a stop in the Azores to take on olives; they ordered a tracer put out on the Queen of England when she failed to take their call at Buckingham Palace; they performed *La Traviata* at La Scala, using cue cards; and they considered a café franchise with radio-dispatched trucks delivering hot omelets and fast-food octopus, before eventually specializing as the House of Toast.

Tom Goulding, who occasionally visited the studio after school, re-called: "Every once in a while they'd throw, like, a curve ball [during the *Backstayge* bits]—something outrageous—to the other guy and just stare at him, like, 'You handle this ball.' And then somehow they'd pick it up and make it work. . . . When they'd start over-voicing and almost tripping over each other, it was hysterical."

They improvised "without pushing," Chris Elliott said. Reaching a punch line was not their ultimate goal. "They would just let the conver-sation go and eventually something funny would happen. And if didn't, it was just funny that they were letting the conversation go as long as it did."

Being a team provided a certain level of comfort, Bob pointed out. "We relied on each other. Once we had established a flow, we knew we could fall back on the other."

"Occasionally something might veer off the wrong way," Chris said, "and the other one would support it enough so that it would have some legs. They always had each other's back in terms of whatever branch they were going out on. . . . The subtext is keeping it funny and interesting, but I think they just intuitively knew how to do that, and how to keep it moving, and how to help each other."

Also improvised was an extended "Trophy Train" whistle-stop tour, during which devoted fans of the team were invited to railroad sidings throughout the Northeast for close-up views of "Bob and Ray-iana." After sometimes crossing as many as eleven sets of tracks, and having to "pay through the nose," the faithful could scrutinize mementos such as Ray's fourth-grade shoes (with jackknife compartment), Bob's graduation tie, and the gearshift knob from his first car. The premise originated on the CBS series as various memorabilia—Bob's bicycle clip, their draft notices encased in plastic—continued to be added. Its original purpose was simply as a goodwill gimmick with local affiliates. Vestiges of the bit extend back to their first network days, when the "nineteen-mule" *NBC Mule Team*, then later, the *Mutual Mule Team*—always accompanied by the sound of galloping hooves and a cracking whip—crossed the country, with listeners in each city advised to bring sandwiches and coffee for the driver. When commenting on the durability of such bits, Ray once told an interviewer,

"We magnify the insignificant. You know, flourishes and bands accompanying the opening of a sandwhich."

"My collection of Bob and Ray-iana," proclaimed Jeffrey Lyons, "could fill the Trophy Train."

By early 1974, the Tom Koch epistolary airlift of material was again revved up. Among others, new Koch contributions included takeoffs on TV's *Mannix*, *Kojak*, and *The Waltons* (familiar to B&R listeners as *Blimmix*, *Rorshack*, and *The Pittmans*, respectively). A handful of his oldies, stockpiled a decade earlier when the WHN show went off the air, required some updating. But not *The Gathering Dusk*, as he explained in a letter to Elliott: "That's probably because the heroine was living in the past in 1964, and is just living ten years deeper in the past now."

GEG legal-beagle Stan Schewel's tenaciousness, whether firing a warning shot at Jim Henson or busting the illicit B&R orange-drink operation, paled in comparison to Bob's ex-wife's attorney and his relentless pursuit of back alimony. "I kind of dulled myself to it," Bob said. "Lee and I expected to get served every other couple of days there for a matter of years." Finally, in April of 1974, Bob continued, it came to the point where Jane's attorney would settle if they got the Sixty-Fourth Street townhouse. "After thirteen years there, we had to get out. It was dramatic for all of us. The kids spent their youth in that house and still have vivid memories of it, particularly the younger ones."

"My mother had tears in her eyes," Bob, Jr., said, recalling his father informing him, Amy, and Chris of the news over dinner. "I never imagined that we'd ever move from that house. So that was a big shock."

With Bob anchored at WOR most days, Lee found an apartment on East Seventy-Second Street for the family. Subsequently the Sixty-Fourth Street townhouse changed hands several times, Bob said. "The last time it was sold, Martin Scorsese bought it."

"It's quite a mess you people have gotten yourself into," Ray Goulding told viewers of their prime-time special, *Bob and Ray's Cure for California*. Produced by KNBC, Los Angeles, and airing July 15, 1975, the show imparted the team's "solutions" to twenty-seven critical problems confronting Southern California, from "earthquakes to avocado blight."

Addressing the issue of rapid transit at one of the canals in L.A.'s Venice area, Ray, as a would-be entrepreneur, told Bob's Word Carr that he hopes to soon be transporting locals to and from work on his fleet of barges, even though, he noted sheepishly, "There's no water in the canal right now." He was simply waiting, he said, for the city council to vote his "$350-million appropriation" to cover flooding the city, plus additional police and ambulances. "There's bound to be a big typhoid fever epidemic," he pointed out, "once the streets were full of water."

Neither Elliott nor Goulding were that familiar with the pressing issues then facing L.A., but the show's writer, L.A. resident Tom Koch, certainly was. The special was shot all over the city, including the lavish Pasadena home of the consulate general of Finland, which NBC rented for part of the production. "Ray was very impressed," said Koch. "I remember him telling me that Finland was the only country that had paid off all its World War I debts." (Even off the air, Ray was a master of non sequiturs.)

An attempt at easing congestion at Hollywood, Beverly Hills, and Sunset Strip tourist sites was covered by Wally Ballou, a passenger on guide Milton Whohack's (Goulding) eight-dollar bus tour of Eagle Rock. Bob, as the environmentally concerned operator of the Deep-Six Oil Company's Santa Monica Bay drilling platform, demonstrated to Ray's Artie Schermerhorn how he prevented the rig from becoming an eyesore. "The new beige drill pipe," he explained, "is in the closet off the foyer, and over there are the turbines in the back hall behind the powder room . . ."

"It is Koch's pen and Bob and Ray's straight-faced delivery that makes *Cure for California* worth the 30 minutes," wrote *The Hollywood Reporter's* advance review.

The program would be just as timely today, except the problems are worse. For those pre-mockumentary times, the concept of wrapping humor around serious issues was a major plunge for a network-owned affiliate whose identity was largely defined by its highly respected news operation. Tom Koch graciously made a point of this during his acceptance speech upon receiving a local Emmy for the show.

Cure for California aired during the WOR series, then in its third year, requiring hit-and-run round trips to L.A., as did the ongoing *Tonight Show* appearances. During one stay, while strolling along the sculpted hedges in the residential flats near the Beverly Hills Hotel, Ray and Liz spotted Groucho Marx walking toward them on the opposite side of the street. But Ray's discomfort when stopped in public had the reciprocal effect of wishing to spare other performers the same agony. Unwilling to invade Groucho's privacy, he and Liz kept walking straight ahead. Then, out of the corner of their eyes, they noticed Groucho, having recognized Ray, suddenly crossing the street and approaching, yelling, "What? You don't know who I am?!" The three then enjoyed a friendly chat.

With a combined eleven children and a never-ending stream of tuitions, Elliott and Goulding increasingly planned for the future by turning to their past. A 1975 HBO one-hour special, *The One and Only*, was based on *The Two and Only*. During the same period, Genesis Records released the album, *Vintage Bob and Ray*—twenty mostly mid-'50s *Monitor* segments, followed not long after by a GEG-produced LP, *Bob and Ray Present Mary Backstayge, Noble Wife*, hand-picked episodes from the WOR series, the latter, in Bob's opinion, the "most continuing, creative effort we made, and the kind of thing we liked to do the most." The album, Ray said, was "a lifetime supply of Mary Backstayge."

In August of 1975, WOR lopped off the three o'clock hour, reducing the program to three hours. It was already the boys' longest local New York run, but they were essentially swimming upstream. "Radio was already becoming fractionalized in New York," Nat Asch said. "We had begun to hear *The Good Guys* on WMCA and all the other crap that existed on WABC. And, for whatever the reasons, ratings on all radio stations, not just WOR, had become less than they had been."

"Money seems to be the thing," Elliott wrote to Koch, informing him of the station's decision to pull the plug on their program. "They're putting in a jock at half the price."

The last show, which aired April 30, 1976, featured highlights of the preceding three years, leading off with a *Mary Backstayge* episode that was still being "written" as it was being broadcast. As the panicked "actors" awaited their pages, its fictional creator and author, Chester Hasbrouck Frisbie (Ray), at a typewriter in a corner of the studio, confessed that he could not come up with one single idea. "I'm in a dry well," he pleaded, seized by desperation. "I am sweating gumdrops for the first time in my literary career."

"Brilliant radio, just beyond anything," Asch said of their three years at WOR.

With another *Tonight Show* booking just a few days after their last show, B&R were off to L.A. Passing a bank of pay phones at JFK on the way to the gate, Lee and Bob overheard a man they didn't recognize shouting into a telephone, "I don't give a shit what happens to *Mary Backstayge*— we're not buying it!"

"I don't know if he was talking to Saltzman, or whoever," Bob said, explaining that during their final weeks the station was trying to work out a syndication deal for the *Backstayge* episodes. "But to hear that at JFK! I didn't even look back."

One of Carson's other guests on that particular *Tonight Show* was Orson Welles. "During a commercial on the couch," Bob said, "he leans over and asks if we're still on WOR. We said, no, we were—to all effect—fired. He said, 'The dirty bastards!'" Ultimately, Bob said, the *Backstayge* segments were syndicated "somehow, somewhere."

Later that spring, when B&R emceed the annual Writers Guild of America, East Awards dinner, the landscape had already started shifting under the three major TV networks. For the first time, one of the top comedy hits was a syndicated program, *Mary Hartman, Mary Hartman*, a soap-opera parody which had been turned down by ABC, CBS, and NBC as too controversial.

Other than savoring a couple of steaks at Barberian's, the boys were not sure what to expect when heading for Toronto as guests on *The David*

Steinberg Show. The CBC series starred Steinberg as the host of his own fictional talk show, supported by a cast of Second City Toronto co-conspirators, including Martin Short, John Candy, and Joe Flaherty, their SCTV days not far off.

"I played what my friends would call a redundancy—an egotistical version of myself." Steinberg explained. ". . . I would do a monologue at the start of the show. And then it would be about what the guest was going to do, and how I either liked that or didn't like that, or kissed their ass or didn't, and like that."

In the fictional "off-air" sequences, Elliott and Goulding, as the guests of the week, were thus integrated into the scripted plot, which embraced the obvious generational overlap. The Second City bunch had no real recollection of Bob and Ray, but being "culture freaks, they knew *of* them," said Steinberg, a native of Winnipeg, "which is sort of the outskirts of Canada."

They were all fellow travelers in the business of satire and making their audiences feel smart, or at least enough so as to be familiar with what is being lampooned. The then-looming SCTV could just as well have been a sister-station of *The Cuckoo Hour*'s KUKU, and both affiliates of Bob and Ray's "Finley Quality Network."

"It wasn't like we'd lost a big star and Bob and Ray were who we brought up," Steinberg said. "Myself, the SCTV guys, we all wanted Bob and Ray. . . . We just picked our favorite people."

During the show-within-a-show portion, everybody, Steinberg recalled, referring to Martin Short and the troupe, were "mouth-open with respect" watching Bob and Ray perform "The Slow Talker" sketch. "The slower it went, and the longer the pauses, the bigger the laughs from the audience," he said. ". . . You could have gone to Second City that night with the two of them at their age and gotten more laughs than any sketch that was on. That's how good it was."

Noting that almost every comedy person he knew from that era was Jewish, Steinberg cited all-time Canadian favorites Wayne and Shuster: "Very gentile-sounding names," he pointed out, "but they were Jewish. And Bob and Ray were WASPY. I don't know what the significance of that is, but it was part of their uniqueness—that sort of cool, McLuhan-istic laid-back [quality] was perfect. . . . They were very real people. And their voices didn't change and their energy didn't change on-camera when they did their material, which is very unusual. . . . It's easy to underestimate the integrity they had, because what they did was very subtle. You had to listen. You had to get it. It was totally unique. It takes a lot of guts to just do what they were doing and be so original like that."

Having enjoyed their dinner at Barberian's Steak House, the following night B&R asked the hotel doorman if he knew of another nearby steak place. Without hesitation, he answered, "Joseph's—two blocks over. Best steak in North America!"

"Ray forever bridled when we remembered that exchange," Bob said. "That the doorman could not just say 'best in Toronto'—or even 'in Canada'—but that he'd include the U.S. in his recommendation."

18

TUESDAYS AND THURSDAYS ONLY

It was just a beautiful trip," Liz said, recalling Bob and Ray's 1978 New Orleans Super Bowl weekend excursion. It included a paddleboat trip down the Mississippi and dinner with the late King Tut—that is, his solid-gold mask and other artifacts from the pharaoh's tomb, then touring the U.S. It was all compliments of American Express, for whom the duo had appeared in a TV spot and print ads. The Gouldings stayed on a few extra days, with Liz reliving an earlier visit during her college years. Especially memorable to her were the city's famous beignets. Only this time, she discovered, they were "ten times better with coffee."

It was Liz who ate the delicious, powdered sugar-coated beignets, but it was Ray who swelled up. He was "quite bloated," she said, "which I didn't really realize. But he would never ever show any pictures of himself from there. . . . In New Orleans he was being careful about what he ate. He knew something was wrong." Very shortly after, Liz recalled, a Bob and Ray commitment in Florida had to be canceled.

In March, the 1978 Cadillac-hosted National Marketing Symposium luncheon at Tarrytown, New York, was to be just another Bob and Ray appearance for a GEG advertising client. However, Ray fell ill. "He'd always had a great appetite and he didn't touch his lunch." Bob said. ". . . I was surprised at that."

The next day, Bob got a call from North Shore Hospital. "Well, you'll never guess," his partner told him. "They're feeding me through my belly-button."

"He knew he had trouble there—kidney trouble," Bob said. "He knew from his family. . . . That luncheon was when it had become unbearable."

Like his mother and his brother Phil, who had died at age thirty-nine, and his sister Mary, at sixty, Ray Goulding, at fifty-six, had suffered kidney failure. "It was devastating," Liz said.

Ray's options were extremely limited. "He had no hope of a transplant, whatsoever," Ray, Jr., said. "Back then, finding a match was so hard. They didn't have the rejection drugs that they have now. Obviously, the best possible transplant would have been from a family member, which he nixed right away. That wasn't going to happen."

Diagnosed with chronic kidney disease, he immediately began five-hour dialysis sessions every Monday, Wednesday, and Friday. By then, easy-to-use home dialysis machines were becoming widely available. Given a choice of having the treatments at home or in a hospital, "He went to the hospital," Liz said. "I would have been willing to have it at home, but he wouldn't do that. He didn't want to tie me down that way and felt more comfortable, I think, at the hospital."

By the 23rd of May, Ray was able to join Bob in co-emceeing the National Fathers Day Committee awards luncheon at the New York Sheraton. It was the first time he had been out of Manhasset for months. Bob recalls that his partner looked "terrible." By September, Ray's health had improved enough for a quick trip to Philadelphia, where B&R were honored by the Golden Slipper Club "for Service and Distinction in the Television Industry."

As precarious as Goulding's condition was, so too was the entire thirty-two-year *Bob and Ray* enterprise, with all engagements now meticulously planned exclusively for Tuesdays and Thursdays. Producers of variety shows, typically requiring guests' presence for a full five-day week, could hardly be expected to embrace such rigid scheduling, nor could potential agency clients in the habit of demanding their time-sensitive spots "yesterday."

Clearly, B&R concluded, a new component to their business model was called for: deception. Ray's illness, it was decided, had to be kept secret. It would not be easy. Then as now, the insular broadcasting and advertising communities thrived on information and gossip, which are often one and the same.

Less scheduling contortions were required for guest-shots on New York-based programs, such as the David Letterman and Regis Philbin shows, and a guest appearance on *Saturday Night Live*. The pair had been idols of many on *SNL*, particularly writers Matt Neuman, Tom Davis, and Al Franken (today, a U.S. Senator from Minnesota). The three, according to Davis, had rolled on the floor with laughter while playing old B&R tapes. "The formulas became imprinted in the minds of Franken and Davis," he wrote in his memoir.

As this particular *SNL* episode aired in December, it featured a holiday-themed *Hard Luck Story* sketch. A reporter (Bob) interviews Parnell Garth (Ray), who happens to be in possession of a scrawny, pathetic-looking Christmas tree. Parnell had traveled all the way from Washington State to New York with the giant Northwest fir tree on his lap, he explained, with the intention of selling it to Rockefeller Center as its annual Christmas tree. However, during the five-day trip he soon discovered, "There's a right way and a wrong way to go through a bus door with this thing."

Though Ray's professional life was substantially curtailed, it was discovered that, with prior arrangements, he could receive treatment away from New York. Appearances on *The Merv Griffin Show*, and continuing Johnny Carson *Tonight Show* bookings, each requiring trips to Los Angeles, still proved challenging. There were not that many places which provided dialysis, said Liz, who coordinated all the out-of-town arrangements through Ray's home-base unit at North Shore Hospital. All the details had to be gone over in advance. He coped with the dialysis sessions as "just something he had to do," Liz said. "He read and watched TV. He had to have paperback books because he couldn't hold them. They had one arm down. He made it seem easy for us so we never realized what it must have done to him."

It was his "routine," Melissa said. "You got used to the sounds. He was up early and had to be ready. You don't miss a day."

～

On Saturday, March 31, 1979, a live, late-night NBC special produced by the *Saturday Night Live* staff, *Bob & Ray, Jane, Laraine & Gilda*, aired in the eleven-thirty time period. With *SNL* regulars Dan Aykroyd, John Belushi, Garrett Morris and Bill Murray given the night off, cast members Jane Curtin, Laraine Newman, and Gilda Radner joined the boys for ninety minutes direct from Bob and Ray's "Finley Quality Network." In addition to fourteen comedy bits were two musical selections by Willie Nelson.

One of the opening features of the show was "The Bob and Ray Story," a brief, mock documentary made up of dummy headlines, film clips, and doctored photographs. One of the many ludicrous claims was that Ray had served his country during World War II by impersonating President Roosevelt. "For three years," Jane, Laraine, and Gilda explained, "he sat on the White House lawn tying up Nazi intelligence operatives who stood vigil, watching him."

"I was really glad when the war ended," interjected Ray in the narration, "so I could get up and stretch."

While rehearsing the segment, Ray caught a glimpse of a monitor and the accompanying video, an authentic photograph of Franklin Roosevelt sitting in his wheelchair on the White house lawn, except the president's face, in keeping with the bit, was replaced with a picture of Ray, complete with FDR's ever-present cigarette holder. Upon closer inspection, Ray noticed that Roosevelt's pant legs were up just enough to reveal his leg braces. That was all Ray—who almost punched an Army officer for an inappropriate remark following FDR's death—had to see.

"We really put up quite a stink over that," Bob said. "Just didn't like the association of doing comedy and a picture of Roosevelt and his braces." The flap was ultimately resolved by effectively extending each pant cuff in the photo a millimeter or so, carefully inking over the braces.

The *SNL* format was made-to-order for Bob and Ray's spoofy commercials, such as their pitch for "Friedolf & Sons, Shoelace Cleaners." This establishment, according to Ray's voice-over, has "never lost a pair of shoelaces in over forty-seven years of operation." Filmed in an actual SoHo shoe-repair shop, the spot had Jane, Laraine, Gilda, and Bob as the shop's employees, all wearing sterile, white lab coats and shower caps. A customer (Ray) has his shoelaces removed with exquisite care; they are then gingerly deposited in steaming liquid. "Your shoelaces," the narration continues, synced to close-ups of each cleaning phase as performed by the girls, "will be disinfected in a secret, patented wash, rinsed and then towel dried and steam-pressed, increasing the lifetime of your shoes four-to-five times." In this case, the visual component enhanced the team's original 1952 radio bit.

On radio, the simultaneous-speaking McBeebee Twins had always been effective. But now, seeing the identically dressed Claude (Ray) and Clyde (Bob) at home with their dates, Patti and Patti (Jane and Gilda) heightened the insanity. When the inseparable twosome momentarily exit to the kitchen, the girls begin to conspire: "Maybe," suggests Patti (Jane), putting the plot in motion, "I can figure out some way to get Clyde in the other room, so that you and Claude can have some time together."

Although Bob and Ray's new "action-adventure movie," *Bullets Never Kiss*, was still being edited, explained Laraine Newman, a preview clip of the "hair-raising chase sequence" was available. Dissolving to film, the boys, as a couple of hoods in overcoats and hats, dart behind parked cars to keep out of each other's sight. Slipping into his car, Ray starts it up and peels out into what is suddenly a jammed side street, stuck behind a line of gridlocked automobiles. Bob, in his car, then pulls on to the same street, a couple of vehicles behind. Without a line of dialog, the entire "chase," accompanied by pounding, climactic music, is intercut with close-ups of the protagonists' increasingly exasperated faces, as both can only creep forward inches at a time.

For the hardcore B&R fan, the special also featured an episode of their *Dragnet* parody, *Squad Car 119*, first performed on Mutual twenty-two years earlier. Dusting for fingerprints at a murder scene in a fancy Mulholland Drive home, Ralph R. Kruger, Jr. (Goulding), remarks that the picture over the mantel "must be the victim's kid."

"It says right under it," replies Sam Finch (Elliott), "Gainsborough's *Blue Boy*."

"Strange they would dress a kid up in a funny suit like that," comments Ralph. He then reminds his partner that the captain had told him to dust the empty glass on the cocktail table. "Hand it to me, will you, Sam?"

"Sure," says Sam, handing it over. "It's sure a nice-looking glass, with those pheasants on the side of it."

"That's funny," says Ralph, examining it closely. "These look like your prints on here, Sam. See, they've got the little loop up here at the top, and the swirl down here."

"They *are* my prints," Sam says. "I handed you the glass, remember?"

"You shouldn't have done that, Sam. It's going to look pretty bad in court. Hope you've got an alibi for three o'clock this afternoon."

Such trusted bits (they had done 151 *Squad Car 119* episodes) came with their own comfort zones, especially in challenging venues. Naturally, each felt that he was the best judge of what would—and would not—work.

One piece of material set off an immediate warning light. The *SNL* staff had prepared a special arrangement for Bob and Ray, together with Jane, Laraine, and Gilda, to perform Rod Stewart's then-current disco hit, "Da' Ya' Think I'm Sexy?" The number featured cutaways from the girls for a couple of B&R duets, just for the lyrics: "If you want my body, and you think I'm sexy, come on, sugar, let me know." The two absolutely refused to do the song. It was just *not* Bob and Ray, they argued. Of course, they were right. It was *not* Bob and Ray. And that is precisely why the number was so hilarious.

"We fought that song," Elliott said, "as much as doing the Broadway show." But they were up against crafty infighters when it came to wrangling over material, namely Al Franken and *SNL's* brilliant keyboard man, Paul Shaffer. "Franken fought for that," Bob said, "and we did it. And then it was fine; it was fun. . . . More people in the years since have come up to me and mentioned that song, and us doing it."

The night was not without *SNL's* usual crises. Between dress rehearsal and airtime, the running order of the show's comedy segments, plus musical guest Willie Nelson's numbers, were completely reshuffled. But, as Bob later wrote to Tom Koch, the boys were thrilled with the overall reaction. Koch responded that he knew it went "extremely well" when he realized he was "awake until one o'clock in the morning."

Following a *Tonight Show* appearance in July, B&R took the rest of the summer off before confronting the next geographical challenge for Ray, a GEG Dr. Pepper bottlers' convention at the Sheraton Waikiki in Honolulu. They were trying to sell the idea of "heated Dr. Pepper," Bob said. "Instead of your morning coffee, try Dr. Pepper hot."

It was a "hectic" experience, Liz said, because dialysis patients were required to report to a certain hospital some distance from the hotel for their initial visit. "We took a bus, trying to find it." After that, he was able to be treated at a more conveniently located hospital. Before returning home, the two couples rewarded themselves with a week in Maui, which, for the Gouldings, necessitated an eighteen-mile drive to dialysis. But the scenery was beautiful, Liz said, recalling the day they spotted a spectacular rainbow. "We stopped the car," she said, "and got out and walked up the hill to see if there was a pot of gold. . . . There was nothing."

Normally, Bob and Ray would not be a producer's first choice as fictional outside characters on sitcoms or dramatic series, especially when appearing together. Their team identity would tend to jar a viewer's suspension of disbelief. But some shows delight in "stunt casting," the practice of deliberately shining a spotlight on certain roles, usually for promotional purposes. Such was the case when the boys portrayed wedding caterers on an episode of ABC's *Happy Days* (not to be confused with the earlier summer variety series of the same name). They later appeared as bird watchers, squabbling over which of the two had been the first to spot "the great western Wallowipper," on an installment of the CBS dramatic series *Trapper John, M.D.* Their *Trapper John* scenes were squeezed into two days of shooting to accommodate five hours of dialysis in L.A.; the *Happy Days* appearance was a little more complicated.

From the initial table read to the filming in front of a live audience, the team, along with regulars Tom Bosley, Marion Ross, Ron Howard, and Henry Winkler, were sequestered in a soundstage on the Paramount lot for five days. On this and similar assignments, given Ray's strict regimen, they had to confide in someone connected with the show, Bob said. "We had to explain before we went all the way out there that here's what would have to happen. . . . They were all completely cooperative. They revised schedules so it worked out." During cast note sessions when Ray was away, Bob added, "I would go and then transmit the changes or whatever to Ray when I saw him."

Ray, Jr., then living in nearby Simi Valley, became part of the week's shuttle service to the dialysis clinic. "I drove to Paramount and took him there," he said, "and Mom picked him up afterward."

"I usually drove him because he was kind of washed-out right afterward," said Liz, who accompanied her husband on all out-of-town trips.

B&R never gave serious thought to joining the industry's permanent California migration. "I think they knew instinctively that they were a different animal," Chris said. "They never felt like they fit in with that crowd, even though they admired many of those people."

The team also met GEG commercial demands with appearances at various advertising and promotional conferences in Chicago, Washington, Las Vegas, and even San Juan, Puerto Rico. "Everything had to be planned," Liz said. "Oh, it was unbelievable." Outbound flights were booked right after a dialysis treatment in New York. Liz carried a hanging suit bag while Ray pulled a rolling suitcase. Recycling all that blood was "draining," she said. "He didn't have the stamina to carry his suit bag and pull the suitcase at the same time. I really can't say that he ever seemed to be drained to other people. Only I was aware of it. . . . He kept up appearances." At home, she said, his normal routine, following dialysis, was to rest in bed for the remainder of the day. The next day he would be fine.

George Carlin's first decade-plus of stand-up was rooted in broadcasting spoofs of wacky newscasts, commercials, and game shows. Carlin did them all—motor mouth DJs, spacey weathermen, airhead sportscasters—nailing the accents and the voices. "Material that went around in circles," he called it, "media material taking off on media form, television about television."

Sound familiar?

Was George Carlin a Bob and Ray fan? "Oh, yeah, sure," said Jack Burns, recalling their *Burns and Carlin* days on KDAY, and later Playboy circuit gigs when one of George's characters was called "Biff Burns"—an "unconscious lifting of the name," Jack said.

"We considered it a compliment," Elliott said. Jack and George even created their own version of Wally Ballou's habit of chopping off the first letters of his name when beginning a remote broadcast, in the trade, an up-cut (Elliott's jab at slow engineers when opening a correspondent's mike).

In Hollywood, the boys had joined George Carlin, Steve Allen, Jayne Meadows, Norm Crosby, and Mark Russell in *A Funny Thing Happened on the Way to the White House*, an HBO election-eve special taped over two days at MetroMedia's studios. A variation of another *Two and Only* piece was melded into the shows election premise. Ray appeared as a sore-loser candidate who squandered all of his life savings on his campaign. "All I have left," he said in his angry election night concession speech "is what I have here in my pocket!"

In contrast to Bob and Ray's influence on George Carlin, Bob Newhart, and a subsequent generation of performers, David Letterman relied on them as a personal social barometer. "If you ever go out with somebody on a first date or something," he remarked on his show one night when introducing the pair, "and you don't really know too much about the person and you want to find out if he or she has a good sense of humor, one quick easy way: If they like Bob and Ray, they're okay."

They had a definite influence on "my calmness," Jonathan Schwartz explained, "my notion that I could do this; I could talk about anything, whether it be sad or funny and make my own voice heard. . . . Bob and Ray played a very important role in that." When writing a piece about the boys for the *Village Voice*, Schwartz found himself walking down Forty-Fifth Street with the two. "I was in the middle of them," he said, "and they were talking, but they did so satirically. Picking up on the rhythm of it, I was hard pressed not to laugh. I don't remember what it was. At first, I thought it was about me. But I've always thought *everything* is about me."

The one-hour CBS late-night pilot, *From Cleveland*, broadcast as a "special," on October 25, 1980, reunited Bob and Ray with Second City stars, this time Joe Flaherty, Eugene Levy, Andrea Martin, Catherine O'Hara, and Dave Thomas. But the real star was the city of Cleveland. CBS had been intrigued with executive producer Rocco Urbisci's nervy, culture-specific concept of a late-night, blue-collar, laughtrack-free sketch show, shot on the streets in Cleveland, about Cleveland. That city's bleak, eroding industrial cityscape would be the ever-present backdrop.

Glamour and show business were not part of the equation, said Urbisci, who, growing up on the city's West Side, had been a B&R fan. Feeling they were a perfect fit for the Second City troupe, he cast them to fulfill what he called "a Wolfman Jack role."

While not exactly a performer Elliott and Goulding could recall ever being compared to, they were not about to question Urbisci's judgment. For all they knew, maybe he had perceived some hidden talent of theirs to which they had both been blind.

Urbisci had been impressed with how the Wolfman's penetrating rasp had so complemented the film *American Graffiti*. He foresaw a Bob and Ray radio show in a similar capacity for *In Cleveland*, to provide, as he put it, the "comedic soundtrack." They were "extremely brave" to trust me, Urbisci said. "They had no idea what the hell I was doing, except I told them what the premise was. . . . You could give them a kernel of an idea and they could expand it into not only a comedic bit, but a funny scene. . . . We'd shoot a piece and then we'd go in and talk about it and they'd make an adjustment. Ray would say, 'Look, I'll say this and you do that'—an improv. . . . Come on, man, these guys invented this stuff."

In one of B&R's segments, Bob was a Cleveland authority on "the aye-aye lemur, a nocturnal primate of Madagascar," which, he explained over and over to Ray as the inattentive interviewer, exists "on a diet of sugarcane and wood-boring caterpillars."

To Urbisci, it was another example of the team's lack of "the division of bad guy-good guy," as he termed it. "Sometimes Bob was the antagonist, sometimes Bob was the protagonist. . . . They could switch back and forth seamlessly. . . . Very droll and very dry and very understated. Nothing was broad, nothing was big rimshots."

All elements of the show were indigenous to Cleveland, yet B&R never set foot in the city. The two were in L.A. for the earlier HBO special, permitting all their "radio" sequences to be shot at the studios of NPR's Santa Monica affiliate, KCRW. Urbisci was not about to fly them to Cleveland he said. "I had heard Ray was not in good health."

While the city's river famously caught fire, the show did not. The one-time special was not picked up as a series.

Introducing the team in November on NBC's new *Steve Allen Comedy Hour*, Steve announced, "I'm a Bob and Ray freak." Since making their first appearance on Steve's original *Tonight* back in '54, it was not unusual for the three to find themselves sharing grooves of the same Coral comedy albums, the pages of *Mad*, or, as—only weeks earlier—guests on the same HBO special. When in New York on various projects in the early seventies, Steve had often visited his oldest son, Steve, Jr., a doctor with the student health service at Stony Brook University on Long Island. During more than one of those trips, he accepted a lift from Ray on his way home to Manhasset. Given how both dreaded small talk, those drives could have seemed like an eternity. Not so, according to Allen's widow Jayne. "It was like therapy for Steve," she said. "Somebody he could laugh at and with."

On this occasion, in Hollywood in 1980, Bob and Ray taped material for three Allen shows, including one on which Ray portrayed Dr. Klaveman of the "New York City Bureau of Terribleness." In a city with so many terrible possibilities, he informed his partner, it was his job as "administrator" to see that they are all "carried out."

After so many California assignments, Toronto, with its manageable distance from New York, was a welcome relief for Ray. The boys were in town in early December to lay down voice tracks for the animated *B.C.: A Christmas Special*, based on the comic strip by Johnny Hart. Any concerns they may have had about another syrupy, warm and fuzzy holiday-genre stereotype—traits not necessarily in the Bob and Ray playbook—had been quickly dismissed upon being told the premise. Sensing that "there's a buck to be made," lead cavemen Peter and Wiley concoct a Yuletide scheme to merchandize rocks as presents. ("Every year we'll sell X amount of gifts to the masses. We'll call it Xmas.")

Ray, as Wiley, points out that, to be successful, their self-created "myth of Santa" must be presented "in a manner deserving of star status."

"You're absolutely right," Bob, as Peter, assures him. "We'll give him a limo with steel-belted radials."

Wiley explains that Santa has to be "believable enough to reject, and unbelievable enough to accept." Then, reflecting on his own words, his conscience suddenly gets the best of him. "I can't help it, Peter," he whines. "I feel cheap."

"Sure, it's a big con," Peter admits. "But think of the happiness and excitement we're giving them. . . . They're going to get rocks."

Launching his new PBS series, *Inside Story*, in May 1981, journalist Hodding Carter III, formerly of both the Lyndon B. Johnson and Jimmy Carter administrations, and newly resigned from the state department, wanted the program to be taken seriously, but not *that* seriously. He and producer Ned Schnurman turned to Bob and Ray for vignettes tied to the program's weekly half-hour focus on scrutinizing the media. They will remove "that sense of self-importance and pomposity," Carter pompously announced upon launching the series. For Ray, the big plus was that no traveling would be required. The team's bits could easily be taped in New York.

On one of the initial broadcasts, B&R did a sendup of TV's then-in-vogue ambush-style reporting. Bob, as the manufacturer of "potentially lethal" ice-cube trays which stick to the bottom of freezer compartments, is suddenly confronted by Ray's Artie Schermerhorn with news that a child "strained several of his internal organs while trying to remove ice cubes."

After the first season, Carter evidently decided the program needed that sense of self-importance and pomposity after all, and Bob and Ray were dropped. It was still a busy year, with sessions for major GEG clients Xerox, Alcoa, Tastykake, and Kentucky Fried Chicken, plus a Bob and Ray induction into the National Broadcasters Hall of Fame. The latter entailed sharing a limo to the ceremonies in New Jersey with fellow honoree Lanny Ross. "We dozed a great deal of the way," Bob said.

The scene involves a handsome playwright, his leading lady (with whom he is not so secretly in love), a producer, and two backers, all of whose futures are riding on the reviews due to hit the stands at any moment. Another *Mary Backstayge* episode, right? No, it was the climactic sequence of the 1982 motion picture, *Author! Author!* The setting was the packed upstairs dining room at the legendary theater-district haunt, Sardi's, and the "diners" on that December 1981 afternoon were paid extras. Director Arthur Hiller was on his seventh take of a complicated tracking shot involving Al Pacino as a angst-ridden playwright, Dyan Cannon as his leading lady, Alan King as the overwrought producer, and, in their second movie, Bob and Ray as brothers Patrick and Jackie Dicker, investors in Pacino's *English with Tears*, "a serious play in a comic mode."

Goulding managed to thread his dialysis sessions around three days of shooting, but his stamina was being put to the test. Recalling Hiller's meticulousness, Elliott said, "He must have done that thirty times . . . *thirty takes!* . . . Ray got terribly tired. He was working despite physical problems."

In the story, Al Pacino and Alan King have a late lunch in a Chinese restaurant. (In reality, it was more like an early breakfast. To accommodate the eatery—Noodletown on Bowery Street—the scene had to be completed before the place opened at nine.) Finally noticing Bob and Ray at the table, a platter of fish bones and carcass in front of them, the distracted, late-arriving Pacino asks, "Who are you guys?"

"We're backing you with a million, three hundred thousand," Ray informs him.

"Of our own money," adds Bob, devouring a second order of spicy sea bass.

Bob and Ray played their scenes "very well," said Arthur Hiller, deflecting all credit for the outside-the-box thinking to Cis Corman, Martin Scorsese's longtime casting director, who had suggested them for the roles.

Aside from their several scenes, Hiller provided the two with only a couple of shreds of information about the movie. "Never did know what the story was," Elliott said. It was by design, a technique preferred by certain directors—Woody Allen among them—hoping to catch fresher, more honest performances. The less actors know, the theory goes, the less inclined they will be to over-think a role.

The device may have worked for *New York Times'* film critic Janet Maslin, who found Bob and Ray "ever-delightful." But, apparently, it did nothing for what she saw as the film's bigger problem: Hiller's lack of a "comic touch or madcap pacing."

Because of B&R's limited knowledge of the plot, when plugging *Author! Author!* six months later on NBC's *Late Night*, they were at a loss when David Letterman asked them if it was a comedy.

"I don't know what it is," Ray answered. "I just know what we've done. . . . Al Pacino—does he do comedy? . . . I'm dying to see it myself."

19

A Night of Two Stars

By 1981, Larry Josephson's early-morning WBAI-FM show had been off the air for nearly a decade. A counterpoint to the typically cheerful wake-up man, Josephson had discovered "a need for someone to be natural, to be grumpy," he told the *New Yorker* in 1967. In truth, he was beyond grumpy. "Gramps" on *Lassie* was grumpy; Josephson was angry.

"Sarcastic, maybe," he acknowledged, adding that "part of it was just having to get up so early and being kind of angry at that. . . . It wasn't Howard Stern, let's put it that way." Making fun of WBAI's counterculture image, and what Josephson termed "theological liberals," he sometimes called the station "*Mr. Rogers* for grown-ups." The six-year series, and another that followed, earned him a measure of acclaim and some impressive reviews in the *New York Times* and the *Los Angeles Times*, the latter describing Josephson as gliding around his studio "like a Jewish Buddha on casters."

Among the subjects on which Larry Josephson held strong opinions (he did not have any other kind) was radio. As a consultant charged with lining up entertainers for the Corporation of Public Broadcasting and NEA-sponsored Airlie Conference at Glen Cove, Long Island, it was Josephson who asked, "What about Bob and Ray?" The team, which had not been heard on radio in five years, readily accepted. The average age of the attendees—mostly young radio producers with some NPR staff—was twenty-five or thirty. "They just ate it up," Josephson said. The time was right, he felt, to bring Bob and Ray back to network radio.

"He came up to the office," Elliott said, "and urged us to think about it. And we did." And not for very long.

"They said, 'Sure kid,' Josephson recalled. "I don't know if in those words, but basically they didn't know who I was. . . . I think they were familiar with me as a New York radio personality. I think I paid them five hundred dollars or something for a six-month option. . . . And I sold it to NPR."

Informing Tom Koch of the new weekly series in April of 1982, Elliott wrote that NPR was hoping they would introduce a new soap-opera feature, one that is "as contemporary as possible . . . recognizable, that is." They were then off for a week to the St. Francis in San Francisco for a McDonald's salesmen convention, a top-dollar booking also featuring singers and dancers, and requiring them to reheat a half-hour's worth of some of their old routines plus a couple of Big Mac tie-ins. This was a far cry from Massachusetts roadhouse gigs and being paid in frozen lobsters and rubber checks.

Not familiar with the hit nighttime soaps—*Dallas*, *Knot's Landing*, *Dynasty*, and *Falcon Crest*—Koch saturated himself "in all of them at once," he wrote to Elliott two weeks later. "Of course, in one week, I didn't get the characters straightened out on any of them." In the end, Koch decided on a parody of the entire genre, which he titled *Garish Summit*. "It seems to me," he informed Elliott, "that establishing the rich family in the palatial mansion with family business, sleazy dealings, lots of intra-family back stabbing, et cetera, sets a stage that the listener will immediately recognize as being 'one of those.'"

With the addition of one or two new characters in each segment, Koch wrote in a later note accompanying the first batch of *Garish* scripts, "I think we now have a large enough cast to confuse ourselves as thoroughly as *Dallas* or any of the others."

The first two *Bob and Ray Public Radio Programs* were taped on May 13, 1982, in front of a live audience at RCA Studio A on West Forty-Fourth Street (today the site of the midtown headquarters of the IRS). Filling out the rest of the half-hours were reprises of vintage features, including *Hard Luck Stories*, *The Do-It-Yourselfer*, and the *Suspense* radio show takeoff, *Anxiety*, among others.

"It just keeps happening to us," Ray remarked to the *New York Times* at the time. "I suppose each new generation notices that we are there."

"The great thing about it," said Bob, "is that it enables us to reuse our old material."

"It's good to go back," Ray added. "On radio it was two of us and an engineer dozing in the control room. You could work in your T-shirt."

Additional shows were added for an initial run of eight episodes, two being recorded every Thursday, allowing for Ray's dialysis. Al Schaffer returned on sound effects, as did, a few shows later, Paul Taubman, by then in his seventies, at the organ.

Ray had "no energy," Josephson said, recalling his dialysis regimen. "He would come in looking sort of all pasty-faced. . . . And then when we started recording, he came alive and was a hundred percent *Ray*." Off the air, they were very laconic, Josephson continued. Bob was a "Manhattan sophisticate and he had friends in show business. I think Ray less so. Ray was more interested in home and Little League and stuff like that. . . . Ray had this dominant personality. Bob was quiet. He took care of the business, the scripts, and whatever business that was involved in their partnership. I never saw any conflict between them—ever. People have asked them why did their partnership last so long, and they said, 'Well, we made each other laugh.'"

Commenting to journalist Glenn Collins upon the NPR premiere, Ray said, "I think he's funny because he laughs at what I think is funny."

"They knew their work was good," Josephson said, but "they didn't brag about themselves." Partly, he felt, it was Bob's New England Yankee background. "They *did* have an ego," Josephson allowed, adding that sometimes "Ray would lose his temper if a script page was out of order or something like that," but then he would just forget about it. "He was quick to forgive. He didn't hold it in. He didn't hold grudges as far as I knew." The two "weren't all-consumed by show business or performing," he explained. "They came to the office or studio, or wherever. They did their work and they did it very well, and people loved them."

The final two shows wrapped just prior to the opening of *Bob and Ray: A retrospective* at New York's Museum of Broadcasting (now the Paley Center for Media) on June 15, 1982. Presented in daily, five-hour segments, the B&R faithful binged on twenty-five of the team's radio and TV programs, clips of their TV guest appearances and ad campaigns, spanning—at the time—their thirty-six years together. When attendance nearly tripled, the exhibit was extended for an additional two months.

Gracing the retrospective's program was an essay by Kurt Vonnegut, Jr., in which the author recalled visiting the duo's studio twenty years earlier, seeking work as a writer. He could still account for every single routine they did that day, as he noted in his 1975 foreword to *Write If You Get Work: The Best of Bob & Ray*, the first published compilation of the team's vignettes. He also remembered not getting the writing job.

"I feel delighted," Goulding said at the reception launching the exhibition. "It's an honor, and it's nice to have it happen when you're alive." Upon the exhibition's closing, a *USA Today* reporter visited Ray's twenty-fifth-floor office and discovered him just staring outside at the panoramic view. "I've been looking out this same window for thirty years," Ray lamented, but "I *still* don't know how to build a skyscraper."

A few months later, Bob, as a labor of love, recorded *The Best of Benchley*, a collection of Robert Benchley pieces, including "The Treasurer's Report" and "The Social Life of the Newt," for Caedmon Records. Heywood Hale Broun wrote the liner notes, pointing out that "Benchley is best when read aloud." At the same time, Ed Graham returned, writing and directing intermittently through the 1980s with B&R on specific accounts, including Tyson Foods and Time/Life. One of the pair's longest-running regional campaigns was for Arizona Bank. In a four-year series of TV, radio, and print ads—including a newspaper comic strip—they portrayed ten-gallon hat-wearing Easterners out West, representing the competing Bank of Bob and Ray.

Another order of NPR shows was taped in late 1983, each with a couple of new Koch bits, or, as Elliott put it in his September 20th request: "One *Garish* and two of anything in column B." One was a semi-regular spot mocking trendy consumer-affairs features, with Bob as product evaluation expert Hoyt Netley reporting on various bargain items, such as ten-year-old canned radishes and sponge-rubber doggie play toys imported from Belgium. Topical new sketches included *Down the Byways*, a parody of the Walter Cronkite news feature *On the Road with Charles Kuralt*. In *Byways*, Elliott, as avuncular Farley Girard, stumbled onto homespun stories like that of a knitting-mill operator (Goulding), who enabled senior citizens to feel "useful and productive" by putting them to work, weaving bolts of cotton fabric in sweatshop conditions. ("The old folks are required to clock in at seven o'clock in the morning and work at their looms for a ten-hour day.")

Around the same time, Larry Josephson was also pulling the strings behind *A Night of Two Stars* (a twist on the title of a 1982 television special, *Night of 100 Stars*). The show, to be presented at Carnegie Hall, was scheduled for two concert performances, May 31 and June 2, 1984. "It took me a year talking them into doing it," he said. "It was incredible. They said, 'Nobody will show up.' They were also worried about having to memorize all the material. . . . They insisted on a very low top of $35, and there were people outside scalping them for $75. . . . The minute I announced it, it was sold out."

At each performance, hearing only the first line of their signature bits, Bob and Ray connoisseurs instantly burst into applause. Nostalgia was the theme, the two announced in their brief opening remarks to the Carnegie Hall audience. Their first bit, an offer from the Bob and Ray Overstock, Surplus Warehouse, like the others to follow, was in reality from the pair's own real-life warehouse, a vast repository of routines from every B&R network and local series, in addition to *Two and Only* favorites. Some of their original scripts were more tattered than Charles the Poet's "manuscripts." They selected a *Mr. Trace* episode from their original 1951 NBC run. They also did a mock bank announcement:

The folks at the Friendly National Chemical Loan and Trust Company have lost the records of the bank—the records of your deposits and withdrawals. Now, if you could come in to our main office and tell us *honestly* how much you have in there, we'd be much obliged. We'll take your word for it.

A more recent feature the team performed, this from the WOR years, was *Dining Out with Bob and Ray*, a parody of on-air restaurant critics. The gourmet recommendations for the Carnegie crowd included Eddie's House of Iceberg Lettuce in Long Island City, the Waiters' Union Practice Hall on Tenth Avenue, and, for the budget minded, the Little Bit of Honduras Bar and Grill, where there is nothing on the menu but bananas, described as "green, yellow, yellow with brown speckles, and brown starting to turn black."

Following the intermission, and introductions of Paul Taubman and Al Schaffer, the two simulated a broadcast of *The Bob and Radio Public Radio Program*.

"We made no pretense," Elliott recalled. "We introduced it as, 'This is how the radio thing looked.' . . . And then we read bits."

The evenings concluded with a trio of the team's familiar soap spoofs, including *Mary Backstayge, Noble Wife*, spotlighting a certain headline-making consumer advocate referred to as "Ralph Crusader." ("Last month alone, over one hundred and ten thousand pairs of socks were recalled because the heels were attached with a 1979 type of stitching that could give way after being in a shoe for only fifteen minutes.")

The concerts were "incredibly successful," Josephson said, noting that the two nights alone made a five-figure profit. "They had fans outside the entrance on their way out, shoving autograph books at them. . . . I provided limos for them to go with their families out to dinner, or wherever, afterwards. Of course, I was left to sweep up the hall—a little self-pity on my part. They did intermittently express appreciation."

"I will never forget that feeling," Collie said. "We went both nights, and I remember as Dad and Ray walked out on stage, the entire audience rose to its feet, clapping. And that was really quite extraordinary."

"Spine-tingling, no doubt about it," said Bryant. "It was phenomenal, wonderful; the reverence for them was really nifty."

"I was applauding appreciatively," Liz said, "and looked down and the pearl on my solitaire ring—a very lovely pearl—was gone. The man in front of me who felt something whiz by his ear said, 'That's certainly giving a lot for your husband!' It flew off my setting and never was found . . . I remember that particularly—a woman would."

It was "the most exciting thing we've ever done," Ray told Johnny Carson a few weeks later on *The Tonight Show*.

The energy in that theater was "tremendous," said Liz. She fondly recalled the night when, getting dressed for the show, her husband walked their daughter Melissa onto the stage and pointed out a tiny dot on the floor where the leg of Vladimir Horowitz's piano was to be placed whenever he performed there. "Ray found that so amusing," Liz commented. "My daughter finds it more amusing that she and her dad stood on the stage of Carnegie Hall and that her dad was in his stocking feet."

~~~

A cruel side effect of Ray's illness was its impact on his appetite. "He wasn't able to eat steak for over a year," Liz said. ". . . Couldn't even look at one." As the dialysis was still a secret, he avoided showing up at Peter Luger's in Great Neck and facing an interrogation from its manager and his close friend, Carl Dickert, as to why he was not ordering his usual rare steak. In time, Dickert began to notice Ray and Liz's absence, and took it personally. He was very hurt, Liz said, because "he thought he'd done something. Finally, we had to tell him Ray was on dialysis."

Maintaining the subterfuge often entailed skillful tap-dancing, usually by Bob, who was at 2545 more often than Ray. In time, they sensed the *Tonight Show* staff probably suspected something as well.

Even since taking part in a cerebral palsy telethon shortly after moving to New York, the boys had accepted a number of charity and benefit invitations. At one of these events, in 1984, they were guests of honor at a fund-raising dinner for the Washington Ear, a non-profit reading service for the blind and physically handicapped. The organization provided both Elliott and Goulding with same-day round-trip tickets to Washington. As the boys arrived at LaGuardia on November 13th for New York Air's Flight 25, they were informed by the gate agent that, since their tickets were "non-revenue," they must show some form of identification. The problem was: neither Bob nor Ray had anything that was considered to be acceptable. Bob offered his voter-registration card, but that and other appeals fell on deaf ears. When traveling to and from air terminals by limousine, both found bulky, credit card-filled wallets to be unnecessary. (This was long before all passengers were required to carry photo IDs.)

The gate agent admitted that he recognized them, and one boarding passenger even offered his credit card to pay for new tickets, all to no avail. Their anguish and frustration rising, the pair tried to reach New York Air's public-relations department through their agent, Lester Lewis, but got nowhere. After watching Flight 25 depart without them, the two guests of honor returned to their homes by cab.

If the gate agent was rewarded for his steadfast adherence to company policy with a promotion to the executive suite, it was short-lived. New York Air folded two years later.

Elliott and Goulding did make it to the second *Night of 100 Stars* gala at Radio City Music Hall. The three-hour, ABC prime-time extravaganza—a benefit for the Actors Fund—took seven hours to tape, finishing after midnight. Guests were then taken by limo up Sixth Avenue for dinner at the New York Hilton. Ray and Liz were in one car, Bob and Lee in another, and, thanks to a seating arrangement mix-up, at separate tables. Ray and Liz were seated with a group of A-list celebrities, including John Forsythe—then starring in *Dynasty*—with whom Liz shared a dance.

"Imagine," she announced after returning to her table, "*me* dancing with somebody who's on TV!"

"Hey," Ray barked, "what do you think *I* do?!"

The Elliotts, meanwhile, were stuck at the far end of the room with intimates of the show's famous husband-and-wife producing team, Alexander H. Cohen and Hildy Parks—yet not intimate enough to be invited to sit at the same table with them. As Bob and Lee and the strangers in their circle of ten waited, the first drinks were slammed on the table. "For the most part," Bob said, "they were what had been ordered." The kitchen staff, it seems, was expecting the night to be over by one o'clock in the morning. "Before finishing the now-warm fruit cocktail," Bob went on, "the salad and chicken and peas arrived together; never mind the mood of the diners." The early morning found Bob and Lee returning to Seventy-Second street, finally crawling into bed around four o'clock.

From time to time over the years, friends would suggest that Bob and Ray try performing abroad. "England would love you guys," they would say. "Your dry, deadpan humor is just what the British go for."

Maybe.

The chance to find out was in the works.

20

THE ENGLISH CHANNEL

It was one-thirty on a chilly November morning when the British Airways flight with Ray, Liz, Bob, and Lee touched down at Heathrow. The foursome was met in the almost-deserted terminal by BBC representatives, who handed them a large envelope with a mumbled explanation as to its contents and an admonition that "it might be wise to keep it shut 'til you get to your hotel."

In 1985, Lester Lewis received an offer for the boys to appear on comedian Bob Monkhouse's popular Sunday-night show in London. The fee was next to nothing, but with airfares and hotel accommodations included, and more than generous expense money—enough, in fact, for a vacation after the show—it was too good to refuse, even with the prospect of playing before an audience that had never heard of them. It was a trade-off, Bob mused. "After all, we'd never heard of Monkhouse, either."

But Monkhouse had heard of them. Bob Monkhouse was a show business-steeped authority on all U.S. comedy performers, possessing a Milton Berle-like familiarity with their routines.

The couples' London quarters, the Hilton Kensington in Holland Park near the BBC's Shepherd's Bush studios, appeared to berth mainly airline personnel. The lobby bustled periodically, signifying flight arrivals or departures. Their rooms were tiny, barely large enough for one person to pass between the foot of the bed and the wall. "But we promised ourselves that wouldn't happen too often," Bob noted.

Ray and Liz joined Bob and Lee with a round of Scotch that Ray had found in a dispenser in the hall. It was then that they decided to open the envelope. It was a "moving moment," Bob observed, when they stared at a large mound of English currency that fluttered onto the bed. After some discussion—and more Scotch—they concluded it must be their per diem money, a "generous hands-across-the-sea gesture, maybe" Bob said, "to relieve us of the tax ramifications had we been paid by check."

"It wasn't even divided," Liz said. "It was just a big envelope of cash. . . . I can remember the two of them counting it out: 'This for you, this for me. This for you, this for me. This for you, this for me' . . . we were hysterical laughing at them, Lee and I."

"Two times in a row," Bob said, "we couldn't get it right, going over it and over it. . . . Finally, we said, 'The hell with it,' and went downstairs."

In the lobby, Bob and Ray woke the clerk, and stashed the money in a lockbox. After a few hours of sleep, the two "crazy Yanks," as Bob put it, returned to remove the envelope from the safe, under the incredulous eye of the very same clerk. "He couldn't figure what was going on," Elliott said. This time, they finally succeeded in counting and dividing the loot down to the last ha'penny.

Between rehearsals and shopping forays, the group met at a restaurant/bar off the lobby. "It was the Crystal Room or something," Liz said. ". . . And we started noticing the same girls were there all the time and we then realized it was a pickup place."

"The hotel told us they were airline stewardesses," Bob recalled.

He and Lee also managed a scenic side trip to Edinburgh by train along the rugged English coast. Their accommodations at the Railway Hotel directly overlooked the railroad tracks. The constant din of in- and outbound trains conveniently freed them of having to rely on morning wake-up calls.

"We went to Stratford and a couple of places—little mini-tours," Liz said. "We would have loved to have gone with Bob and Lee but couldn't because of dialysis. . . . But, in London, it was walk-in dialysis." After the Elliotts' Scotland excursion, Ray and Liz related some of their London adventures, including a tour of Madame Tussaud's Wax Museum. Aware of his slowly waning health, Ray summed up their visit: "It was all we could do to get out of there," he said. "They wanted to make me part of the exhibits."

As for the Monkhouse appearance, B&R chose "The Raconteur" and "The Slow Talker," both of which, like several Two and Only pieces, enjoyed a long shelf life. The dress rehearsal, in front of a studio audience, did not "go well at all," Elliott said. Adjustments were quickly made—for

Monkhouse. On the air, his setup was more focused—better preparing the Brits to be whisked off to Bob and Ray fairyland. "It's just amazing," he added, "that it has taken forty years to bring them to London." It worked. The laughs were long and loud, though perhaps not reaching the heights of Liz and Lee's watching their husbands trying to divide the expense money.

Back at 2545, Hartford Insurance sought GEG's help with a pressing image problem: the company, with its ever-present giant stag trademark, was perceived as being just another huge, impersonal institution—a problem made all the more difficult because it was true. B&R were not deterred; they had come up against the truth before. To humanize the outfit, eight thirty-second TV spots were filmed, featuring Bob as Wally Ballou interviewing Ray in various occupations. In the guise of each character, he would refer to the appropriate coverage he had with Hartford, prompting Ballou to interject, "Oh, the company with the moose."

"It's a stag," Ray replied.

GEG specialized in such challenges. After all, they had also helped introduce Borden's Pudding on a Stick. Fortunately, they had completed the Hartford campaign, as well as thirty-second Pizza Hut spots directed by David Steinberg, before Ray fell on a patch of ice and broke his humerus at the shoulder. The pain was brutal: he could not sleep for a long period of time, during which he lost fifteen pounds. Then, in the late summer of 1986, he developed a nagging throat condition. It was serious enough to push back scheduled guest-shots and another season of the NPR series.

The last thirteen programs were taped in November and December— as before, two every Thursday—but this time, in deference to Ray, at a smaller recording studio in the Graybar Building, and without a studio audience. "It was hard for him," Josephson said, "to do the audience thing." Plus, by then, Ray's falsetto had taken a toll on his vocal chords. "Often times," he once said, "I've left the studio with my voice in a sling."

Audio cassettes and, later, compact discs of the NPR shows were marketed by Larry Josephson in connection with GEG on his *Bob and Ray* website. Additional volumes from various B&R series were added incrementally, consisting of content from their syndication library. Material also came from devoted fans who over the decades, taped, collected and traded the routines like audio baseball cards.

The Bob and Ray Public Radio Program, comprised of wall-to-wall bits, ran on and off for five years, winning the Peabody Award for Elliott and Goulding (their third), and Josephson, who produced the thirty-one half-hour shows. At the Hotel Pierre ceremonies, Bob accepted on behalf of his partner, as the event fell on a Wednesday.

Happily for Josephson's former WBAI listeners, the success did nothing to dampen his "grumpy" reputation. "Larry Josephson," Ray once remarked on the air, "has known the thrill of victory and the agony of defeat. And he still can't decide which he likes best."

As in any producer-talent relationship, there are going to be "tensions," Josephson said of his B&R experience. "There were moments of difficulty where they didn't think they got enough money, or whatever." When negotiating with their attorney, Stan Schewel, Josephson said his lawyer found them "very difficult to deal with. It's sort of, 'If you don't like it, take your business to another *Bob and Ray* company.'" Basically, they "weren't that needy; they weren't that anxious to work," Josephson stated. ". . . And they deserved deference, too. They were stars in my mind. . . . Maybe there were sometimes where Bob felt or Ray felt I wasn't responsive. I'm not a show-biz type; I'm not a Broadway type."

While not, perhaps, a show-biz type, on his website, Josephson—to Elliott's consternation—proclaims himself to be Bob and Ray's "producer for 28 years and counting," more than two and a half decades after completing the last show. "That offends the most," Bob said. "Proprietorship, like he discovered us." Similarly, online solicitations by Josephson for "contributions" do not sit well with Elliott. "It's embarrassing," he said, though acknowledging, Larry "does appreciate what we do, I'll give him that."

The two have not exactly burned up the telephone wires, talking to each other in recent years, although, Josephson said. "Lately Bob has sent me several warm letters." He's a colleague, he explained, not a personal friend. "I've never been inside their homes." (Given how few times Bob and Ray were in each other's homes, Larry Josephson can't feel too bad.)

In June 1987, the team was at the Waldorf Astoria to accept the Orson Welles Award for Creative Excellence at the Twentieth Annual ANA/ RAB (Association of National Advertising / Radio Advertising Bureau)

Workshop. But when their *Night of Two Stars Live at Carnegie Hall* was nominated for the Grammy Awards' Best Comedy Album category the same year, Ray decided the last thing he needed was another round-trip flight to L.A., only to sit for over three-hours in the stuffy Shrine Auditorium in his tux, with a one-in-six chance of winning (against fellow nominees Steven Wright, Bette Midler, George Carlin, Bill Cosby, and Rodney Dangerfield). Then, reflecting on the same odds, Bob decided that it was the last thing *he* needed, too. Neither made the trip. (Cosby won.)

"I know," Mark Goulding said about his dad, "he never wanted to let Bob down. I bet there was a lot more work that they could have done, but my dad's dialysis situation kind of stopped it from happening. . . . I'm sure it kind of weighed on him and stressed him out. It wasn't like he was done with five hours of dialysis and ready to go. The rest of the day was more or less shot."

"He'd grab a soup at the deli on the way home," Tom Goulding said. "He was just a trouper. . . . I was always impressed, the way he persevered through that. It was really hell."

As Mark recalled, "Friends who worked at the deli told me my dad would come in and just kind of lean on the counter with his head on his forearm, just kind of bracing himself. Then," he added, "he'd come home and crash; he was just kind of wiped out. . . . Obviously, it got more draining the older he got, but this went on for years and years and years."

To help pass the hours at the hospital, Ray kept the dialysis unit entertained with serialized, soap-opera scenarios, featuring the attending staff members as characters. Then, at home in the evening, he would relate these fictional stories. "He invented this entire second family," Melissa recalled. The stories were "so clever and the characters were so real, so ridiculous, and just so funny."

"He was a wonderful grandfather, and great with babies," Ray, Jr., said. "They would reach out for him to hold them whenever they saw him. He would play with them—even on his bed when he got home from dialysis. My kids have very fond memories of 'Pop Pops.' Tommy's kids also adored their 'Gramps,' as did Melissa's daughter, Rebecca."

Tom's son recalled his grandfather's backyard "magic bush." When Tom and his family would visit, he commented, "There'd be a toy or surprise hidden in the bush. 'Let's go check the bush!' The joy and anticipation were special."

In time, to lessen the number of out-of-own dialysis treatments, Ray's doctors scheduled back-to-back sessions on two consecutive days, the last one just prior to his departure from New York. This worked especially well for one-shot *Tonight Show* trips, thus eliminating any treatments in L.A. But sometimes it took a toll. As guests of Garrison Keillor on *The Prairie Home Companion* at the World Theater in St. Paul, in May of 1987, Goulding's voice was noticeably raspy. "He did not look well," Bob said, "though never complained to any extent."

He was "showing it," Liz said, referring to the effects of double dialysis sessions. "He had had to do two fast ones, and then get on the flight, and then get up there."

In his foreword to *The New! Improved! Bob and Ray Book*, the third published collection of their scripts, Keillor had "imagined what it would be like to meet them in person." The opportunity presented itself when B&R and their wives were invited to an after-party at his house. But, following the broadcast, the boys were suddenly thanked and then, with apologies, informed that the party had been canceled. The foursome, according to Bob, could not help but feel that Ray's shaky appearance had somehow made Keillor uncomfortable.

"It was a little strange," Liz said. "We did speculate because we didn't know. Ray didn't think he showed anything. Of course, he also lost his wallet on that trip and that was causing him some frantic moments."

As special guests on the 1988 CBS sitcom, *Coming of Age*, Elliott and Goulding were back in California for a week on the sprawling Universal lot. Set in an upscale Arizona retirement community, the series starred Paul Dooley and Phyllis Newman.

Having just viewed his DVD of B&R's episode, executive producer Barry Kemp felt it was "arguably the best" of the entire series, short-lived though it was. It was plain to see, he said, that Ray was "having a very difficult time trying not to laugh because Bob is cracking him up. . . . Those were the best takes we got because there were several breakups. They were just flat-out funny. . . . Everybody from the writing staff to the cast was very excited to have them on. . . . We all had a history with them—some of us maybe slightly more distant than others. Obviously, they're icons."

In the episode, Ray, as Colonel Pat Peck, in full military dress uniform adorned with an impressive display of fruit salad, was the intractable president of the residents' association. He played the character with the authoritative tone of a man used to being in command and not being questioned. Bob, as the colonel's brother, Peter, was the association's sergeant-at-arms. A man apparently accustomed to doing the colonel's bidding, Peter had a quieter, but equally steadfast, demeanor. "He tried to appear stoic," Kemp noted, "but you could see him trying not to crack Ray up."

The two were that episode's antagonists, intent on thwarting the tenants' desire to have cable TV installed. It was a challenge for both. We were "hampered," Bob said, trying to make the audience laugh, all the while focusing on the significance of their scenes in relation to the rest of the storyline. He added that memorizing dialog had become very difficult.

"Interesting perspective," said Kemp, informed of Bob's reaction. "You never would have known it looking at the show."

But, then, keeping others from "knowing it" is part of a performer's job.

Staying at the Sheraton Universal adjacent to the studio enabled Ray to grab some rest following dialysis at Cedars-Sinai Hospital. He did look "kind of frail," Kemp said. "We were aware that there was some health issue, but not the particulars. Even though you could tell he had lost some weight, gosh, his voice was strong. I certainly bought the fact that he was a colonel. . . . Had the show survived, we undoubtedly would have brought them back because they would have been part of that community."

"We went to the dress rehearsal with him," Ray, Jr., said, "and he had trouble walking. And, of all things, my father could walk miles when he was in good shape. And that was kind of hard for us to see. It's sad when you see the guy who used to scare the bejeebers out of you with the raising of his voice, now becomes a frail, older man. And he wasn't that old."

By the last half of the eighties Ray had slowed down considerably. Taping the NPR shows was a grind. In 1988, two proposed Smucker's radio spots for the Lois Wyse agency did not sell. A couple of weeks later, at a GEG taping session, Ray's voice was "bad," Elliott remembered. "It was something in the nature of an audition, and I don't know whether he knew. *I* knew at the time nobody was going to buy this, and we passed it off as a touch of the flu or something."

On the 17th of June, Ray underwent surgery at North Shore to stop internal hemorrhaging. The doctors gave him a 20 percent chance of surviving the procedure. Somehow he did, and upon his return home on July 1st, Liz told Bob that her husband was down to 143 pounds.

"He worked unbelievably long," Bob said, "and put up with dialysis for twelve years. I was amazed at how much he could do. He would get tired very easily toward the end. And he would still take the subway."

"He never complained about it," Liz said. "Never made anybody feel it was an effort, no matter how he felt."

"He just didn't," Melissa agreed. "I think that's really remarkable."

Taking the subway also meant trudging through the crowded, subterranean concourses of Grand Central Station, plus connecting to the Long Island Railroad at Woodside, Queens.

Ray managed to reward himself along the way, stopping for clam chowder at the Grand Central Oyster Bar, or a favorite French bakery to bring home a couple of baguettes, Mark recalled. "He loved food—that was his thing. . . . I don't know if it was Bryant or me who was getting ready to go jogging, and my dad said, 'What are you doing?' And I said, 'Going to run a couple of miles.' And he said, 'What are you going to do that for?' Somehow, fitness wasn't his thing." The entire Goulding family, Mark explains, has this kidney and heart issue. "It's like we have this somewhat loaded gun that my dad watched his parents and siblings die from. . . . And I don't want to load that gun. . . . I'm getting on a big health kick."

Ray was unable to join Pat Weaver, Henry Morgan, and others at an October 1988 dinner in Washington, at the opening of the Museum of Broadcasting exhibit at the National Portrait Gallery. Bob represented the team, simply attributing his partner's absence to ill health. He did this again, a few months later in Los Angeles—accompanied by their original

TV accomplice, Audrey Meadows—at the museum's *Evening with Bob and Ray* presentation, and again a month after that, at the opening of the MGM studios at Disneyworld in Florida.

Though the two kept in contact, there developed, as Bob put it, a "kind of tacit acceptance" of the fact that Ray would probably not be able to work, at least in the foreseeable future. With Ray's encouragement, Bob went it alone on a few ventures, the first being an episode of *Newhart*, in which he portrayed the star's father.

"It was either at my suggestion," Bob Newhart said, "or they said, 'How would you feel about Bob Elliott playing your father?' I said, 'Yeah!' right away . . . I looked forward to when we weren't shooting and I could just sit in a director's chair next to Bob and ask him about *Bob and Ray* and *Monitor* and all that went on."

In 1989, Bob contributed "rebuttals" to his son Chris's book, *Daddy's Boy: A Son's Shocking Account of Life with a Famous Father*, a send-up of *Mommie Dearest*, Christina Crawford's scathing expose on her late adoptive mother, Joan Crawford. In June, Bob filmed scenes for the Bill Murray feature, *Quick Change*, essaying the role of a cowardly bank guard. (Watching Elliott's understated performance, wrote the *New Yorker*'s Terrance Rafferty, is "like sitting in on a master class.") Bob also made multiple appearances on *American Radio Company of the Air*, a new Garrison Keillor radio series.

By late 1989, Ray was being transported by ambulance to dialysis sessions. As he was no longer coming to 2545, the team gave up their thirty-four-year Graybar Building stronghold, one of more than eighty properties—including the Empire State Building and the Flatiron Building—owned or controlled by Helmsley-Spear, Inc.

"We're fans," read the firm's letter, cheerfully letting GEG out of a lease with three years remaining, plus a hefty rent. But, then, the letter had been precipitated by one from Elliott, who, having first been turned down by the building manager, wrote directly to Harry S. Helmsley, the eighty-year-old, multibillionaire head of the real-estate empire and devoted husband of Leona, the just-crowned "Queen of Mean."

"I laid out the real, true sob story that it was," Bob said, "and it got to him. I was just grateful that the letter never found its way to Leona." Bob packed up everything: Ray's desk went to his house, and Bob's to his office at the East Seventy-Second Street apartment. GEG's two Ampex tape machines found new homes at the company's museum in Redwood City, California.

The following year, Bob and Lee were transplanted to L.A. when Chris's series, *Get a Life*, was picked-up by the then-new Fox network. Bob was cast as the bathrobe-wearing father of Chris's character, a thirty-year-old paperboy who lived in an apartment above his parents' garage. Bob was also asked to play his signature character, Wally Ballou, on Al Franken's NBC series, *LateLine*. Upon hearing his up-cut sign-on, "—allou reporting from—" the staff and crew burst into laughter. In the control room, a young, ambitious network suit suggested to director Ken Levine that he ask Bob to do it again with just a tad more nasal inflection. "Look," Levine recalled telling the staffer, "with all due respect, I'm not going to go out there and tell Bob Elliott how to do Wally Ballou."

The last days of his life, Liz said, Ray knew he was dying. Following dialysis on his birthday, he told the hospital unit, "This is goodbye. I'm not going back." Dependence on an ambulance and a wheelchair was "existing, not living," he said. He told the family not to be upset, Liz continued. "'You know,' he said, 'God's got a big show for me and He said He wants me to emcee it and I need to rehearse. So I've got to get up there.' So he kind of broke the ice with the kids and made fun of it."

Raymond Walter Goulding died at home on Saturday morning, March 24, 1990, four days after his sixty-eighth birthday. "To be honest," said Ray, Jr., who twenty years later would be diagnosed with the same disease and has himself been on dialysis, "I don't know how he did it for twelve years; I really don't. I mean, he knew this was his life from here on out."

At her father's wake, Melissa had the magazine sketch of the lighthouse that her father had given her when she was in junior high, and which the two had playfully traded back and forth for years. "I tucked it into his pocket and it was a little sacred moment between us," she said. "It was so significant because it was something we always shared, and it was the last passing of the picture."

All six of the Goulding children gave readings at the funeral service, which was held at St. Mary's in Manhasset. "The one thing we didn't do, and sometimes I wish we had," said Ray, Jr., "was to extemporize and just say something about our father. But we never did. I think we all might have wanted to, but that would be more personal than out in public."

"Liz had asked me if I would like to say anything," Bob remembered, "and I would have, but I couldn't. It was such an emotional thing."

Adding to the emotion for the family was the presence of thirty-nine-year-old Barbara, having been diagnosed with multiple sclerosis, and, noted Liz, not "standing too steadily" as she gamely tried to get through the Twenty-third Psalm.

Initially, Barbara had had "neurological concerns," Bryant explained. "It took them a long time to figure out that she had it. . . . While we were all emotional, her emotions led to physical challenges. . . . From my dad's death on, her multiple sclerosis got dramatically worse. I think the emotional toll of that was huge."

Barbara's battle ended at age forty-three, on August 22, 1994. "I'm thankful," Liz reflected, "that Ray did not have to live through the utter devastation of her loss, and I'd like to think of them together now."

Recalling the motorcade to the cemetery along Northern Boulevard, Larry Josephson said, "Every intersection was blocked off as the cortège passed so they didn't have to stop for lights, or something. That, I think, says a lot about how Ray was thought of in his community. That amazed me; I was impressed by that."

The distance was "about twelve miles," Bryant noted. "An unforgettable twelve miles."

Inevitably, some incidents related to Ray's passing produced laughter, including an initial meeting between the family and the funeral director, who, Ray, Jr., said, had "no idea who Dad was. And all the kids and my mother were sitting there and he wanted to find out more about this Ray Goulding. And we were just talking about [the fact that] he liked the Red Sox, and he was on the radio, and dah-dah-dah. We were there a good hour. And as we were coming out Bryant is the one who said, 'Hey, how come no one mentioned Dad's temper?'"

At the cemetery, the thought was expressed among Ray's sons that if the Red Sox ever were to win the World Series, they should all meet at their dad's grave. "We talked about that," Ray, Jr., said. "But, back then, it was a pipe dream." When the Sox finally accomplished the feat in 2004, he added, "We were on the phone that whole night."

"That was big," Tom said. "I'm kind of embarrassed that I'm a sixty-year-old idiot and my heart's still hanging on my sleeve like that. . . . It was almost as if we didn't want to gather for the game because you didn't want to jinx it."

"Only in retrospect," Liz said, "have I realized what it must have meant for Ray to give up so much of his life with so much still planned to do. He never let our family feel the impact of his illness, and so we all took our lead from him and took it in stride as Ray seemed to do. . . . Ray never complained about his hardship. He worried specifically about what it would do to Bob and his career."

"It was a marriage, let's face it," Bob said. "It was a very close thing that you can't compare to anything. . . . If it had been reversed, I think he would have felt the same."

Bryant told the *New York Times*: "I think Dad spent as much time over the years with Bob as with my mother."

Though the sadness can now be put away slowly, Bob wrote to Tom Koch a few days later, the memories can not. "We had such great times for so many years that any rough spots we may have faced have faded into nothing. It was, indeed, a fortuitous bit of fate that brought us together in the first place, and a lucky star that shone over us both that allowed us to chalk up a forty-four-year association!"

Jack Sidebotham and his wife, Bernadette, were somewhere having a drink when they learned that Ray had died. Sidebotham suddenly found himself doodling on a cocktail napkin. The finished drawing was a cartoon depicting Harry Piel, a tear on his cheek, standing next to a gravestone marked, "R.I.P., Bert." Coming from the open grave was a caption balloon of Bert saying, "Lighten up, Harry."

Though not quite sure if Liz would find it appropriate, with Bernadette's encouragement, he went ahead and sent it to her. "She called me," he remembered, "and said she had loved it and had copies made for all the family. It rests on a shelf in her living room today."

‐‐〜

In the winter of 2004, Lee Elliott began experiencing dizziness and balance problems, precipitating a series of tests at Lennox Hill Hospital. She eventually received a diagnosis of hydrocephalus. After a spirited, nearly decade-long battle, she died at home in Maine, on April 26, 2012, with her family at her side. She had her "wry smile and was rolling her eyes" until the very end, Amy said. "She didn't want to leave the party."

Bob now resides full-time in their summer home. It's what they had always wanted, said Collie—the privacy and isolation. At least now there is a generator. "They had times up there where everything went out and it was just horrendous. . . . Trees down and nobody could get out to them."

Bob's days are filled with two active brother-and-sister miniature schnauzers, Bert and Harriet, the *New York Times* crossword puzzle, and the *Post*'s Sudoku. It seems he is always within a few days of a visit from another of his adult children and grandchildren. With his son Chris, and Chris's daughters, Abby and Bridey's successes, Bob is the patriarch of three generations in the business of comedy. And judging by the ink-clogged centers of the small *e*'s and capital *B*'s in his fifty-year-old Olympia Manual Standard typed letters, he appears to be holding his own in a two-decade tussle with his kids against learning the computer.

But when it comes to Bob and Ray, Collie said, "As modest and unassuming as Dad is, he has a finger on the pulse of everything they did."

ACKNOWLEDGMENTS

Like all of Bob and Ray's work, this book, too, is the product of a collaboration; one spanning several years during which I have been the beneficiary of the generosity and patience of Bob Elliott and Liz Goulding. In personal interviews, and in letters, e-mails, and countless phone conversations, both extended unfailing kindness, support, and limitless amounts of their time. Liz's discerning reflections and anecdotes were invaluable. Bob escorted me through all aspects of the team's forty-four year partnership. Whether relating their successes or disappointments, he was equally candid; no special provisos as to content were ever requested. Bob also made available voluminous files of B&R correspondence, clippings, scripts and recordings—though I sometimes wondered if this was merely to head-off my interminable questions. He also provided numerous photographs which compliment these pages.

I am similarly indebted to Ray's sister, Ann King, for her vivid recollections of her brother's childhood years growing up in Lowell, and again later when serving as the team's secretary. I owe special thanks to both families—Ray, Jr., Tom, Bryant, Mark, and Melissa Goulding, together with the Elliotts: Collie, Shannon, Amy, Bob, Jr., and Chris—for their perceptive insights and guidance. I am also deeply grateful to Ed Graham for his council and introspective observations, particularly with regard to the GEG advertising and animation business.

Many fellow artists, executives, and craftsmen with whom Bob and Ray were engaged on one project or another graciously agreed to be interviewed. For sharing their comments and reminiscences, I thank Joe Alonzo, Nat Asch, George Atkins, Marion Brash, Jack Burns, Jack Carter, Joe Cabibbo, Dick Cavett, Fred B. Cole, Milton DeLugg, Mort Drucker,

Al Feldstein, Stan Freberg, Joseph Hardy, Arthur Hiller, Larry Josephson, Les Keiter, Barry Kemp, Ruth Kennedy, Tom Koch, Cloris Leachman, Norman Lear, Johnna Levine, Ken Levine, Grey Lockwood, Jeffrey Lyons, Jayne Meadows, Nick Meglin, Bob Newhart, Keith Olbermann, Bill Persky, Carl Reiner, Jack Riley, Peter Roberts, Jonathan Schwartz, Harry Shearer, Jack Sidebotham, Mike Smollin, David Steinberg, Grant Tinker, Ciro Torchia, and Rocco Urbisci. In addition, my gratitude for an abundance of favors is extended to author and Boston media authority Donna L. Halper, Essanay Silent Film Museum historian David Kiehn, Miles Kreuger's Institute of the American Musical, Game Show Network television historian David Schwartz, and Ron Simon, radio and television curator at the Paley Center for Media.

Acknowledgments are also owed Ben Alba, Bill Allen, Steve Allen, Jr., MD, Woody Allen, Kaye Ballard, Hank Behar, Bruce Benderson, Eugene Bergmann, Jill Bernstein, Roz Bernstein, Gloria Bremer, Robin Commagère, Jim Cox, Warren Debenham, Butch D'Ambrosio, Chauncey Doud, James Gavin, Lois Balk Gibson, Penelope Glass, Richard Hayes, Andrew Hunt, Fritz Jacobi, Ross Klavan, Mark Lashley, Brandi Brice Pollock, Dan Pollock, Paul Pumpian, Carl Samrock, Tony Sauber, Bernadette Sidebotham, Kathryn Sigismund, and Karl Tiedemann. I am beholden also to David Letterman for writing the foreword; to Ralph Shirak for his firsthand accounts of the realities facing the 104th Infantry in Lorraine and the Ardennes; to Dan and Carol Gillespie for their technical assistance with many of the photos, in addition to their undying encouragement; and to Stu Miller for literary representation of the highest order.

A bow, too, to some close friends, each a highly respected veteran in the business of creating comedy: Charlie Hauck, who read a very early chapter, and later, Ron Clark, and my writing partner for forty years, Elias Davis (who once walked nineteen blocks through a blizzard to watch Bob and Ray broadcast at WOR) for their incisive comments, criticisms, and suggestions on the manuscript. At Applause, I thank Jaime Nelson; copyeditor Lon Davis for catching my grammatical errors—that is, the ones that slipped past Ron and Elias—and Marybeth Keating for her advice and cheerful guidance throughout the entire editing process. Lastly, I owe special thanks to Group Publisher John Cerullo for his initial response to the project; it all started with John.

BIBLIOGRAPHY

UNPUBLISHED SOURCES

Besson III, Major John J. "Operations of Company D, 104th Infantry Division in the Attack of December 22–24, 1944," Staff Department monograph, Infantry School, Fort Benning, Georgia, 1949–1950

Bob Elliott Script Collection (private)

Earle Doud Script Collection (private), courtesy of Chauncey Doud

Gene Klavan Papers (private), unpublished memoir, 2004, courtesy of Ross Klavan

Larry Josephson Papers (private), Johnny Carson correspondence

Vic Cowen Script Collection (private), courtesy of Terri Collin

LIBRARY AND ARCHIVAL SOURCES

Academy of Motion Picture Arts and Sciences, Margaret Herrick Library, *Variety* archive, "The Bob & Ray Show" reviews, July 4, 1951, July 18, 1951, November 28, 1951, July 9, 1952, October 15, 1952, and April 29, 1952; "Happy Days" review, July 10, 1970; "The Jonathan Winters Show" review, February 24, 1965

Boston Public Library, Hotel Touraine Collection, the *Boston Globe*, September 8, 1897, March 19, 1898, and March 25, 1898

Donna L. Halper Research Archive, Boston media history, John Matheson obituaries, the *Boston Globe* and the *New York Times*, March 28, 1940

Miami-Dade Public Library, Tatem Wofford file

RADIO/TELEVISION ARCHIVAL SOURCES

Archive of American Television

Karl Tiedemann Collection (private)

Keith Olbermann Collection (private)

The Paley Center for Media

Sheryl Smith Collection (private)

Tom Goulding Collection (private)
UCLA Film and TV Archive
Vic Cowen Collection (private)

BOOKS

Allen, Fred. *Treadmill to Oblivion*. Boston: Little, Brown, 1956.

Amburn, Ellis. *Subterranean Kerouac: The Hidden Life of Jack Kerouac*. New York: St. Martin's Press, 1999.

Armbruster, Ann. *The Life and Times of Miami Beach*. New York: Alfred A. Knopf, 1995.

Barber, Red. *The Broadcasters*. New York: The Dial Press, 1970.

Bilby, Kenneth. *The General: David Sarnoff and the Rise of the Communications Industry*. New York: Harper & Row, 1986.

Biondi, Joan. *Miami Beach Memories: A Nostalgic Chronicle of Days Gone By*. Guilford, CT: Globe Pequot Press, 2007.

Brooks, Tim, and Earle Marsh. *The Complete Guide to Prime Time Network TV Shows*. New York: Ballantine, 1979.

Burrows, Abe. *Honest, Abe*. Boston: Little Brown, 1980.

Buxton, Frank, and Bill Owen. *The Big Broadcast: 1920–1950*. New York: Viking Press, 1972.

Caesar, Sid, with Bill Davidson. *Where Have I Gone? An Autobiography*. New York: Crown, 1982.

Carlin, George, with Tony Hendra. *Last Words*. New York: Free Press, 2009.

Cole, Hugh M. *U.S. Army in World War II, European Theater of Operations, The Ardennes: Battle of the Bulge*. Washington, D.C.: Office of the Chief of Military History, Department of the Army (no date).

Conway, Lorie. *Boston The Way It Was*. Boston: WGBH Educational Foundation, 1966.

Cox, Jim. *Radio Speakers*. Jefferson, NC: McFarland, 2007.

Davis, Tom. *Thirty-Nine Years of Short-Term Memory Loss*. New York: Grove Press, 2009.

Dunning, John. *On the Air: The Encyclopedia of Old-Time Radio*. New York and Oxford: Oxford University Press, 1998.

Dworkin, Susan. *Miss America, 1945: Bess Myerson's Own Story*. New York: Newmarket Press, 1987.

Elliott, Bob, and Ray Goulding. *From Approximately Coast to Coast . . . It's The Bob and Ray Show*. New York: Atheneum, 1983.

———. *The New! Improved! Bob & Ray Book*. New York: G.P. Putnam's Sons, 1985.

———. *Write If You Get Work: The Best of Bob and Ray*. New York: Random House, 1975.

Everitt, David. *King of the Half Hour: Nat Hiken and the Golden Age of TV Comedy*. Syracuse, NY: Syracuse University Press, 2001.

Frank, Gerold. *Judy*. New York: Harper & Row, 1975.

G3 Section, 26th Infantry Division, ed. *26th Infantry Division: The "Yankee" Division in W.W.II*. Wels, Austria (no date).

Gavin, James. *Intimate Nights: The Golden Age of New York Cabaret*. New York: Limelight Editions, 1992.

Gelbart, Larry. *Laughing Matters*. New York: Random House, 1998.

Goldman, William. *The Season: A Candid Look at Broadway*. New York: Harcourt, Brace & World, 1969.

Harris, Michael David. *Always on Sunday: Ed Sullivan: An Inside View*. New York: Meredith Press, 1968.

Henry III, William A. *The Great One: The Life and Legend of Jackie Gleason*. New York: Doubleday, 1992.

Hill, Doug, and Jeff Weingrad. *Saturday Night: A Backstage History of Saturday Night Live*. New York: William Morrow, 1986.

Jaker, Bill, Frank Sulek, and Peter Kanze. *The Airwaves of New York*. Jefferson, NC: McFarland, 1998.

Kendrick, Alexander. *Prime Time: The Life of Edward R. Murrow*. Boston: Little Brown, 1969.

Kiehn, David. *Broncho Billy and the Essanay Film Company*. Berkeley, CA: Farwell Books, 2003.

Klavan, Gene. *We Die At Dawn*. Garden City, NY: Doubleday, 1964.

Lax, Eric. *Woody Allen: A Biography*. New York: Alfred A. Knopf, 1991.

Lee, Peggy. *Miss Peggy Lee: An Autobiography*. New York: Donald I. Fine, 1989.

Lewis, Jerry, and James Kaplan. *Dean & Me: A Love Story*. New York: Doubleday, 2005.

McCabe, John. *Mr. Laurel and Mr. Hardy*. Garden City, NY: Doubleday, 1961.

Meadows, Audrey, with Joe Daley. *Love, Alice: My Life as a Honeymooner*. New York: Crown, 1994.

Moldea, Dan E. *The Hoffa Wars: Teamsters, Rebels, Politicians, and the Mob*. New York: Paddington Press, 1978.

Moore, Deborah Dash. *To The Golden Cities: Pursuing the American Jewish Dream in Miami and L.A.* New York: Macmillan, 1994.

Nachman, Gerald. *Raised on Radio*. New York: Pantheon Books, 1998.

———. *Seriously Funny: The Rebel Comedians of the 1950s and 1960s*. New York: Pantheon Books, 2003.

Palladino, Major General Ralph A., ed. *History of a Combat Regiment 1639–1945:104th Infantry Regiment*. Baton Rouge, LA.: Army and Navy, 1960.

Paley, William S. *As it Happened: A Memoir*. Garden City, NY: Doubleday, 1979.

Passman, Arnold. *The Deejays*. New York: Macmillan, 1971.

Reidelbach, Maria. *Completely Mad: A History of the Comic Book and Magazine*. Boston: Little, Brown, 1991.

Richmond, Peter. *Fever: The Life and Music of Peggy Lee*. New York: Henry Holt, 2006.

Robertson, James D. *The Great American Beer Book*. Ottawa, IL and Thornwood, NY: Caroline House, 1978.

Simon, Neil. *Rewrites: A Memoir*. New York: Simon & Schuster, 1996.

Sklar, Rick. *Rocking America: An Insider's Story*. New York: St. Martin's Press, 1984.

Smith, Sally Bedell. *In All His Glory: The Life of William S. Paley*. New York: Simon & Schuster, 1990.

Sterling, Jack, with William C. Vance. *So Early in the Morning, or My Topsy-Turvy Day*. New York: Thomas Y. Crowell, 1958.

Thompson, Harry. *Peter Cook: A Biography*. London: Hodder and Stoughton, 1997 (sourcing: Cook, Lin. *Something Like Fire*. London: Arrow Books [an imprint of Random House], 2003).

Tinker, Grant, and Bud Rukeyser. *Tinker in Television*. New York: Simon & Schuster, 1994.

Weaver, Pat, with Thomas M. Coffey. *The Best Seat in the House: The Golden Years of Radio and Television*. New York: Alfred A. Knopf, 1994.

ARTICLES

Ames, Walter. "Bob, Ray Returned to KHJ After Fans Stir Up Protest." *Los Angeles Times*, April 12, 1957.

Amory, Cleveland. "The Dick Cavett Show." *TV Guide*, September 28, 1968.

"At Laughably Low Prices: Bob and Ray Spoof Radio, TV Idiocies." *Life*, May 19, 1952.

Balliett, Whitney. "Their Own Gravity." *The New Yorker*, September 24, 1973.

———. "Two-Man Show," *The New Yorker*. July 5, 1982.

Barnes, Clive. "Bob and Ray on Broadway." *New York Times*, September 26, 1970.

"Barry Predicts Long Span for Radio at NBC Conclave." *Billboard*, October 28, 1950.

"Blue 'Tap Day' Finds Chet LaRoche Wooing Key Y&R Men." *Variety*, October 4, 1944.

"Bob & Ray As Kukla TV Mates." *Variety*, November 21, 1951.

"Bob and Ray on Commercials, or Why Square Wheels Don't Roll." *Television Magazine*, February 1961.

Bolt, Jack. "By Any Other Name, Bob and Ray Spell Fun." *National Observer*, October 21, 1963.

"The Boys from Boston." *Newsweek*, September 10, 1951.

Champlin, Charles. "Slow-Curve Humor of Bob and Ray." *Los Angeles Times*, September 17, 1983.

———. "Cold Turkey." *Los Angeles Times*, March 5, 1971.

Clark, Edie. "Bob & Ray: The Two and Only." *Yankee*, September 1987.

Clark, Mike. "The Inimitable Bob & Ray, by the Book." *USA Today*, September 25, 1985.

"Closing Time," *New Yorker*, January 3, 1983.

"Cold Turkey." *Playboy*, May 1971.

"Cold Turkey." *Daily Variety*, January 29, 1971.

"Cold Turkey." *Boxoffice*, February, 8, 1971.

Collins, Glenn. "It's Bob and Ray Time—Again" *The New York Times*, June 13, 1982.

Crosby, John. "Comedy from Boston." *New York Herald Tribune*, July 30, 1951.

———. "Zanies rrom Boston." *New York Herald Tribune*, December 28, 1951.

———. "Bob and Ray After Midnight." *New York Herald Tribune*, May 18, 1953.

Elie, Jr., Rudolph. "Reserved for Radio." *Boston Herald*, July 5, 1947.

"FCC Orders WORL Closed." *The Boston Globe*, April 24, 1947.

"Five-Way Pick-up." *Billboard*, August 19, 1944.

Gardner, Hy. "The Early Bird on Broadway." *New York Herald Tribune*, July 2, 1951.

Gill, Brendan. "Japes and Capers." *The New Yorker*, October 3, 1970.

Gilmour, Clyde. "Lone, Magnificent Palm in Vast, Dreary Desert." *Toronto Telegram*, February 13, 1965.

Gehman, Richard. "Mr. Elliott (Bob) and Mr. Goulding (Ray)." *Cosmopolitan*, August 1956.

Goldstein, Richard. "Obituary: Don Herbert." *New York Times*, June 13, 2007.

Gould, Jack. "NBC Cuts Kukla, Fran and Ollie to 15 Minutes, Making Way for Team of Elliott and Goulding," *New York Times*, November 28, 1951.

———. "NBC 'Monitor' Scans All." *New York Times*, June 13, 1955.

Graham, Robert. "Singer Appointed Sister's Guardian." *San Francisco Chronicle*, August 23, 1963.

Grimes, William. "Obituary: Clive Barnes." *New York Times*, November 19, 2008.

Hews, Henry. "Boys in the Attic." *Saturday Review*, October 10, 1970.

"Holy Cow, They're Back." *Newsweek*, July 6, 1959.

"Inside Story." *Newsweek*, March 23, 1981.

"Inside Stuff." *Variety*, May 6, 1953.

Jensen, Elizabeth. "Remembering a Forgotten Newsman." *New York Times*, October 18, 2008.

Kalem, T. E. "Kidders of the Cliché." *Time*, October 19, 1970.

Kehr, Dave. "Obituary: Claude Chabrol." *New York Times*, September 12, 2010.

Kerr, Walter. "Very, Very Funny Men." *New York Times*, October 4, 1970.

Kroll, Jack. "Funny Gentlemen." *Newsweek*, October 5, 1970.

"Kukla Frowns at NBC, But Okays Trim to 15 Mins." *Variety*, November 14, 1951.

"Leder Revamps WINS, Names New Personnel." *Broadcasting-Telecasting*, March 15, 1954.

"The Loveable Hucksters." *Newsweek*, December 29, 1958.

Maslin, Janet. "Pacino in 'Author! Author!'" *New York Times*, June 18, 1982.

MBS Unveils Sales Plan in Chicago." *Broadcasting-Telecasting*, April 23, 1956.

McCue, Danny. "Making People Laugh." *Encore*, December 7, 1987.

Maeder, Jay. "Best of Big Town." *New York Daily News*, December 21, 2001.

Messina, Matt. "Bob and Ray Come Back in Cluttered Radio Show." *New York Daily News*, July 31, 1962.

Mitchell, Sean. "Gotham Grump." *Los Angeles Times*, March 1, 1992.

Morse, Jim. "Hearing is Believing." *TV Radio Mirror*, March 1960.

Mott, Patrick. "Bob and Ray's Cure for California." *The Hollywood Reporter*, July 15, 1975.

"NBC Gives Sked 'Summer Cleanup.'" *Variety*, May 2, 1951.

"Nightclubs: The Sickniks." *Time*, July 13, 1959.

"Obituary: Jackie Miles." *New York Times*, April 27, 1968.

"Pearson's Windfall." *The New Yorker*, December 30, 1950.

Peck, Stacey. "Al Lohman & Roger Barkley Q&A." *Los Angeles Times*, November 16, 1980.

Petit, Don. "Erickson Had Wofford Share, Papers Reveal." *Miami Daily News*, June 9, 1950.

Prideaux, Tom. "Cyanide in Custard." *Life*, December 4, 1970.

"Radio Follow-Up." *Variety*, May 20, 1953.

Rafferty, Terrence, "The Current Cinema," *New Yorker*, July 30, 1990.

Sandomir, Richard. "Jerry Seinfeld on 'Who's on First?'" *New York Times*, July 10, 2012.

Scheuer, Philip K. "Leona Thinks Her Singing Horrible." *Los Angeles Times*, September 5, 1958.

Schmidt, Sandra. "Bob, Ray in 'Two and Only.'" *Los Angeles Times* (no date).

Schneider, Ben. "Tatem Hotel is Purchased by N.Y. Men." *Miami News*, August 3, 1956.

Simon, John. "The Two and Only—Let's Hope So." *New York*, October 12, 1970.

"Spiel for Piel." Time, May 21, 1956.

Spillman, Ron. "Leg Cramp Halts N.Y. Postman's New Attempt to Swim Channel." *Jet*, September 9, 1954.

"The Stepchild." *Time*, April 18, 1949.

"Storer's $10 Million WMGM Buy Okayed." *Broadcasting-Telecasting*, December 18, 1961.

"The Talk of the Town." *The New Yorker*, June 17, 1967.

"Talkers Extraordinary." *Newsweek*, August 27, 1962.

"This Week's Stars in the Night Clubs." *Boston Traveler*, March 2, 1949.

Trumbull, Stephen. "Little Augie's Status Tops Hotel Case," *Miami Herald*, March 11, 1948.

Weiss, Patricia. "Bob and Ray Go Stag." *Hartford Courant*, May 25, 1986.

"When Film Comics Were in Flower." *Oakland Tribune*, May 17, 1963.

"Who's Who Cooks." *Good Housekeeping* (no date).

Wilson, Earl. "It Happened Last Night." *New York Post*, July 2, 1951.

"Wofford Hotel to Be Renamed." *Miami Daily News*, October 4, 1950.

INDEX OF BOB & RAY PARODIES

INDEX